FIRESTORMS
OF
REVIVAL

FIRESTORMS
OF
REVIVAL

How Historic Moves of God Happened—
and Will Happen Again

Updated Second Edition

BOB GRIFFIN, SR.

XULON PRESS

Xulon Press
2301 Lucien Way #415
Maitland, FL 32751
407.339.4217
www.xulonpress.com

Paperback ISBN-13: 978-1-6628-2134-9
Ebook ISBN-13: 978-1-6628-2135-6

Dr. Bob Griffin's *FIRE STORMS OF REVIVAL: Historic Moves of God: How They Always Happened—and Will Happen Again* is dynamite. This solid and scriptural study is molten lava. Griffin's passion for revival in our time is set in an actual locality and marks out the track in very specific terms. In every generation, we need a fresh statement on the nature and necessity of spiritual awakening. J. Edwin Orr, Brian Edwards, and Stephen Olford have shared in days gone by. I believe this readable volume will make such a contribution today. Strongly endorsed, every church leader in every local church should have a copy.

—Dr. D. L. Larsen, Professor Emeritus of Preaching
Trinity Evangelical Divinity School, Deerfield, IL

The fires of revival throughout history are a glorious reminder that it is God's mission in the world. As a missiologist led to Christ during the Jesus People Movement, I have encountered the amazing impact of revivals in the USA, East Africa, Indonesia, and the Solomon Islands. As Dr. Edwin Orr reminded us years ago at Fuller Seminary, revival is a powerful force in the spread of the gospel. Bob Griffin provides us a clear biblical, historical, and practical understanding of the nature of revival. His wide reading of other works on revival are evident throughout the book. This is a book to be read prayerfully in anticipation of revival!

—Doug McConnell, PhD, Professor of Leadership and
Intercultural Studies
Fuller Theological Seminary

Grateful as we are for all the dedicated ministries being carried on around the world, we know that everywhere, and especially in our own country, there is a desperate need for a mighty work of the Holy Spirit. So from our hearts we cry, "Will you not revive us again, that your people may rejoice in you?" (Ps. 85:5). While some believers are engaging in fervent intercession for a deep-seated, widespread spiritual awakening, most of us are moving along in life's usual groove. Not Bob and Connie Griffin! They have been spearheading a Christ-exalting movement in the city of Rockford, Illinois. And here in this soul-stirring book, Bob shares with us his and Connie's passion. He tells about revivals in years gone by, spelling out the biblical principles which have been powerfully operative in those great stirrings of church and society. Destined to be a classic in its *genre,* this book will prove a personal catalyst to its readers.

—The late Dr. Vernon Grounds, Chancellor
Denver Seminary

Bob Griffin is a scholar and a student of revival. He has not only read broadly but has also been involved in the excitement, disappointment, enthusiasm, and down-to-earth human involvement that God uses to bring new life to congregations and communities. This book provides us with much needed insight into God's work in the twenty-first century. Everyone interested in revival will want to read this important contribution.

—Jay Kesler, President Emeritus
Taylor University, Upland IN 46989–1001

Dr. Bob Griffin chronicles here God's irrefutable promise for health, healing, and revival in our world, our cities and our lives. Bob documents God's faithfulness throughout history to his 2 Chronicles 7:14 promise, identifies commonality in these sweeping movements of the Holy Spirit and points the way to revival in our own days. Compelling!

—Rick Kroeger, President
Kroeger World

This is a book pastors, prayer leaders, and City Reachers will find instructional yet inspirational, historical yet applicable, biblical and practical. It may be the one resource they have each been looking for that will feed and fuel their own souls while offering their prayer groups and vision teams a biblically based summary of the who, what, where, when, why, and how of authentic revival. This is the book you can use to turn a stagnant prayer meeting into a strategic, revival-hungry group. It is a source for the preacher who has a burden to teach the powerful truths found in the revivals of scripture and history. *Fire Storms of Revival* serves prayer leaders who want their members to pray, prompted by a longing for revival. Bob Griffin has produced a book that is both deep in knowledge and wide in scope.

—Phil Miglioratti
National Pastor's Prayer Network

I have read many books on Revival, but none more comprehensive than *Fire Storms of Revival*. The historical documentation from the Old Testament to the present is clearly recorded and defined. While it is comprehensive, it is also very concise. For instance, *"Revival will not cross the bridge until unity is well under construction."* Dr. Bob brings a beautiful blend of what we can do and what the Holy Spirit will do. This work could well become the textbook on revival for students to use. It is the most exhaustive study of the subject I have ever read. I recommend it to everyone.

—The late Rev/Dr. Don Lyon, Senior Pastor
Faith Center, Rockford, Illinois

Have you ever wondered why all of those mainline denominations with so many rich traditions and all of those highly educated clergy and laity are dying off so quickly? After over three decades as a pastor in one of those mainliners that continues to move so rapidly to the sidelines of influence upon American and global cultures, I have found the antidote, Bob Griffin's *Fire Storms of Revival*, which is the practical as well as erudite review of the biblical, historical, and pneumatic ingredients of revival's recipe. Dr. Griffin, an uncommonly discerning pastor and scholar on the cutting edge of ecclesiastical evolution, has provided the most complete guide to cooperating with the reviving movements of our Lord to prepare His bride for His glorious return. Coming from the mainline experience, I am encouraged and challenged by Dr. Griffin's passion for holiness, spiritual discipline, and authentic ecumenism as personified in Jesus and prescribed in the Bible as the medicine for what ails churches.

—Dr. Robert R. Kopp, Author; Pastor
First Presbyterian Church, Belvedere, Illinois

Here is a book that will draw you into the lessons learned from great moves of God in history and today. In 1995, my wife and I started a journey to discover what God was doing to awaken His Church across our nation. We have had the privilege of visiting over twenty major cities in the USA. We have seen firsthand an obvious new move of pastors and marketplace leaders beginning to come together across denominational and cultural lines for prayer, church growth by conversion, and social justice. These spiritual leaders are simultaneously beginning to pastor the Church of their city that meets in many locations. In *Fire Storms of Revival*, Bob has captured the time-tested principles that better welcome and sustain a historic move of the Holy Spirit over a city. It is practical and inspirational. You will be convicted and uplifted to pick up the torch to light revival fire in this hour. Bob has thoroughly searched the scriptures and history to give us practical and proven principles. Take these steps and apply them.

—Rev. Tony Danhelka, Cofounder/President
Riverwoods Christian Center, Chicagoland City-Reacher

The most effective way to increase our spiritual appetite and faith for revival is to consider what God has already done. Biblical and historic revivals are plentiful, and we have a responsibility as God's people to prepare ourselves for His visitation in our day! Bob's book is an important tool to consider again God's pattern for revival and the biblical principles that draw His presence near to desperate people. This book will ignite a fresh fire and faith in your heart to seek God for another spiritual awakening in our nation.

—Rhonda Hughey, Author
Director, Fusion Ministries

Sensitive to the lateness of the hour, Dr. Bob Griffin sees an American church that is divided, underpowered, and yielded to the materialistic and sinful culture of this age, a culture heavily shaped and influenced by Satan who understands that his time is now very short. Bob knows that only a genuine, heaven-sent revival will change this into a sanctified bride, dressed in white linen. Therefore, with regard to the Old Testament period, the New Testament period, and the church age, Bob has done a masterful job in presenting the common denominators of historical revivals and the resulting changes in society, in the economy, in the lives of individual believers, and also in the spiritual life, ministry, and witness of the Church. God has given Bob magnificent insight to His big picture for the ages. Bob's research has been detailed and insightful, and his conclusions are both relevant and uplifting to the gatekeepers and intercessors who stand in the gap before Him, praying for America, and saying "Come quickly, Lord Jesus."

—Frank Shappert, President, Shappert Engineering, retired
past Board Chairman, Renewal Ministries

Bob Griffin has produced a book that is both deep in knowledge and wide in scope. He has much to teach us about the revivals of the past—a past that extends to ancient times in Israel. But he also offers us some wonderful practical lessons about what we can do here and now to prepare the way for much-needed new "firestorms of revival." We must move beyond our "encrusted institutionalism" to a posture of fervent spiritual humility, characterized by tears of repentance, powerful biblical preaching, and a renewed commitment to the cause of the Gospel in all of its clarity and power.

—Richard J. Mouw, PhD, President Emeritus
Fuller Theological Seminary, Professor of Faith/Public Life

This book is dedicated to Connie Griffin—my wife, my best friend, and my partner in ministry. Second, it is dedicated to the city of Rockford, Illinois, and to all who are interceding with Connie and me for area-wide transformation, a sweeping revival of the Church, and a Great Awakening in which thousands come to faith in Jesus Christ—our Savior, Lord and soon-coming King.

ACKNOWLEDGMENTS

I GRATEFULLY ACKNOWLEDGE THE outstanding profes-
sors who mentored and inspired me at Trinity International
University. Special mention goes to Dr. David Larsen who coached
me through my doctoral program. He shares not only my love for
the Church of Jesus Christ and the city of Rockford, Illinois, but
also my passion to see a sweeping revival of the Church and another
Great Awakening in our day. Special thanks goes to many friends
and colleagues who read the manuscript and gave helpful sugges-
tions and endorsed this effort.

My heart is thankful for Connie—my wife and partner in the
gospel—who has displayed patient endurance through the years of
my ministry and maturing (I still have a long way to go). I deeply
appreciate her steadfast strength and commitment, especially
in the later years as God called us out of our comfort zone and
into the faith adventure of Rockford Renewal Ministries (RRM).
The renewal ministry and this book would have been impossible
without Connie. We have served side by side in ministry, and she
read and edited the book manuscript before anyone else saw it.

I will forever be grateful to my friends and the publishers and
editors at Creation House who coached me through the first edition of *Firestorms of Revival* in 2006, and for the publishing team at
Xulon Press who creatively worked with me to publish this updated
second edition.

TABLE OF CONTENTS

Will you not revive us again, that your people may rejoice in you? Show us your unfailing love, LORD, and grant us your salvation. I will listen to what God the LORD says; he promises peace to his people, his faithful servants—but let them not turn to folly. Surely his salvation is near those who fear him, that his glory may dwell in our land. Love and faithfulness meet together; righteousness and peace kiss each other. Faithfulness springs forth from the earth, and righteousness looks down from heaven. The LORD will indeed give what is good, and our land will yield its harvest. Righteousness goes before him and prepares the way for his steps. (Ps. 85:6–13)

Introduction

I SAT IN A small lakeside cabin in Wisconsin, praying and listening to God's still, small voice. It was a day I set aside to be with God, my adoptive heavenly Father. The sun was bright, but a cold, strong winter wind blew snow across the woods and the path to the door. As I asked God for a sweeping move of revival across our area, He lovingly assured me, "Be still and patient, my son. The wind of My Spirit shall blow again as at Pentecost."

The wind continued to howl through the woods and shook the cabin. Through the large window in front of me, I watched the trees bend in the gusts, the smaller ones nearly snapping while the larger ones stood strong against the wind's mighty power. I was thankful for the warmth from the potbelly stove in the corner of the cabin.

My heart cried, "Oh God, bring the wind of your Holy Spirit soon. Bend your Church back to passionate obedience and fiery first love. Oh Father, do it again like Isaiah prayed: 'Oh, that you would rend the heavens and come down, that the mountains would tremble before you! As when fire sets twigs ablaze and causes water to boil, come down to make your name known'" (Isa. 64:1–2).

God Has Told Us What to Do

When will the wind of the Holy Spirit blow across the land? God is ready. He is waiting on His Church to prepare the way. God told us what to do after He made one of His most incredible visitations in Israel's history, at the dedication of Solomon's temple. After the construction of the temple was complete, the stage was set for God to fill the house. In grand fashion, Solomon offered a lengthy prayer to dedicate the new temple (2 Chron. 6). As he poured out his heart to God, he asked Him over and over to hear Israel's cry and forgive her when certain disasters came as a result of the people drifting into sin, idolatry, and rebellion.

Second Chronicles 7:1 says that when Solomon finished praying, God's glory fell like a firestorm from heaven and consumed the sacrifices: "When all the people of Israel saw the fire coming down and the glorious presence of the LORD filling the Temple, they fell face down on the ground and worshiped and praised the LORD" (2 Chron. 7:3, NLT). Two weeks of great celebration followed this phenomenal event. The new temple was spectacular. God's presence—His glory—so filled the house that the people couldn't stand. With faces to the ground, they worshiped God. When Solomon returned to his palace—probably excited and exhausted—God spoke to him in the night and answered the questions and concerns he had expressed in his prayer of dedication. What would happen in dark and difficult times? Would God meet the people of Israel in times of great need? Would He answer when they cried out to Him at this great temple? Would He help them? Would He restore them?

Solomon knew tough and terrible times would come. It was a matter of *when*, not *if*. There would be times of spiritual decay and drift. God's people would turn away from Him in sin and rebellion. It would be bad economically, spiritually, socially, and militarily. Graciously, God spoke to Solomon: "*If* my people, who are called by my name, will humble themselves and pray and seek my face and turn from their wicked ways, *then* will I hear from heaven and will forgive their sin and will heal their land" (2 Chron. 7:14, emphasis added).

This text stands throughout history as God's instructions for His people when things turn bad. Although it is specific to Israel, its truth can be seen anytime God's people anywhere drift away from Him. When life turns dark and difficult, if they humble themselves, seek Him, pray, and repent, God will respond according to His promise. This thread is woven into the history of Israel, and it is also evident in the New Testament and post-biblical history. An Old Testament scholar will explain later how God's promise extends to His people for all time.

Back to the Basics

The fire and winds of revival come when God's people return to Him in first love, with all their heart, soul, and mind, the first and greatest commandment—The Great Commandment (Rev. 2:4; Matt. 22:37–38). Think of first love as lots of time together and conversational intimacy—like lovers. Couple that love with loving others as you love yourself (Matt. 22:39). Jesus instructs us to go much further when He says, "Love one another as I have loved you" (John 13:34). He was tortured and killed in love for us. In the same chapter, Jesus washed His disciple's trail-dirty feet as an example of how we are to love others (v. 13).

Love for God includes growing obedience to our Great Commission, reaching and growing other disciples: "Go and make disciples of all nations, baptizing them in the name of the Father and of the Son and of the Holy Spirit, teaching them to obey everything I have commanded you. And surely I am with you always, to the very end of the age" (Matt. 28:19). We have all the power we need to obey. "You will receive power when the Holy Spirit comes on you; and you will be my witnesses in Jerusalem, and in all Judea and Samaria, and to the ends of the earth" (Acts 1:8). It is not enough to only attend a gathering of fellow believers on weekends. God's people must know Him, love Him, and with dedication and vision, mobilize into their communities with His light and love.

According to comprehensive surveys, the authentic Church in America has diminished to between 7 and 9 percent of the population. She has become a subculture.[1] Author and pastor, John Dickerson, defines the authentic Church as those "trusting in Christ alone for eternal salvation and valuing God's Word [the Bible] as the true standard for belief and practice." He describes what is happening with the remnant to which we belong:

- The fuel of American evangelicalism—dollars—is disappearing and will dwindle over the next three decades.
- We're losing millions of our people—about 2.6 million per decade, just from one generation studied.
- The evangelical church is not winning new believers fast enough to keep pace with rapid population growth in the United States.
- While these forces eat away at the church internally, the external climate is turning against evangelicals. The fastest-growing subcultures in the United States express a militant antagonism against Christians who take the Bible seriously.
- What's left of a smaller, shrinking, strapped church is also splintering and splitting itself over politics and postmodern views of God and the Bible.[2]

Back in 2000, the Church began to take notice of her decline. Popular teachers, Elmer Towns and Warren Bird, concluded, "Consensus is that congregations, instead of making a redemptive impact on their surrounding neighborhoods and cities, are irrelevant and inconsequential." [3]

In his compelling book, *Irresistible: Reclaiming the New that Jesus Unleashed for the World*, Andy Stanley writes: "It's no secret the religious landscape in America has shifted. Fewer and fewer Americans are self-identifying as Christians, while more and more are identifying as religiously unaffiliated. You've heard by now, this group has been nicknamed the "Nones" because they check "None of the above" on religious affiliation surveys. According to Pew Research Center's "2014 Religious Landscape Study," nearly a quarter of Americans claim no religious affiliation, representing a seven-point jump in just seven years. Nones represent nearly 23 percent of Americans. Think about that—23 percent. That's just under fifty-six million people. Young Americans are more likely to be religiously unaffiliated than older Americans, with millennials comprising 44 percent of Nones. Translated: "Millennials are walking away from the faith they grew up with in record numbers." [4]

Andy turns to the former *National Review* editor, John O'Sullivan, for a troubling definition of post-Christianity. "A post-Christian society is not merely a society in which agnosticism or atheism is the prevailing fundamental belief. It is a society rooted in the history, culture, and practices of Christianity but in which the religious beliefs of Christians have been either rejected or, worse, forgotten." [5]

Only One Church

There is something central to the Church that has been neglected. We have strategies and materials to help us share the gospel, but with some exceptions we do not have that for which Jesus prayed that we would embrace—*unity*! Could it be any clearer that the Church in every region is to be unified?

> My prayer is not for them alone. I pray also for those who will believe in me through their message, that all of them may be one, Father, just as you are in me and I am in you. May they also be in us so that the world may believe that you have sent me. I have given them the glory that you gave me, that they may be one as we are one—I in them and you in me—so that they may be

brought to complete unity. Then the world will know that you sent me and have loved them even as you have loved me. (John 17:20–26)

The apostle Paul was passionate about the unity of the Church. He wrote: "I urge you to live a life worthy of the calling you have received. Be completely humble and gentle; be patient, bearing with one another in love. Make **every effort to keep the unity of the Spirit** through the bond of peace" (Eph. 4:1–3). Although there may be many congregations in an area, there is only one Church. Through unity, our cities and our nation will know "the Father sent His Son" (John 17:20–23). That's the Gospel! In our unity the love of Jesus will be on display! Imagine the impact of a unified regional Church mobilized in loving service and redemptive impact. Think about the significance of a unified regional Church gathered from time to time, worshipping, praying, and seeking God's face.

Eight of Paul's letters are written to cities or regions. In each one of them, he urges unity. After all, it's what Jesus told the Church to be—unified. (See Rom. 12:3–16; 15:5–9; 1 Cor. 1:10–17; 3:3; 10:17; 11:17–16; 12; Gal. 3:2 6–29; 5:22–26; 6:2–5, 9–10; Eph. 4:1–7, 11–14; Phil. 1:27; 2:1–18; Col. 3:12–17; 1 Thess. 5:9–22.)

We must intentionally remove the religious and cultural barriers that have kept the Church divided in disobedience and long-standing defiance of what Jesus prayed for and Paul taught. Not only did Jesus pray for unity in John 17, He said, "If a kingdom is divided against itself, that kingdom cannot stand [including God's kingdom]. If a house is divided against itself, that house cannot stand" (Mark 3:24–25). Matthew 12:25 adds: "Every city or household divided against itself will not stand." The Church has not stood strong in unity, but she has always had the ability to answer Jesus's prayer for it. Strange, isn't it? In obedience God's people can answer Jesus's prayer.

For some, the connotation of unity is to force all Christian groups to be identical, to lose their historic distinctives. For these, it will be helpful to think of harmony, the blending of diverse instruments, notes, and melodies into a beautiful symphonic masterpiece as we follow the Divine Maestro. Regional gatherings for prayer, worship, and fellowship could adopt this perspective. Regional leaders praying together could create city-reaching strategies and work together to accomplish them. With God-led direction, ponder the impact of the Church mobilized across a region. In these days when the Church is only 7 to 9 percent of America and often facing hostility toward Christian faith, loving acts of care and concern are what pave the way to an openness to the Good News of life in Jesus Christ. It's like one church I know that tells her people, "Let's love our city until they ask why!"

In 2020, a strong coalition of national Church and mission leaders launched a movement called "All.America." In each region or city, it was called, for example, "All.Chicago." It was a nondenominational, nonprofit initiative designed to serve all churches, groups, organizations, and individuals within the body of Christ. The passionate hope was that All.America would become a movement to help the entire Christian community accomplish the Great Commission. It was not meant to compete with other initiatives but, rather, to complement them. All.America was an initiative of "*call2all.*" Some of the leaders sensed that, given the decline of the Church, God was giving her a "reprieve" (see https://allamerica.org).

God wanted us to love Him with every fiber of our being. He sacrificially loved us first, not wanting anyone to perish (Deut. 6:5; Mark 12:30; Matt. 22:37; Luke 10:27). He commissioned us to go into our world with the gracious good news of the Gospel (Acts 1:8; Matt. 28:19–20). This "going" into our world has seemed to be much more biblically predominant than what we have often heard: "Come to church." Haven't we been taught go "to church," to go into the world and make disciples, and to love our neighbors as ourselves?

In revival, or a historic move of God, the number of those who gather for services will no longer be the measure of success, although in revival, churches are usually packed with people seeking God. There will be great regional excitement over the redemptive impact of the Gospel, people coming to faith in Christ, growing in Him, and mobilized as redemptive agents. Pecking order pride and competition among clergy and congregations will diminish. Certain religious forms and rituals external to the Bible will be drained of their significance. The Church will no longer embrace what Jesus spoke against, encrusted ways of doing things (Mark 7:5–16). He confronted the religious establishment of his day: "Why do you break the command of God for the sake of your tradition? You nullify the word of God for the sake of your tradition. You hypocrites" (Matt. 15: 3, 6–7a).

The regional Church must get back to majoring on what unites her and minoring on issues that tend to divide her. When she begins to take seriously her need for revival and begins to unify, repent, and pray, she will begin to flourish. Her cities will be transformed. First love for God will burn with passion again. It's time to return to our first love (Rev. 2:4). St. Augustine, who died in AD 430, teaches us how to view regional Church fellowship, "In essentials, unity; in non-essentials, liberty; in all things, charity." [6]

Word Pictures That Could Help

Would you agree that the Church is to be more like an army than an audience, or like a training center, where new recruits are equipped to be soldier-saints and mobilized disciples? Could it be that the Church is to be more like a hatchery for new followers of Jesus, planting fish in every lake, pond, or stream, rather than a beautiful aquarium, housing attractive fish that swim aimlessly? She's not to be a grand yacht or cruise ship, is she? Isn't she is to be a cargo ship sailing out of port with lots of lifesaving equipment and carrying precious food and cargo to dying people? There is a large poster in a friend's office of a grand sailing ship in full sail, battling a terrific storm at sea. What really catches one's attention is the inscription on the bottom. "Ships are safe in the harbor, but that is not what ships are for." It's credited to John A. Shed. It's a picture of the Christian life.

Something Missing

What do people sense when they enter our churches? Considerable attention is given to welcoming guests, as a team helps them find parking. "First impressions" teams serve to warmly greet visitors as they enter the doors. Great programs are offered in a variety of areas to meet important needs, especially ministries for kids. However, Rhonda Hughey, in her book *Desperate for His Presence*, suggests something is missing. She wonders if God is present, that is, His manifest presence. There is something beyond the presence of Jesus indwelling His followers individually. "For where two or three gather in my name, there am I with them" (Matt. 18:20). Do curious people looking for God sense Him through exhilarating worship music, through encouraging and compelling teaching, and through God's people loving and caring for those who come? After identifying the sin that shuts out God's presence, she writes: "As the Church grows more and more compromised and disconnected from Jesus...two things happen: true believers will leave the empty institutionalized Church in pursuit of life and intimacy with Jesus, and others will remain, determined to shape and mold it after their own image." [7]

Hughey believes that the Western Church is a subculture rather than a counter-culture. A subculture reflects the value system and worldview of the primary culture and cannot be an agent of change. God's kingdom culture must reflect love and unity among believers, humility, meekness, holiness, encouragement, and God-centeredness. This stands in contrast to what we know as "church splits." It's serving and giving, rather than wanting to receive. It's about living by faith in generous sacrificial living, and even suffering for the sake of God's kingdom. Hughey says, "The Church has become a well-trained institution, and the reality is that we are capable of functioning without the manifest presence of God. That is alarming." [8]

It's time for revival, a historic move of God. It's time to so embody the love of Christ that people are drawn to Him through us. "Mercy triumphs over judgment" (James 2:13). It's time to model grace and gentleness that is "evident to all" (Phil. 4:5), along with the fruit of the Holy Spirit in Galatians chapter five. Through love and a passion to live out God's Word, the Church will reflect Jesus in our towns and cities. Revival and area-wide transformation will invade our towns on three strategic fronts: unified, repentant prayer, humble intentional relationships of unity in diversity, and redemptive action—the Church mobilized to meet the crying needs of the city.

This book is the story of revival, the story of how revival always happens, and how it will happen again. It's about a *firestorm* of loving redemption across our towns and cities as the Church is renewed and mobilized.

When I was a young farm boy, my family cooked our food and heated our home with wood-burning stoves. I gathered wood and built many fires. I knew how to place discarded paper in the stove, then kindling, and finally the larger pieces of wood. I knew how to light the fire. Sometimes I had to blow on the early flames to get it going. The Church has built the fire of revival like that—laying down the paper of humility and the unity of the Church, adding the kindling of prayer, the wood of teaching and repentance, and passionately seeking God's face. God has lit the match. The wind of the Holy Spirit has created a hot burning firestorm. When God's people have done their part, He has done His.

Why This Book?

Why this passion for revival? Recalling that surveys say there is little difference between the Church and her surrounding culture, that she is marginalized and in serious decline, I am deeply concerned. Increasingly, I sense the Church has lost her redemptive impact. I saw frightening cultural trends. For example, on I-65 in Indiana, a billboard announces: "One out of three high school students will graduate this year with a sexually transmitted disease." Sensuality and secularism are increasingly pervasive. Pew Research finds: "One-in-four parents living with a child in the United States today are unmarried. Driven by declines in marriage overall, as well as increases in births outside of marriage, this marks a dramatic change from a half-century ago, when fewer than one-in-ten parents living with their children were unmarried (7%)." [9]

Desperate for revival and the transformation of our cities, I had been asking: "Is there hope? What was God's response when passionate prayer and repentance began to spread among His people? Was there a pattern that would help me trace God's response?" Similar to King Solomon's prayer, I asked, "Oh God, what will you do in our time?"

An Old Testament scholar had affirmed that the instructions for revival were in 2 Chronicles 7:14. It had motivated me to begin facilitating a movement of prayer gatherings in our area. Shortly after we began, my wife, Connie, and I were called by God to launch Rockford Renewal Ministries. About the same time, I faced the deadline to choose the major topic for my final doctoral work. I was going to research "The Impact of Life Coaching" in churches, but with this new passion, I chose to study historic moves of God. I needed to know how they happened. I discovered ten characteristics that could be traced throughout Scripture and post-biblical history.

I am writing to share them with you. I want to light a *firestorm* of historic revival. First, however, I will tell you the story of our revival journey. I love to tell this story, but if you can't contain your urge to get into the book, jump ahead to the first chapter and join me in chasing revival fire through time.

Our Story, the Birth of Citywide Prayer

In 1994 the Evangelical Free Church of America established a National Prayer Accord. As a part of the strategy, groups of three churches in each city were encouraged to meet quarterly for combined prayer for revival in the Church and the transformation of their cities. When the plan was presented to the staff of the Evangelical Free Church where Connie and I were serving in Rockford, Illinois, I volunteered to lead the effort. I called the pastor of a large Assembly of God church across the street, and he was enthusiastic about praying together. At last, two very diverse congregations were going to pray and work together. What about a third church?

Months earlier I had met with fellow clergy, city officials, and the mayor to hear Dr. Ray Bakke, a Christian urban specialist, speak about the urban crisis in America. He had led a church in Chicago for a number of years and had written books on city transformation. After Bakke's talk, the group discussed why cities deteriorate and what needed to happen for our city to be transformed. At the conclusion of the meeting, a pastor suggested that we pray. Our city was in deep social and economic trouble. Homicides were off the chart—more per capita than Chicago. The local school district was under federal control, having been convicted of inequitable treatment of students from the west side of town, where the population was primarily African American and Hispanic. Businesses had been moving out of the city, and families had been moving outside the city limits because of rising taxes needed to meet the government's requirements to reorder the school district. Economically, Rockford had been in the top ten cities of her size in the 1980s, but things had changed drastically.

When God led me to pray aloud, I began to share the pain I was feeling. Gripped with sadness for our city, I began to weep softly and could not continue to pray. An African American pastor slipped in beside me, took my hand, and prayed until I regained my composure. At that moment, it hit me like a ton of bricks: This is what needs to happen in this city: pastors of different races and denominations praying and weeping together. In that moment I whispered to God, *Our city is desperate. I am just one small person, but if there is any way You want to use me to help bring revival and restoration to this city, Oh God, I am available.*

I had volunteered in the city council chambers to do anything I could to help the city. I told the church staff I would coordinate our denomination's prayer initiative. As the Assembly of God pastor and I discussed what church we could ask to join us for prayer, it grabbed me. Call the African American pastor who had taken my hand, shared my concern, and joined me in prayer. I called him. When he checked the suggested date for the first prayer meeting, he exclaimed, "That's Brotherhood Sunday. Could we meet at our church?" It was arranged. The two larger congregations of several thousand each—predominantly Caucasian, Pentecostal and non-Pentecostal—gathered at Pilgrim Baptist, a predominantly African American church of several hundred. We met on the west side of the Rock River that had divided the city from her inception. Many drove to the meeting from the east side. Others, who were afraid to drive into the west side at night, were taken in church busses.

People came from all across town, and God showed up. Pilgrim Baptist was packed, and people were turned away. The local press heard about the gathering, and a young woman from the newspaper asked for an interview after the service. The next morning, the prayer gathering had captured front-page headlines and was the lead article. A large picture showed people of great diversity worshipping and praying together. What had been organized for three congregations became citywide. A steering committee of four African American and three Caucasian pastors was formed. I was asked to coordinate the effort. As time passed, the committee grew to include representatives from all those who considered themselves evangelical (orthodox) Christians: Protestant, Catholic, African American, Caucasian, and Hispanic—both male and female.

Concerts of Prayer were held quarterly (except for summer), beginning in February, 1995. The largest crowd—about fifteen hundred people—met in a downtown theater. At the twenty-fifth city-wide gathering on October 4, 2002, a crowd of over nine hundred read a litany together, crowning Jesus Lord and King over the city (See appendix I). After the climax of the twenty-fifth Concert of Prayer Gathering, some of the leadership, especially, Connie and I, felt the unified, area-wide Church needed a more regular and visible expression. As a result, in January 2003, GRIPP—Greater Rockford in Prayer and Praise—was born. Meetings were scheduled across the area—north, south, east, west, and central—on the third Friday of each month. The gatherings were simplified to keep the meetings free from a parade of leaders, a tight schedule, and a formal order of service. GRIPP was intentional about diversity, and in each church it was simply praise, repentance, and passionate prayer for revival.

Rockford Renewal Ministries Begins

Early in the history of the prayer movement, the Concert of Prayer steering committee held a breakfast for pastors. Since I was leaving to minister in India, I could not attend. However, I was asked to produce a video that told the story of how the Concerts of Prayer were born, and also cast a vision for the revival of the Church and the transformation of the city. At the breakfast meeting was a pastor who led a weekly church prayer meeting of about two hundred people. His prayer group had been asking God to raise up someone full-time to facilitate the revival efforts for the area-wide Church. As he watched the video, God quietly said to him, "This is the one for whom you have been praying."

When I returned from India, this young pastor made an appointment to see me. Entering my office, he introduced himself and reported what God had spoken. I was surprised if not shocked. "Lord, what does it mean? Were you speaking?" I tucked this experience away and proceeded with my pastoral ministry, including the work of facilitating citywide prayer meetings. In December of 1996, Connie and I left our church positions to seek God's direction for a new chapter in our lives. We began extended times of prayer. Our assumption was that God would lead us to pastor a congregation. The search began. Two months after our resignation, a businessman in the city asked to meet me for lunch. He knew about me through a mutual friend, and after we became acquainted, he began to share his passion for revival. He was confident that God was bringing revival to Rockford. The citywide Church would need someone to facilitate it.

Then he dropped a bomb. God had spoken to him, and he believed that Connie and I were to stay in the city to lead the prayer and revival effort full time. If we would, he would be on a board of directors and help financially. This was the second person who had spoken about us staying and serving in the city. Not long after this lunch meeting, God met me in an early morning "burning bush" experience. I was praying, listening, and writing in my journal. I sensed God was speaking. It was brief and clear:

"Renewal Ministries—for the healing of hearts, help for the Church, and hope for the city."

My best understanding was that God wanted Connie and me to continue helping people with broken hearts—especially leaders and pastors. He wanted us to call the Church in the city to passionate prayer for revival according to 2 Chronicles 7:14. As the Church obeyed God's instructions to seek his face in humble, repentant prayer, revival would come. With revival, the deep wounds in the city would be healed. She would be transformed. (In 2013, *Transform Rockford* was born when more than 1,300 people attended a community meeting and learned the "brutal facts" about the city. Many responded to a call for action, a vision to transform the city socially and economically.)

Connie was praying that God would direct us to a lead pastor position where we could use our gifts and experience. Neither of us wanted to stay in Rockford. We were ready to move. This strange word from God was far from what we thought God was doing in our lives. It was a significant stretch for us. It would mean creating a ministry and raising financial support, one of our least favorite things to do. Had I heard from God, or was it too much morning coffee? Connie agreed to pray about it and ask the Lord for a clear call and confirmation. Weeks later she came into my study one morning to tell me that God had confirmed the call while she was praying.

We still wanted to make sure. It would be foolish to begin a new faith ministry, and humanly impossible without God's call and the confirmation of His people. We knew of no other ministry like this. We also knew it would draw enemy fire, especially in a city where the Church was deeply divided and the enemy had well-established strongholds. In the past, we had traveled internationally under Barnabas International, ministering to pastors and missionaries. Although we had raised financial support then, it was common knowledge that support for a home ministry was more difficult to raise. We needed the confirmation of God's people.

We decided to hold a banquet downtown at the City Club. Since we had been facilitating city-wide Concerts of Prayer for two years, we had worked with many Christians across the city. We needed their confirmation and support. Ninety-two pastors, city leaders, and friends met together for a great meal in April 1997. Pastors from different ethnic groups gave leadership to the evening. An African American soloist sang the popular song, "To Dream the Impossible Dream." [10]

After dinner, Connie and I shared our story. We asked people to pray together at their tables for confirmation that God had spoken and called us to this new adventure. Individual response cards were on the tables. When the cards were collected, they were very positive. An offering was taken to pay for the evening, and it exceeded expenses by $1,500—start-up funds. We asked a pastor in the city to close the evening with prayer. As he began to share his excitement, he spontaneously asked pastors to gather at the front to commission us for the new work. Connie and I knelt before them. We had heard from God.

Rockford Renewal Ministries was born. The following morning we engaged an attorney to prepare incorporation papers. We prayerfully created a board of directors and asked a team of friends to pray for us and for revival. A vision statement sprang quickly from our hearts, and our mission statement followed naturally. We would call the Church in Rockford, Illinois, to prayer and repentance for revival. A fourteen-point revival strategy was developed to make the vision a reality. (See appendix II)

> **THE VISION OF ROCKFORD RENEWAL MINISTRIES** is a sweeping revival of the Church of Jesus Christ in the city of Rockford, Illinois and a great awakening across

the city, both accomplished by effectual, fervent prayer and personal and corporate holiness.

The Mission of Rockford Renewal Ministries is to call the Church of Jesus Christ across the city to repentance and to seek God through humble prayer for revival and a Great Awakening according to 2 Chronicles 7:14. The results shall be personal and corporate righteousness, people and congregations on fire for God and His kingdom, and dramatic social change—the transformation of the city.

I had been working on a doctoral degree at Trinity University in Deerfield, Illinois, and I needed to select the topic for my final paper shortly after we launched the ministry. I had planned to write on lay counseling—life coaching. I asked God, "How has revival happened? Was there a pattern in the Scripture? Was there a pattern throughout Church history? Were they the same? I wanted to understand these things if Connie and I were to serve this new calling." It didn't take long to decide to write my major doctoral paper on historic moves of God—revival. I needed answers; my doctoral committee readily approved the topic.

God Accomplishes His Kingdom Work

I finished my doctoral degree while Connie and I launched the ministry. We pursued our vision and mission for fifteen years, working side by side as partners in ministry. Like many married couples, we are individually very different, but we learned to complement each other. I was president; Connie was chief executive officer; both of us shared the jobs of secretary and janitor.

GRIPP (Greater Rockford in Prayer and Praise) continued. We facilitated weekly prayer meetings across the area in strategic locations: the jail, the court house, city hall, the school district office, the marketplace—at a corporation office—and two at our office in the heart of the city. We continued to cast the vision and call the Church to unity, repentance, and prayer. I had the opportunity to speak regularly, including in African American, Caucasian, and Hispanic churches.

We often invited pastors and their spouses to our home for dinner with no other agenda than to help them become acquainted with others of denominational and racial diversity. The evenings ended with great joy as we held hands around the table and prayed for each other and for our city. Significant friendships were formed, and racial and denominational divisions faded before our eyes.

Second Chronicles 15:7 pushed us forward in dark and difficult times of discouragement: "But as for you, be strong and do not give up for your work will be rewarded." We were correct in our assumptions. We attracted enemy fire, but God sustained us, especially when we confronted the darkness first hand. Raising support for a local ministry was difficult, but God faithfully provided for us. More and more pastors and Christian leaders grasped the critical importance of area-wide Church unity, prayer, and repentance. The call and promises of God encouraged us, and His Word reminded us how He accomplishes His kingdom work. "Not by might nor by power, but by my Spirit, says the Lord Almighty. What are you, O mighty mountain? Who despises the day of small things? Before Zerubbabel you will become level ground...Who despises the day of small things?"—(Zech. 4:6–10).

In 2012, we stepped aside from Rockford Renewal Ministries to turn the ministry over to younger leadership. We had worked the simple strategy that God gave us, and our board stood with us month after month, year after year. God had provided an ideal office in the heart of the city and a beautiful older home well suited to hosting city leaders and pastors. At one dinner meeting, we hosted the mayor, the chief of police, and a leading judge, and their spouses. There were many miraculous gifts from God through the years.

Small Clouds on the Horizon

Our vision has not changed—revival will come. No one has ever known how long it will take for historic revival fire to fall, or exactly when it will happen, but we know that "The Lord is faithful to all his promises" (Ps. 145:13). A firestorm of revival could very well sweep Rockford, jump to Chicago, and then move across the nation. We have watched God do amazing things. The downpour of rain that came as a result of Elijah's prayers began with "a cloud as small as a man's hand" (1 Kgs. 18:44). Elijah had told his servant to go look for clouds six different times before the small cloud appeared on the horizon. We have already seen many small clouds of God at work. (If you would like to look toward the horizon, request my list at bggriffin42@gmail.com. It's several pages of amazing things God has done, called "God at Work.")

Here are three exciting things God has done:

First, the Rockford School District had been convicted of inequitable treatment of minorities on the city's west side. It came under federal control. The prayer movement and Rockford Renewal Ministry was birthed during this time. Negative rhetoric filled the local paper month after month. Taxes increased to pay for the remediation of the problems. Housing values declined, and people began to move out of the city limits. The school board was polarized. Today the district has been removed from Federal control and has become one of the leading districts in Illinois. It has been led by committed and gifted Christians.

Second, a direct correlation cannot be made, but as mentioned above, and with so much concerted prayer, it's clear to us that God has been at work. In October of 2013, a coalition of nonpolitical leaders established a vision and grass roots organization: "Rock

River Regional Transformation." Three million dollars of private funds were designated for the effort. Hope has been burning brightly for Rockford to be a "Top 25 community by 2025—a great place to live, work, and raise a family!" The city has made great progress and again, the wise and gifted CEOs so far have been gifted followers of Jesus.

Third, after I completed my doctoral studies, I had a burning desire to publish my findings in a readable and academically sound book. I began to rework my doctoral project into a manuscript. After several years of writing, the manuscript was ready. It took months to find a publisher. Finally, *Creation House* contacted me; they wanted my book. I was extremely excited—to say the least! However, a looming obstacle settled over the publication. Because I was an unknown author, I would have to pay $30,000 to get it published. The cost was far beyond our ability to pay. "Stand by," I told them. Within a few weeks we received $50,000 from my long-time mentor, the late Dr. Frank Freed and his wonderful wife, Evelyn. It was one of the most exciting miracles of our revival journey. They had been supportive of our ministries for a long time. We paid for the book. At the tenth anniversary of RRM, Evelyn and Frank established an endowment for our ministry so we could help other city-wide ministries when they were in need.

There has been more to this story. Frank was pastoring a thriving congregation when I first met him. I met Frank when I was finishing my undergraduate studies in social science and history. He asked me to join his church staff to lead a youth choir. In time, the position became full-time. My wife, Connie, became the church secretary. I thought I had reached the apex of service until the day Frank said I needed to attend graduate school to prepare for much greater opportunities and impact. The church sent us off to school with wonderful gifts and an encouraging going-away celebration. He became the most significant mentor in my life, the one who launched me into pastoral ministry.

Frank was "Jesus with skin on" to me—as I like to say—and the father I never had. He believed in me and celebrated my gifts and calling. Evelyn and he were dear friends and encouragers over many years. I was able to celebrate his life and our father-son relationship at his home-going celebration in 2015. Evelyn has continued to be a special friend to Connie and me.

This book is the product of my doctoral study on revival and my heart's passionate cry for it. How does revival come? How does "the fire of God fall" across a region or nation? There is a clear pattern, accompanied by consistent characteristics. I invite you to join me in tracing the footprints of God's Spirit—or shall I say, the Holy Spirit's trail of smoke and flame—across the history of revival. I want to light revival fire in your heart.

Chapter 1

A RUMBLING IN THE DISTANCE

G OOD NEWS IS tucked away in biblical and post-biblical
revival history. God has proved Himself faithful through the
centuries (Ps. 89:8; 1 Cor. 1:9). Out of dark and difficult times, when
His people follow the instructions of 2 Chronicles 7:14, He responds
with great spiritual renewal among His people and amazing social
and economic change. All major moves of God through history are
birthed out of difficult times. It's like God's people begin to weep
out of one eye as they observe the darkness, and smile out of the
other eye as they remember God's promise. They seek Him, repent,
and pray. "God is faithful to all his promises and loving toward all
he has made" (Ps. 145:13).

The Church of Jesus Christ has been drifting, slowly at first, but
picking up speed. Secularism and sensuality have been spreading
like a virus across the Western world. America has nearly matched
Europe with its secularism and small percentage of orthodox or
evangelical Christians. The Church, committed followers and servants of Jesus, has declined to only about 7 to 9 percent of the
American population. I believe the Church could rise up and begin
to follow God's renewal instructions. Unless Jesus returns, before
it happens, another Great Awakening or a historic move of God,
a firestorm of revival could be just around history's corner. Why?
Would not God answer the many who are praying and seeking

God "for such a time as this" (Esth. 4:14)? Could He not use the COVID-19 virus pandemic that hit the world in March 2020, to draw more of His people to prayer and repentance for a move of His Spirit? Could the stage already be set?

What's the Concern?

Jesus has made the revival instructions clear, but His Church has not always followed them. She has not been known for loving care and action, despite the bottom line from our Savior: "Love the Lord your God with all your heart and with all your soul and with all your mind. This is the first and greatest commandment. And the second is like it: Love your neighbor as yourself. All the Law and the Prophets hang on these two commandments" (Matt. 22:37–40). With the first coming of Jesus, the New Covenant of love was birthed. It was to be the mark of the Christian, how to act, speak, and think in our world. In other words, it was the fruit of the Holy Spirit that we were to reflect in our culture, or closer to home, with friends and neighbors. The extent or nature of our love was defined for us by Jesus: "As I have loved you, so you must love one another" (John 13:34). Serve and die loving others.

In the National Association of Evangelicals publication, *Evangelicals*, published in the fall of 2015, Richard J. Mouw reminds us that we have a special calling like Israel had:

> When the ancient people of Israel were carried off into captivity in Babylon they wondered how they could maintain their identity as worshipers of the one True God. They had no temple in Babylon ...But when the prophet Jeremiah brings a word from the Lord to them he gives them no excuse to despair. They are to "seek the peace"...of the city in which they are now living in exile ...A similar command was given to the New Testament

church: "Live such good lives among the pagans that, though they accuse you of doing wrong, they may see your good deeds and glorify God on the day he visits us" (1 Peter 2:12). We have new reasons these days to be reminded that we wait for the Lord's return as "exiles." But that is not a basis for retreat to the margins of our culture. To be sure, these are bad times. There is a new and overt hostility toward biblical Christianity...so bad that it is much like the world into which the gospel first came ...And it was in that world where the Lord announced at Pentecost he was pouring out his "Spirit on all people...." The result was that the cause of the gospel flourished. It can flourish, by God's grace, in our own day. [11]

I attend a large Christian fellowship that is intentional about meeting the needs of their community. (If you request "God at Work" above, I'll send you my current list: bggriffin42@gmail.com) In secular culture, I don't believe there is anything as compelling and attractive as sacrificial love in action. God's love, light, and the redemptive servanthood that Jesus modeled speaks volumes to a lost and hurting culture. During the Black Plague, it was the followers of Jesus that took great risks to minister to the needs of the sick and dying. They were the ones who buried the dead. It was the reputation of the Thessalonian church: "We remember before our God and Father your work produced by faith, your labor prompted by love, and your endurance inspired by hope in our Lord Jesus Christ" (1 Thessalonians 1:2-3). They were following the instructions of Jesus (John 13:34–35). Their love and care were compelling.

There is concern about the serious decline of the Church. Could it be that she is losing her passion for being a loving, caring, redemptive force, and becoming institutionalized and self-focused like ancient Israel? As the Western world is picking up speed in the downward slide into sensuality and secularism, what is happening in the Church? In the early 1990s and before, alarm began to be raised by Church leaders. Ten churches in America were either stagnant or dying. Up to 4,000 churches were closing their doors every year, while only 1,500 new churches were started. The United States ranked as the third largest unchurched nation in the world. North America was the only continent where Christianity was not growing. In proportion to the United States population, there were less than half as many churches in 1998 as there were in 1900. The trend has been picking up speed.

Alexander Tyler, a Scottish history professor at the University of Edinburgh, wrote a commentary in 1787 about the fall of the Athenian Republic, 2,000 years earlier. This was about the time America's thirteen original states adopted their new constitution, written by people who at least honored the God of the Bible and believed it was the Word of God. They were a people seeking freedom and democracy. Where has America landed on the list below, and how much responsibility has been laid at her feet? America was birthed at number one. Tyler wrote:

> A democracy is always temporary in nature; it simply cannot exist as a permanent form of government ...The average age of the world's greatest civilizations—from the beginning of history—has been about 200 years. During those 200 years, these nations always progressed through the following sequence:
>
> 1. from bondage to spiritual faith;
> 2. from spiritual faith to great courage;
> 3. from courage to liberty;
> 4. from liberty to abundance;
> 5. from abundance to complacency;
> 6. from complacency to apathy;
> 7. from apathy to dependence; and

8. from dependence back into bondage. [12]

What we say we believe is not what we believe! What we *do* is what we believe. "Wisdom is proved right by her actions" (Matt. 11:19). "Do not merely listen to the Word and so deceive yourselves. Do what it says" (James 1:22). How is the Church doing? We have the weapon of prayer. We have the model of Jesus living, loving, and teaching in an oppressive Roman culture. He doesn't confront Rome, but He comes to build His kingdom in it. How? Jesus gives us the Great Commandment and the Great Commission. We have truth that sets people free. We have the incredible potential of a unified Church. It's what our leader, Jesus, and the Bible, teach us in John 17. It's what the apostle Paul teaches us in Ephesians 4. To follow biblical teaching is as revolutionary as it was in the first century.

Can You Hear a Storm Brewing?

Listen! There's a storm brewing in the distance, but there is good news—a rebirth of hope, an increase of prayer, and the beginnings of change. God is patient and unique, and unexpected events continue to happen. Over centuries of time, we can trace the heart of God as He hears His people calling out in prayer and repentance, and He answers. This is the exciting news tucked away in the history of revival. Prayer movements have been springing up in cities across the nation and the world for well over twenty-five years. Intercessors for America (https://www.facebook.com/IFAPray/) has been mobilizing many to pray online across the nation. Could it be that the Church in her decline has been stirring and is on the move?

Alongside churches that are closing their doors, mega congregations with thousands in attendance have been born. They have changed former ways of "doing church" to reach and transform the culture they serve and are not associated with denominations but are led by gifted leaders who plant congregations that form a network of fellowships and relate to a central leadership team and teachers. Some have seen it as a return to a more apostolic New Testament leadership. Others have concluded it is a fresh approach, a new move of God's Spirit being birthed alongside aging and dying denominations and the closing of old, difficult to maintain church buildings. It is often a new effort to worship with music that unchurched people can appreciate and to teach biblical truth with language that unchurched people can understand. Many of these fellowships have been serving the social needs of their cities. One observer has even called it a "Revolution" [13]

There is a clear pattern of revival throughout history. When things turn dark and difficult for God's people, the instructions are clear. God tells us what to do (2 Chron. 7:14). When God's people obey His instructions, revival comes. It's time to embrace this text and follow God's instructions.

Winds

The late Bill Bright, founder and president of Campus Crusade for Christ, (now CRU, Inc.), began a monthly newsletter in 1994, called "Fasting and Prayer." He had been fasting for forty days. Bright's passion was to urge participation in annual fasting and prayer conferences. Several thousand attended a conference in 1997, and as Dr. Bright looked forward to the 1998 conference in Houston, Texas, he wrote: "Millions of people want to participate in this conference—either on site or by satellite links around the nation." [14] God's people were beginning to break through apathy, to begin to pray and seek His face. Interestingly, Rockford Renewal Ministries, the prayer movement in Rockford, Illinois, was birthed in 1997.

Other movements sprang up about the same time. The Promise Keepers men's movement swept across America in 1997. Well over one million men gathered in the nation's capital for a solemn assembly of prayer and fasting for revival. I was there with my youngest son, Jonathan. At one time, with faces on the ground, over a million men called out to God for revival. We will never forget the experience. It marked our lives. Men's ministries have been birthed from those days, and congregations have been more intentional about ministering to men.

The National Day of Prayer, first established by the Congress of the United States in 1775 and signed into law in 1952, has become a significant event with millions joining the prayer meeting by video broadcast. Believers from many backgrounds have gathered in their cities to pray on this day. Groups across America, like in our city, have held regular city-wide prayer meetings for revival in the Church and the nation. Houses of prayer have been established.

Books on revival and prayer continue to be published and read. In the literature on revival, prayer is the central key, and before you reach the end of this book, it will have been reinforced. Brian Edward's book, *Revival: A People Saturated with God*, is in its fifth printing. Edwards surveys many of the revivals in history to discover common features and to inspire Christians to pray. In his second chapter, "Before Revival," he claims that urgent prayer is the most significant cause of revival. "You cannot read far into the story of a revival without discovering that not only is prayer part of the inevitable result of an outpouring of the Spirit, but from a human standpoint, it is also the single most significant cause." [15]

Edwards grabs the reader's attention when he quotes great revivalists and revival preachers. For example, Matthew Henry, the Puritan leader, commented on Zechariah 12:10: "I will pour out on the house of David and the inhabitants of Jerusalem a spirit of grace and supplication," remarking, "When God intends great mercy for his people, the first thing he does is to set them a-praying." Edwards includes a great word from John Wesley: "God does nothing but in answer to prayer." He adds a statement from Arthur Pierson, for many years the editor of *The Missionary Review*: "From the day of

Pentecost, there has been not one great spiritual awakening in any land which has not begun in a union of prayer, though only among two or three; no such outward, upward movement has continued after such prayer meetings have declined." [16]

Korean Pastor, Paul Yonggi Cho, grew a mega church of prayer. As early as 1984, when his church was growing at the rate of twelve thousand people each month, he wrote *Prayer: the Key to Revival.* [17] Prayer was the key to church growth in Korea. Korea did not have one viable Christian church of any size in 1900. Prayer was the catalyst for a massive move of God in that nation. Korea has been able to claim the largest Methodist church, the largest Pentecostal church, and the largest Presbyterian church in the world.

From the pen of Dutch Sheets came *Intercessory Prayer: How God Can Use Your Prayers to Move Heaven and Earth.* In the introduction of Sheets's book, C. Peter Wagner summarized the growth of the prayer movement, saying that the modern prayer movement began around 1970. It had been growing in Korea for decades, but it also began to spread worldwide.[18]

Mission America was born out of an International Congress on Worldwide Evangelization in Lausanne, Switzerland, first held in 1974 and again in 1989. The congress produced "The Lausanne Covenant." It was and remains a doctrinal statement and commitment between Christians from one hundred fifty nations of the world, to unify to reach the world for Christ. [19] Their first brochure included a quote from the late Evangelist Billy Graham saying: "As we approach the dawn of a new millennium, our country stands in great need of a genuine spiritual awakening." Mission America created "Celebrate Jesus 2000" with a goal to pray for, and share Jesus with every person in the nation. The goal was not reached, but great progress has been made. The birth of "All.America" and "All.World" in 2019, mentioned in the introduction, was the next wave of this effort. It reflected a growing passion for revival and for turning America back to God and to reach the peoples of the world with the Gospel. Major ministries gave leadership to the movement, including, Go 2020, America Prays, CRU, First Priority, YWAM, Impact World, American Bible Society, Every Home for Christ, and others. Among the leaders of these ministries, there was a strong sense that America and other nations were being given a *reprieve*, a time to seriously spread the Gospel, to obey the Great Commandment, and the Great Commission. There was a consensus that it was time to:

o   Pray for everyone in the world, nations, and cities;
o   Connect everyone to Jesus;
o   Serve social needs in the name of Jesus;
o   Connect everyone to the Bible; and
o   Connect everyone to Christian community. [20]

This exciting movement in our city was called All.Rockford. Leaders met in March 2020 to organize their engagement. Shortly after that meeting, the COVID-19 pandemic began to spread world-wide. Activities of all kinds came to a halt or at least were affected negatively. "Non-essential" businesses were closed. People were told to only leave their homes for necessary food and supplies. It seemed like the enemy was trying to shut the movement down, but God's power has always trumped Satan's. He has often used the darkest of times to birth revival. Understanding the promise of 2 Chronicles 7:14, I began to ask God to use this crisis to birth a massive move of His Spirit across the world and her cities. The pandemic could be used to birth a move of God.

Another initiative of Mission America was to identify and encourage "City Reachers." Before God called Connie and me to form Rockford Renewal Ministries, we had never heard of such people. However, early in our ministry, we learned that's what we were. Others like us were being called. We were invited to a meeting in Colorado, and without an agenda, we sat around tables to share God's calling and what was happening in our cities.

These are challenging days, but this is not the time to slack off or give up. It is time to intensify our prayer efforts. It is time to increase our intentional efforts for the unity of the Church. Although God has every right to discipline His Church, His mercy triumphs over judgment (James 2:13). We must continue to follow the instructions of 2 Chronicles 7:14. We cannot let a pandemic distract us, but instead attract us to new passion and vision. The Church must embrace bulldog tenacity. Bulldog's noses are set back far enough so they can grab someone's leg, hold on for a long time, and still breathe. Pacing in our efforts is important, but our passion must not wane at this critical juncture in history. *Listen! Can you hear the wind of the Holy Spirit in the distance?*

Chapter 2

TRACKING THE STORMS

THE FILM, *TWISTER*, is a nail-biter! Highly motivated, risk-taking scientists chase tornadoes because, in theory, we can know how to deal with these monsters if we understand them. However, one gets the idea that this is as much about adventure as it is about science. Still, it's helpful science—I think. Study the storms. Create theories. Test them. What conditions generate them? How can they be managed? How can early warning systems be built and disasters avoided?

Tracking the history of revival, the powerful wind and fire of the Holy Spirit, is like tracking tornadoes. How does revival come? What conditions generate it? Is there a consistent pattern? Does the move of God's Spirit in recent history follow the move of God's Spirit in the Bible? Let's track these firestorms together. It's a great adventure.

The timing of both tornadoes and revival is unpredictable. Although God's people can prepare for revival, we can't put God in a box, and we can't dictate how He will work. Like storm chasers, people in revival settings do some strange things, what some may call excesses. They are easily caught up in the power of the Spirit's storm. Each revival is distinct, and yet there are similarities. If we can identify the characteristics, if we can understand what brings on the storm—the fire and wind of revival—we can prepare for it.

If we can understand why revivals fade, maybe we can keep them burning longer.

History demonstrates how revival has happened and how it will happen again. The Old Testament is a great starting place to trace the move of God. Time and again, God's people drifted into rebellion or were sucked into the cultures that surrounded them. When things became unbearable, they began to seek God, repent, and once again obey him. Revival came, and they enjoyed the covenant blessings of God and fulfilled His exciting redemptive purposes. Psalm 106 is one of the sad summaries of Israel's up-and-down history. Read it and weep. Look at the Western world today. Weep again.

In the New Testament, after four hundred years of biblical silence, God sent a storm chaser, his prophet, John the Baptist. God's people had become encrusted with tradition and dangerously detached from His purposes. With passion and power, John preached repentance. He stayed on the outskirts of the city where people flocked to hear him. Many were baptized in the Jordan River to symbolize their repentance. It was revival. Jesus came on the scene. He taught about the kingdom of God and showed them how to live. He sacrificed His life in death by yielding to a hideous Roman crucifixion promoted by God's people. He arose from the dead, conquering Satan, death, and hell. He was caught up to the Father's right hand after promising the coming of the Holy Spirit.

As one hundred twenty followers of Jesus met in unity and prayer, the Holy Spirit burst onto the scene. Tongues of fire appeared on their heads. Talk about a historic move of God! Mighty rushing winds—a storm of massive proportions—swept through Jerusalem with a roar. People were drawn to the scene. It happened to be a high holy day, and people from all over the known world were in the city. As they gathered, they heard the good news about Jesus the Messiah in their own language. Three thousand received Him as their Savior and Messiah. It was New Testament revival. Similar moves of God's Spirit followed.

We can know how the fire ignites. Twelve moves of God can be found in the Old Testament and eight in the New Testament. Major revivals of more recent history follow the same pattern. Let's track these firestorms. The lists of revivals we will study are as follows:

Old Testament Revivals
As They Appear in the Scripture in Chronological Order

1. Jacob—Genesis 35:1–15
2. Moses—Exodus 32–33
3. Samuel—1 Samuel 7:1–13
4. Elijah—1 Kings 18 Asa
5. Joash—2 Kings 11–12Elijah
6. Hezekiah—2 Kings 18:4–7; 2 Chronicles 29–31 Jehoshaphat
7. Josiah—2 Kings 22–23; 2 Chronicles 34–35 Joash
8. Asa—2 Chronicles 15:1–15 Jonah (scholarship date, 722 BC)
9. Jehoshaphat—2 Chronicles 17:6–9 Hezekiah
10. Zerubbabel, Haggai; Zechariah—Ezra 5–6 Josiah
11. Ezra, Nehemiah—Nehemiah 8–10; 12:44–47 Zerubbabel, Haggai, Zechariah
12. Jonah in Nineveh—Jon. 1–4 Ezra, Nehemiah

New Testament Revivals

1. Awakening under John the Baptist Matthew 3:1–12
2. The revival at Pentecost Acts 2:1–4, 14–47
3. Revival in the church Acts 4:23–37
4. Revival that grew out of fear Acts 5:1–16
5. The revival that grew out of persecution Acts 7:54–8:25
6. The revival with Cornelius and the Gentiles Acts 10:23–48
7. The Pisidia Antioch revival Acts 13:13–52
8. The revival at Ephesus Acts 19:1–22

Post-biblical Revivals

1. The First Great Awakening 1726–1756
2. The Second Great Awakening1776–1810
3. The New York City Prayer Meeting Revival1857–1858
4. The Welsh Revival1904
5. The Azusa Street Revival1906–1909

Ten themes have characterized the firestorms of biblical and post-biblical history. In my reading and research, I have not found exceptions, only variations on these themes:

1. Revival occurred in times of personal or national crisis and great spiritual need, and in times of moral darkness and spiritual decline among God's people, Israel, or his Church.
2. Revival began in the heart(s) of one or more consecrated servants of God, who became the agent(s) God used to lead His people back to faith and obedience.
3. Prayer was central to revival. Leaders called out to God in prayer, passionately seeking His face in repentance and in the confession of their personal and national sins. They ignited prayer among God's people.
4. Revival rested upon the powerful proclamation—preaching and teaching—of the law of God and His Word. Many of the revivals were the result of a return to the Scripture.
5. Revival in the Old Testament reflected the work of God the Father to awaken his people, Israel, to a restored relationship with Him, to obey Him, and serve his redemptive purpose. Revival in the New Testament and post-biblical history reflected the work of the Holy Spirit in miracles and in the equipping of people for ministry. It resulted in the spread of the gospel and the growth of the Church.
6. Revival was marked by a return to the worship of God.

7. Revival led to repentance and the destruction of idols and ungodly preoccupations, and to turning away from personal and corporate sin.
8. Revival brought a return to the offering of blood sacrifices in the Old Testament and a concentration on the death, resurrection, and return of Jesus Christ in the New Testament—celebrated in the Lord's Supper.
9. Revival resulted in an experience of exuberant joy and gladness among the people of God.
10. Revival was followed by a period of blessing and area-wide transformation that produced spiritual, social, and economic reform.

This is how revival fire ignites and spreads. We have much more to learn as we chase God's firestorms. The story of Israel's history and the Church of Jesus Christ is the story of drift, a condition that sets up the first characteristic of revival. Because of God's mercy and grace, He calls His people back to Himself time and again, back to their first love (Eph. 2:4). Most often, they are suffering the terrible consequences of their sins when He sends someone to call them back to obedience and intimacy with Him.

God will not allow His redemptive purposes through His people to be thwarted for long. What is His call? It follows His words to the Churches of Laodicea: "'Here I am! I stand at the door and knock. If anyone hears my voice and opens the door, I will come in and eat with him, and he with me" (Rev. 3:20). This is the key to revival. Obedience to God's instructions in 2 Chronicles 7:14 "opens the door." It is time for America to open the door, to follow God's Word, and to enter in.

> *God's plan was never to allow us to be passive bystanders, but to give us a strategic and fulfilling part to play, to be an important part of His great redemptive plan. It has never changed.* —Bob Griffin

Chapter 3

WEATHER PATTERNS AND GOD'S HEART FOR REVIVAL

IN 2004, SEVERAL severe tropical storms hit the coast of Florida like consecutive punches from a hard-hitting boxer. In some areas, people were just getting on their feet, dealing with loss and assessing the damage, when another storm hit. Were the storms a shift in the weather patterns? Did the jet stream change?

At the end of 2004 a violent earthquake in the Indian Ocean spawned one of history's most destructive tsunamis, causing damage into the billions of dollars and taking the lives of over 300,000 people. On January 6, 2005, *CBS Evening News* aired a special report, asking about the role of God in the quake and the resulting killer waves.[21] Was He behind this natural disaster? Was it a freak of nature? There was no conclusive answer, only a range of opinions from theologically diverse perspectives. Scientists were asked if there was any way to predict and track such phenomena. Were patterns available? The scientists who were interviewed reported that small efforts were in place, but those who were watching for tsunamis were caught by surprise.

We can count on some weather patterns, especially those that follow the seasons, spring, summer, fall, and winter, but within those, there's a lot of forecasting that we depend on to shape our activities. What patterns can be traced before a "firestorm of revival?" What conditions spawn a mighty rushing wind of the Spirit? What's the pattern of restoration? Before we examine the ten characteristics of God's firestorms, it is important to look at some theological meteorology. There are seasons of spiritual drought and great storms of spiritual renewal. As we study to know God, we learn about His heart for redemption and for the renewal of His people. God is sovereign, and yet He allows mankind considerable freedom, even to change the course of history. In dark and difficult times, revival comes when God's people return to him.

The Bible records a great cry for revival in Psalm 85:6. "Will you not revive us again, that your people may rejoice in you?" Notice the word *again*. God answers the prayers of His people for revival when they follow His instructions.

Another passionate call for revival comes from the prophet, Isaiah. Out of desperation he prays, "Oh, that you would rend the heavens and come down, that the mountains would tremble before you! *As when fire sets twigs ablaze and causes water to boil*, come down to make your name known" (Isa. 64:1–2). The prophet was desperate for a firestorm in his day. God had intervened in the past and had answered the desperate prayers of His people. "Do it again!" He was writing in dark and difficult times. Would God answer as He had in the past? How long would God be patient with the pattern—His people flourishing, then drifting; disaster; repentance; then spiritual, social, and economic restoration as they repented, humbled themselves, and returned to Him? Again and again, apostasy was a dark thread woven through the redemptive history of God's people.

We appear to be closing in on such a time in America and the Western world. What can we anticipate from God in our time? We must embrace Isaiah's prayer, his cry for our time. God will answer us if we persist in repentance and passionate prayer.

What will a revived Church look like? She will be passionately fulfilling the Great Commandment—to love God with all we are and have, and love others as we love ourselves—our vision and passion (Matt. 22:37–39; John 13:34). She will be passionately fulfilling the Great Commission—speaking God's truth clearly and lovingly, not in anger, judgment, or condemnation, but in the power of the Holy Spirit (Acts 1:8; Matt. 28:19–20). She will carry the mark of the Christian, love, the oil that lubricates the truth.

There is a problem when the Church measures herself by herself—size, programs, media, or other churches nearby—rather than by the New Testament, and fulfilling the Great Commandment and the Great Commission. She must embrace the unity of John 17 and Ephesians 4 to be a mobilized force for God, good and loving her cities. A better measurement is to ask how many people are coming to Christ, embracing God's great love, and growing in their faith.

Another evaluation point is to ask how closely God's people reflect Jesus. The Church will never see her cities transformed until her people are growing into the likeness of Jesus, until the fruit of the Holy Spirit (Gal. 5:23–24) and the Beatitudes (Matt. 5:1–12) characterize God's people. Rhonda Hughey, writes, "The issue isn't about having enough Christians to do Kingdom business; rather, the issue is finding Christians who have passed through the fire and now look, talk, and smell like Jesus." [22]

What Is Revival?

Revival is to take something back to its original purpose. What is God's ordained purpose for His people and human history? Let's push the rewind button all the way back to the beginning. When God created us, He gave us dominion over the creation (Gen. 1:26–28; Ps. 8:3–8).

> Let us make man in our image, in our likeness, and let them rule over the fish of the sea and the birds of the air, over the livestock, over all the earth, and over all the

creatures that move along the ground. So God created man in his own image, in the image of God he created him; male and female he created them. God blessed them and said to them, "Be fruitful and increase in number; fill the earth and subdue it. Rule over the fish of the sea and the birds of the air and over every living creature that moves on the ground." (Gen. 1:26–28)

God created people in His image for relationship with Himself. In the Garden of Eden, they walked freely in the cool of the day with God. There was only one tree in the garden that gave them the opportunity to disobey, to exercise their free will, and break their relationship with their Creator. They were clearly warned about the dire consequences of eating the tree's fruit. To do so would mean death, spiritual separation from their Creator, and breaking their intimate sin-free fellowship with Him. The deceiver, Satan, questioned God's instructions, and they exercised their free will to disobey. Forced to leave the pristine garden, Adam and Eve struggled to live under the curses shaped by their sin and to be targets of Satan's nefarious purposes. This enmity between God and mankind has played out across human history and across the heart of every person.

God revealed His gracious care for people by clothing Adam and Eve before they were removed from the garden (Gen. 3:21). He promised a redeemer: "And I will put enmity between you and the woman, and between your offspring and hers; he will crush your head, and you will strike his heel." Jesus fulfilled this promise in His death and resurrection. He defeated Satan, death, and hell. He opened the way for mankind to be restored to God, their Creator.

From the beginning, God's plan was to give us a strategic and fulfilling role to play in redemption. As we embraced God's salvation, we became His redeemed redemptive agents, one of life's greatest privileges. It has always remained the most exciting reason to live, to get out of bed each morning to be a part of what God was doing in the world. The Israelites were called to this purpose when God established a covenant with Abraham, the first agent of God's redemptive purpose. Sad to say, the history of God's chosen people became a tragic roller-coaster ride. Twelve times they drifted in and out of their relationship with God and their service for Him. Their acts of repentance were followed by His restoration, His blessings, and His covenant promises. They returned to redemptive service, and God's plan marched on with new force. Then they drifted from Him again and suffered spiritual, social, and economic decline, even so far as to sacrifice their babies to idols (Ezek. 16:15–29).

God's covenants with Israel found their ultimate fulfillment in the coming of Jesus, Israel's Messiah. He was the eternal Son of God in human flesh, God incarnate, the Savior, the Son of David, and the "I AM," the self-existent one. Demonstrating His deity with phenomenal signs, wonders, and miracles, He proclaimed the Good News of God's kingdom and modeled it by the way He lived. Toward the end of his three short years of ministry, the religious and political tide turned against Jesus. He was brutally tortured and crucified on a Roman cross. A large bolder sealed the entry to the borrowed tomb in which He was buried, but the grave couldn't hold him. Death died in His magnificent resurrection. Fellowship with God and eternal life were the gifts He provided for all who would accept His death as the sacrifice for their sin (John 3:16, 1:12; Eph. 2:8–9).

After Jesus's return to the right hand of the Father, the Church was born and took up God's redemptive kingdom cause. In obedience to his instructions, the early Christ-followers met to wait in the upper room. They gathered together in unity and prayer. Just as He promised, they were clothed with power from on high. The Holy Spirit came like a mighty rushing wind, and tongues of fire rested on their heads. He came with power and gifts to serve God's kingdom cause. All of His followers became redemptive agents.

With Jesus as their head, they were the second incarnation—His body, living and active on earth again.

The pattern of drift in the Old Testament, could be seen in the first century. The church in Galatia had slipped back from grace into Jewish legalism. Paul wrote to correct them. In the letters to churches in Revelation 2 and 3, most of the churches could be affirmed in some areas. All but two, Smyrna and Philadelphia, had drifted into error or had become cool in their love for God. The church in Ephesus lost her first love. Some in Pergamum were embracing the teaching of Balaam and the Nicolaitans. Some in Thyatira were being drawn into sexual immorality by a prophetess named Jezebel. The church of Sardis had a reputation for doing good deeds and being alive, but God saw their hearts. They were dead. Perhaps they were like the church in Laodicea that was known for good deeds but was lukewarm spiritually. In about AD 95, the apostle John wrote to these churches calling them back to obedience and a passion for serving God's redemptive purposes.

The story moved forward through the centuries, from spiritual vitality and spiritual impact to drift and disobedience, or just apathy about God's plan. When things became bad spiritually, socially, and economically, if they humbled themselves, prayed, sought God for restoration, and repented, restoration—revival came.

What is revival?

> **Revival is a spontaneous spiritual awakening by God the Holy Spirit among His people. It comes in answer to their humble prayers as they passionately seek His face and repent of their sins. The awakening results in deepened intimacy with God, passion for Him, holy living, evangelism, and citywide or area-wide transformation, expressed through social reform.**

The Hebrew Word

The word commonly translated "revived" or "revival" in the Old Testament is the Hebrew word, *chayah* (*khaw-yaw*). Its primary root meaning is "to live," or to make alive, and includes "quicken, recover, repair, and restore (to life), to revive." The prayer for revival in Psalm 85:6 sums up the result: "Will you not revive us again, that your people may rejoice in you?" It's a snapshot of revival. Habakkuk uses the word in a similar prayer (3:2): "Lord, I have heard of your fame; I stand in awe of your deeds, O Lord. Renew them in our day." The King James Version translates renew as "revive."

Revival in the Old Testament brought Israel back to God and to her redemptive calling, just like God promised in 2 Chronicles 7:14. The Old Testament sacrifices were a picture of the perfect Lamb of God who would, one day, come to pay for the sins of Israel and the whole world. Through this sacrificial system, their eternal salvation was by grace through faith in God's promise of a Savior, the Lamb of God, sacrificed for the salvation of all peoples.

In contrast, the Church has looked back by faith to the death and resurrection of the Lamb, the Messiah, Jesus Christ, slain before the foundation of the world. Both Israel and the Church were to proclaim God's redemption, live in intimacy with Him, and serve His redemptive purposes.

God's People, Israel, on a Mission

God's people Israel were on a mission, just like the Church today. Revival in the Old Testament, was critical to the accomplishment of God's plan of redemption. Much was at stake when Israel drifted from God and neglected her calling. They had an eternal God-given identity and a unique destiny that they agreed it. God kept his part of the covenants with His people, but His people didn't keep theirs.

God promised Abraham that all the nations of the earth would be blessed through Israel. She was a missionary nation long before Jesus and Paul in the New Testament. Isaiah the prophet wrote: This is what the LORD says, "In the time of my favor I will answer you, and in the day of salvation I will help you; I will keep you and will make you to be a covenant for the people, to restore the land and to reassign its desolate inheritances, to say to the captives, 'Come out,' and to those in darkness, 'Be free!' They will feed beside the roads and find pasture on every barren hill" (Isa. 49:8–9).

The people of Israel were the servants of Lord (Lev. 25:42, 55; Isa. 54:17), a picture of Jesus the Messiah—the Servant King. Redemption was foreshadowed through their sacred life of sacrifices, festivals, and temple services. They were to demonstrate the nature of God and His redemptive purpose through their community of faith. In Galatians 3:15–16, Paul the apostle, wrote that the promise made to Abraham and to his seed was Jesus Christ. Jesus perfectly fulfilled God's plan and purpose for Israel. He was the nation personified, its perfect expression. Servanthood and service were perfected in Him. The priesthood reached perfection in Him, the Great High Priest. He was the Son of Man, the Messiah of Israel, sent from God the Father. God's revelation reached its apex in Jesus, and history found its ultimate meaning, the redemption of the fallen world.

Solomon's prayer at the temple dedication rehearsed Israel's mission. It said the foreigners who did not belong to Israel were to hear of God's great name and come from a distance to pray to Him. Solomon instructed:

> As for the foreigner who does not belong to your people Israel, but has come from a distant land because of your name...when they come and pray toward this temple, then hear from heaven, your dwelling place, and do whatever the foreigner asks of you, so that all the peoples

of the earth may know your name and fear you, as do your own people Israel, and may know that this house I have built bears your Name. (1 Kgs. 8:41–43).

The fulfillment of God's promise to Abraham is described in Zechariah 2:11: "Many nations will be joined with the Lord in that day and will become my people. Zion's King will proclaim peace to the nations. His rule will extend from sea to sea and from the River to the ends of the earth." In Malachi 1:11, God declares, "My name will be great among the nations, from the rising to the setting of the sun."

The redemptive plan of God is a grand symphony that is played through both the Old and New Testaments. Paul the apostle rehearses the music:

Consider Abraham: "He believed God, and it was credited to him as righteousness." Understand, then, that those who believe are children of Abraham. The Scripture foresaw that God would justify Gentiles by faith, and announced the gospel in advance to Abraham: "All nations will be blessed through you." So those who have faith are blessed along with Abraham, the man of faith. (Gal. 3:6–9)

I once sat under the teaching of the late George Ladd, theologian and professor of theology, and one of the Church's most informed students on the kingdom of God. Ladd taught that Israel had been the possessor of the kingdom of God. Until the coming of Christ in human flesh, God's redemptive activity in history had been channeled through them as a nation. The residual blessings of God on earth were poured out on Israel and channeled through them. Gentiles could share these blessings only by entering into relationship with Israel. The time came for God to show his redemptive activity through the New Covenant. The kingdom of God visited men in the person of God's Son and brought them a fuller measure of the blessings of His divine plan. The kingdom in its new form was given to all those who would receive Jesus as Christ and Savior. These new people were the Church—"a chosen race, a royal priesthood, a holy nation" (1 Pet. 2:9). [23]

God's People, the Church, on a Mission

If we want a complete view of revival—a theology of revival—it is necessary to consider more than just the accounts of revival. We need to understand more about how God works in response to His people and the dark thread of "driftitis" that is so pervasive throughout their history. Why does God continue to pursue them? Frances Thompson, an English poet, calls God "the Hound of Heaven." This is the old, old story—a gracious story of God's love. [24]

The dark thread that runs through redemptive history, also runs through the heart of every person. It is the thread of our fallen nature, the evil in the heart of every individual that we inherited from Adam and Eve. It's in our DNA.

History's Big Picture

Before God created mankind, He created Satan with an element of free will and enough choice to be destroyed by his own pride. Satan declared, "I will be like the most high." He was driven out of the presence of God to earth (Ezek. 28:17). As the prideful god of this world, he has tried to destroy the work of God. Tragically, God's people—also created with a free will—have been attracted to pride. It has been like an old pop lyric, "I'll do it my way." Satan became the embodiment of evil, all that is opposed to God and His holiness, righteousness, goodness, and love. Satan became the personification and perpetrator of evil.

Other angels, some of high rank, joined with him. They were identified with Satan in Ephesians 6:12 as "principalities...powers...rulers of the darkness of this world...spiritual wickedness in high places" (KJV). They have served Satan's evil opposition and his overt and subtle promotion of sin night and day, seeking to draw people into bondage and away from God's truth and freedom. Satan has been out to devour and deceive those created in God's image (1 Pet. 5:8). However, God's truth has empowered Christ's followers to discern the enemy's deceitful ways and has set them free. We have been given the power to resist him, and when we do, he must flee (James 4:7). God's authoritative truth, the Bible, and the powerful name of Jesus, have empowered us to discern and defeat our enemy. God's truth has been the power to set us free (John 8:32).

God made us in His own image, not as robots, but with personhood and free will. When Satan tempted Adam and Eve to use their free will to sin against God, they chose to break the pristine intimacy that they enjoyed with God in the perfect environment of the Garden of Eden. We inherited the problem and went down with them. In perfect justice, holiness, and righteousness, God had to expel Adam and Eve from the garden. Not only did mankind fall, but nature did as well. We inherited not only a sinful nature, but we inherited a sin-cursed earth.

What if our sin and the curse of the earth were the end of the human story? The good news is that God set out to accomplish the redemption of those He created, to restore them to loving intimacy with Himself, and to provide an eternal new heaven and earth for them.

The great story of redemption rolls through time, reaching its apex in the life, death, and resurrection of Jesus. It is the Gospel, the Good News. Without the shedding of blood, there is not, and never has been, remission for man's sin (Heb. 9:22). Jesus is the Lamb of God sacrificed before the foundation of the world (Rev. 5:12; 13:8), once for all (Heb. 10:26). He is the payment for the penalty of our sin, and we must personally accept His payment. Jesus bridged the gap that sin brought between God and His creation. He established the possibility for a relationship between God and man. By embracing his provision of salvation, the redeemed followers of Jesus have joined the great army of kingdom agents who have served God's eternal purposes in the world. They have been the agents of redemption. This good news story has been summarized in two of the best-known biblical texts:

> For God so loved the world that he gave his one and only Son, that whoever believes in him shall not perish but have eternal life. For God did not send his Son into the world to condemn the world, but to save the world through him. Whoever believes in him is not condemned, but whoever does not believe stands condemned already because he has not believed in the name of God's one and only Son. (John 3:16–18)

> For it is by grace you have been saved, through faith— and this not from yourselves, it is the gift of God—not by works, so that no one can boast. For we are God's workmanship, created in Christ Jesus to do good works, which God prepared in advance for us to do. (Eph. 2:8–10)

This is the Gospel, the Good News. It's this message that the Church of Jesus Christ is to take to the entire world in every generation. One's response of repentance and personal faith in Jesus Christ provides forgiveness for the sin that separates everyone from Him (Eph. 2:8–9; Rom. 10:9–12). All fallen and sinful generations need this salvation (Rom. 3:23; 6:23). The Good News doesn't end there, though. Receiving Christ as Savior and Lord has a wonderful bonus. The Holy Spirit of God comes to indwell those who trust in him as their Savior. His presence creates a new spiritual nature and empowers them with wonderful spiritual gifts (Eph. 4:7–13; 1 Cor. 12:4–11; Rom. 12:3–8). The Greek root word *charis* is translated "grace." [25] We are able to grace others through the gifting of the Spirit. With these tools, every redeemed person is called to serve God's redemptive purpose until Jesus returns. They are His bride, the Church (Matt. 28:16–20; Acts 1:1–11).

One of the best-written philosophies of life for the followers of Jesus comes from the apostle Paul, and he defines maturity for us in Philippians 3:7–15 (emphasis added):

> But whatever was to my profit I now consider loss for the sake of Christ. What is more, I consider everything a loss compared to the surpassing greatness of knowing Christ Jesus my Lord, for whose sake I have lost all things. I consider them rubbish...not having a righteousness of my own that comes from the law, but that which is through faith in Christ. I want to know Christ and the power of his resurrection and the fellowship of sharing in his sufferings ...Not that I have obtained all this, or have already been made perfect (mature), but I press on to take hold of that for which Christ Jesus took hold of me ...One thing I do: Forgetting what is behind and straining toward what is ahead, I press on toward the goal to win the prize for which God has called me heavenward in Christ Jesus. All of us who are *mature* should take such a view of things.

Paul understood that knowing Christ and capturing God's purpose for his life was his highest good and ultimate fulfillment. Notice, so you don't get discouraged, that Paul hadn't arrived yet or become perfect. Paul spoke for all of us who have embraced Jesus as our Savior and Lord and want to be God's redemptive agents in our lost world day by day. He taught us to lay down the past and press on to God's high calling. *This process or spiritual journey is maturity.* Our perfection has never been in the picture.

Who Initiates Revival?

As we consider the theology of revival, we must ask an age-old question: Does revival come as a result of our obedience to 2 Chronicles 7:14, or does God initiate it? The answer is a mystical "yes!" The text is conditional: if—then. God will not respond unless we repent and seek His face. On the other hand, given our human bent to sin, it seems that we would never take the initiative.

God gave Israel the Promised Land. It was a gift, but she had to form an army and fight for it. She had to wage aggressive battles at the cost of sacrifice and loss. We were called to serve God, to love those around us, and share the Good News, but it has always been God who has drawn people to salvation (John 6:44–65; 12:32). From the Bible, we have known that apart from God, we can do nothing (John 15:5). God has empowered and directed our service and accomplished His purpose through us.

Dr. David Larsen, the chair of my doctoral committee, blends our responsibility with God's sovereignty, God's activity and initiative, and ours. He quotes Isaiah 64:1: "Oh, that you would rend the heavens and come down, that the mountains would tremble before you!" Then he writes:

> Among the issues widely discussed in relation to revival, one stands above all others: From where does revival come? We long to see and experience that supernatural visitation which Scripture and history excite us to seek. To listen to Jonathan Edwards the answer seems clear: God does it! To read Charles Finney the answer seems clear: It is up to us! The Scriptures make it clear that there are spiritual laws governing revival and that if we

29

conform to the rules we shall experience the desire of our hearts. Each viewpoint conveys needed truth. All of us must recognize that revival lies within the sovereignty of God. God must do it! This truth preserves us from despair and an overwhelming burden when things are dry. God sees all and knows all, and hope for revival depends upon Him. But that is only one aspect of the reality. Just as we must maintain the tension between divine sovereignty and human responsibility, between the "three-ness" and the oneness of God, between the divine and the human natures of our Lord in the hypostatic union, so we must maintain both God's divine initiative and the significance of our response to Him. Second Chronicles 7:14 does say, "If my people...." There are conditions for revival ...Even the most ardent Calvinist preaches that prayer is necessary preparation for revival. We must affirm both divine sovereignty and human responsibility in revival. [26]

G. Campbell Morgan, adds. "We cannot organize revival, but we can set our sails to catch the wind from heaven when God chooses to blow upon His people once again." [27] In *Rain from Heaven,* Arthur Wallis writes:

Revival can never be explained in terms of activity or organization, personality or preaching ...It is essentially a manifestation of God ...We cannot explain or understand Him in His holiness and sovereignty, and for that reason we cannot really completely understand revival. The wind blows where it wills. Though we do not understand its vagaries we may still 'trim the sail' and work with it. To move with God in the day of His power means understanding and conforming to those principles by which He has chosen to work. [28]

Revival comes in God's time when His people have fulfilled certain conditions. "Return to me and I will return to you" (Mal. 3:7). God's promise is conditioned on obedience as in 2 Chronicles 7:14—If you will...then I will. From there, it becomes a matter of God's timing. There is creative tension between our part and God's. If we move too far in the direction of God's sovereignty, we could easily become apathetic. If we go too far in the direction of our responsibility, we could easily become crushed by it.

The Doctrine of Revival

A common body of belief accompanies historic revival, and it helps to have scholars like J. Edwin Orr lay it out for us. He gives us a formal statement that shaped the move of God in revival during the eighteenth and nineteenth centuries. It reemphasizes basic New Testament teaching. According to Orr, it is the original doctrinal statement of the Evangelical Alliance in 1846, a unified fellowship of biblically orthodox Christians who wanted to strengthen global mission movements and networks. Here is the statement. [29]

I. The divine Inspiration, Authority and sufficiency of the Holy Scriptures, and the right and duty of Private Judgment in the interpretation thereof;

II. The Unity of the Godhead, and the Trinity of Persons therein;

III. The utter Depravity of Human Nature, in consequence of the Fall;

IV. The Incarnation of the son of God, His work of Atonement for sinners of mankind, and His mediatorial Intercession and Reign;

V. The Justification of the sinner by Faith alone;

VI. The work of the Holy Spirit in the Conversion and Sanctification of the sinner;

VII. The Resurrection of the Body, the Judgment of the world by the Lord Jesus Christ, the Eternal Blessedness of the righteous, and the Eternal Punishment of the Wicked.

According to the history of post-biblical revival, there was no departure from these statements. "It was so widely adopted," says Orr, "that it led to a practice of fraternal fellowship having the force of a major doctrine."

All things considered, the nineteenth-century Awakening represented no great discovery or rediscovery of doctrine. Its theology was largely that of the New Testament stated in the language of the reformers and the Revivalists of an earlier century. The real contribution of the Awakening was its application of these doctrines in the evangelization of the great mass of unchurched at home and the heathen abroad [30]

Earl Cairns, in *An Endless Line of Splendor: Revivals and Their Leaders from the Great Awakening to the Present*, states:

> All revivalists, whether Calvinists (God's Sovereignty) or Armenians (man's free will), affirmed the sovereignty of God as Creator and Redeemer. They emphasized God's holiness and justice, before which sinful man must quake as the Israelites did before Sinai. No revival leader had difficulty with the idea that all men are sinners. They believed everyone was guilty of original and actual sin. [31]

Theological differences between Wesley and Whitfield, and Finney and Nettleton, did not stop them from agreeing on the main doctrines of biblical faith. They disagreed in love and went on preaching salvation." [32]

Three Igniting Sparks

When I was much younger, camping was a special treat. It usually had to do with fishing, and I was usually skunked—no fish! After a brief effort at fishing without success, I would go catch little crabs or climb rocks. Campfires were the greatest. We cooked fish—not mine—over an open fire. One of my memories was a serious caution about the campfire. "Be careful around the campfire and be careful to watch that sparks do not hit the tent. They can burn the tent and all our gear, or even worse, ignite dry brush, even begin a forest fire."

What does God use to light fire in His people, to ignite the dry brush of an apathetic Church? In this case, revival is like a forest fire, a "firestorm" of the Holy Spirit. Three sparks—pain, proclamation, and prayer—seem to be particularly incendiary and are frequently used by God. All three are equally involved in the birth of revival, and they are central to the ten characteristics of revival.

Pain

Difficult circumstances were what Solomon asked God about in 2 Chronicles 7. Israel's history shows that they began to call out to God at the low state of their spiritual condition. When life was falling apart and circumstances were dark, they began to look for answers in the law of God. The same kind of setting has drawn the Church back to prayer and the Word of God. They humbled themselves, called out to Him in passionate prayer, and turned from their sinful ways (vs.14). God heard from heaven, forgave their sin, and healed their land. The same kind of circumstances have drawn the Church back to prayer when they obeyed this historic revival text. Revival was birthed out of painful difficult circumstances. There appear to have been no exceptions.

Prayer

Prayer has always been central to revival. R. A. Torrey wrote, "There have been revivals without much preaching, but there has never been a mighty revival without mighty prayer." [33] Prayer has been the most consistent spark that ignites revival. Charles Spurgeon said, "If we are importunate (passionately persistent) in prayer, it must happen again ...Preaching is beginning at the wrong end. Instead thereof, we ought to hold meetings of prayer." [34]

In his book, *Eight Keys to Revival*, Lewis Drummond says that leaders have stressed prayer or intercession almost to a fault. He continues: "But still we do not pray, or at least we do not pray very much ...But if we will pray, if we will get before God personally, if we will develop prayer groups, if church leaders will organize a vital prayer ministry...then God will surely show us His plan...a vital means of producing spiritual awakening. God is far more ready to give than we are to receive." [35]

Brian Edwards writes powerfully about the importance of prayer in revival:

> Historically the church has prayed its way to the outpouring of God's Holy Spirit ...You cannot read far into the story of a revival without discovering that not only is prayer part of the inevitable result of an outpouring of the Spirit, but, from a human standpoint, it is also the single most significant cause. Those whom God uses in revival are men and women of prayer. That is their great priority. And this is true of a community also. If we really want God in revival, we must ask for it. Praying for revival is not enough: we must long for it, and long for it intensely. [36]

In her book, *Flames of Revival,* Elana Lynse, identified the cycles of revival as cycles of prayer. For example, her study led her to believe that the Moravian Prayer Vigil of 1727 could be accredited with the Frelinghuysen revival in New Jersey, the ministry of Jonathan Edwards in 1734, and the ministries of Wesley and Whitfield in 1739. She identified fifty years of Concerts of Prayer beginning in 1792 and concluded that they produced the frontier revival of the 1800s, the formation of missionary societies, the ministry of Charles Finney, and the beginning of the YMCA in 1840. Lynse links the New York prayer meeting revival of 1857 and 1858 to the ministry of Spurgeon, the beginning of the Salvation Army, D. L. Moody's ministry, the beginnings of the China Inland Mission, and an era of great lay ministry expansion. She identifies prayer as central to "the year of the Holy Spirit" and marks 1905 as its beginning, a worldwide awakening sparked by prayer and the birth of the Pentecostal movement. Finally, Lynse points to 1914 as the beginning of a significant prayer cycle that resulted in rally evangelism and the ministries of evangelists like Billy Sunday and Billy Graham. This extends even to the Jesus Movement, the counter cultural revival in the 1960s and 1970s. [37]

As a result of his research, Stephen Olford, wrote in his book, *Heart-Cry for Revival,* "I came to the conclusion that the two outstanding conditions for revival are unity and prayer." [38] James Burns, the editor of "The Laws of Revival," says, "Even as spiritual life is receding there begins to gather a power and volume to return to God. Growing dissatisfaction grows with decline ...Gradually, the number of people praying increases...more urgent and more confident ...[It] is not the cause of a revival, but the human preparation for one. By prayer we prepare the soil." [39]

J. Hudson Taylor wrote, "The spirit of prayer is, in essence, the spirit of revival." [40]

Proclamation

Proclamation—the effective preaching and teaching of the Word of God—is the third spark that God has used to fire revival. The truth of God sets those in the Church and nonbelievers free (John 8:32). "The Word of God is alive and powerful, sharper than a double-edged sword. It skillfully penetrates as fine as a laser to divide even the soul and the spirit and the joints and marrow of a person. It judges the thoughts and attitudes of a person's spirit. Everything is laid open before it; even the thoughts and attitudes of a person's spirit; nothing is exempt from exposure" (Heb. 4:12–13). Great revivals are known for great preaching and teaching from people, such as Isaiah, Jeremiah, John the Baptist, Peter, Paul, Barnabas, Finney, Whitfield, Moody, Edwards, Palmer, and Nettleton.

As pain increases and prayer movements increase, may the solid truth of God's Word stoke the fire. "Oh God, let the sparks fly!"

Chapter 4

OLD TESTAMENT FIRESTORMS

I T'S A GREAT honor and encouragement to be chosen for a special purpose or position. I recall the excitement of being chosen first chair trumpet in high school. I remember the honor and enjoyment of being selected for a much-desired university ministry, and on several occasions, being chosen for pastoral positions. I remember the thrill when Connie said yes to my proposal of marriage. Out of all the other possibilities, she chose me.

In a much more important and historically significant sense, the nation of Israel was chosen to be God's special betrothed, the nation through whom Jesus their Messiah would come. As I have already shown, the people of Israel were God's redemptive agents through Old Testament history. It's a stormy history—the story of Israel's call, her promises made to God, and her repeated drift toward other lovers. She is finally declared a prostitute people (Ezek. 16:15; Hos. 4:10–11; 5:4). With the backdrop of theological patterns, look with me at revivals in the Old Testament. We will examine the up-and-down pattern of Israel's relationship with God, from glorious manifestations of His presence to ignominious low periods of apostasy. Arthur Wallis, who wrote *Rain from Heaven*, describes Israel's pattern of drift:

Decline and decay, inherent in human nature, are not confined to the physical and moral realm, but appear in the spiritual also. We see it in the history of Israel. We see it in New Testament times. We see it in the subsequent history of the church. God has seen fit to counteract this ever-present tendency by seizing the initiative, and working at times in unusual power. In this way ground has been recovered from the enemy, and the spiritual equilibrium restored. [41]

The story of Old Testament revival began in Genesis 35:1–15. This is where Jacob returned to Bethel, which means "House of God." God had met him there in Genesis 28:1–22 and promised that all the nations of the earth would be blessed through him. Now, as Jacob prepared to go to Bethel again, he acted on God's instructions for his household to get rid of their foreign gods and to purify themselves (vs. 2). After he returned home, God changed his name to Israel, "struggles with God" (vs. 10). God confirmed to him the covenant promises He had made to Abraham (Gen. 17:1–8).

Fast forward to the book of Deuteronomy, which means "repetition of the law." Skim some of the early history with me to set the stage for Israel's up-and-down struggle with God. In Deuteronomy, Moses gives careful instructions for God's people as He prepares to transfer the leadership to Joshua. Beginning in Deuteronomy 1:5, Moses delivers his farewell address and carefully reviews Israel's covenant with God. In the territory of Moab, where the Jordan River flows into the Dead Sea, the people reaffirm it. Woven into the book of Deuteronomy is a tapestry of God's love for His people, and in their better moments, their love for Him. Moses calls God's people to a radical commitment of worship and obedience. If they obey and live out their love relationship and calling with Him, He will bless them abundantly in every area of life. If they disobey, they can expect just the opposite, the covenant curses in Deuteronomy 28.

In chapter 31, Moses prepares Israel for difficult times. As they move into the Promised Land, he tells them that God will deliver the nations and the land into their hands. Moses tells them to be strong and courageous (vs. 6), not terrified or afraid. God would go with them, and He would not leave or forsake them. Sadly, God warned Moses of the pattern that would repeat itself through Israel's history. "These people will soon prostitute themselves to the foreign gods of the land they are entering. They will forsake me and break the covenant I made with them ...I know what they are disposed to do, even before I bring them into the land I promised them on oath" (Deut. 31:16, 21).

In Deuteronomy 32 and 33, Moses blessed each of the twelve tribes before he dies. Another great leader, Joshua, stepped into Israel's leadership. The book that bears his name tells how the nomadic Israelites conquered the Promised Land. The first major battle was an overwhelming victory for Israel and her leader. The people took the walled city of Jericho with an unusual military strategy given by God. Massive walls fell before the nomads. With amazing creativity, God demonstrated that He was in charge.

From this high point, Israel, confident of victory, sent a small army to take the city of Ai. It is here that the nation learned, or relearned, a powerful lesson; sin does not pay. Snubbing his nose at God's instructions and covenant, Achan had become enamored with the spoils from the victory at Jericho and had hidden some in his tent. As a result, Israel lost what should have been an easy victory. Thirty-six died.

Recognizing that something was very wrong, that perhaps God had not kept His promise of victory, Joshua tore his clothes and fell face down before the Lord. The elders of Israel followed suit. How did God respond? "Stand up! What are you doing down on your face? Israel has sinned ...That is why the Israelites cannot stand against their enemies ...I will not be with you any more unless you destroy whatever among you is devoted to destruction ...You cannot stand against your enemies until you remove it. (Josh. 7:6–13)

Achan's sin was so severe, and the loss so great, that God required his life to be taken. With a lesson well learned, Joshua and the nation moved forward across the promised territories. With God going before them, they experienced great victory and growing prosperity. In chapters 23 and 24, Joshua, like Moses before him, told God's people farewell with reminders of God's faithfulness. They were to remember that it was God they served, who led and blessed them, and who had established His covenant with them, a covenant to be honored, obeyed, and never forgotten.

Again there is a warning, "If you forsake the Lord and serve foreign gods, He will turn and bring disaster on you and make an end of you, after he has been good to you" (Josh. 24: 20). This is the same thing God told Jacob when he returned to Bethel. The people of Israel held on to foreign gods, but the people responded, "We will serve the Lord."

I wish good news followed the life and leadership of Joshua, but it didn't. The next book, Judges, told the sad story about centuries of Israel's unfaithfulness to the Lord. Chapter after chapter reported their apostasy, their surrender to the allurements of Canaan, and their rebellion, all provoking God's discipline. Under difficult circumstances that follow His discipline, the people made urgent appeals to Him for help. As they repented and returned to God, He embraced and forgave them. The Covenant was renewed and the people were blessed. It was revival. God raised up leaders—judges—who in God's power and wisdom threw off Israel's enemies and restored the land to peace and prosperity.

Only the grace and mercy of God spared Israel from being totally wiped out and absorbed into the surrounding nations. A sad commentary summarized Israel's condition. "In those days Israel had no king; everyone did as he saw fit" (Judg. 17:6; 21:25). The book of Judges highlights the pattern of revival in the Old Testament. Israel went through an up-and-down cycle six times. The first cycle sets the pattern with Othniel (Judg. 3:7–11), and five more judges follow. They begin with this tragic commentary: "Israel did evil in the eyes of the Lord" (Judg. 2:11), and by God's grace conclude with, "the land had peace" (Judg. 3:11). The cycle can be summarized as apostasy, oppression, distress, deliverance, and blessing.

How Does Revival Come?

By the time King Solomon took the throne as Israel's new king, he understood Israel's pattern of decline. He knew their history. Solomon knew that life for Israel would not always be as glorious and exciting as their temple dedication was in 2 Chronicles 5–7, one of the high points of their history and relationship with God. In his prayer of dedication, he asked God what would happen when bad times came. As already highlighted, after two weeks of the temple dedication festivities, Solomon returned to his home, probably elated and most likely exhausted. As he slept, God spoke to answer his questions, the instructions for revival:

> If my people, who are called by my name, will humble themselves and pray and seek my face and turn from their wicked ways, then will I hear from heaven and will forgive their sin and will heal their land. (2 Chron. 7:14).

Notice again, God didn't answer with *if* things get bad, but *when* (NIV). It was what to do when they realized that they had pulled up anchor from their God and were in dangerous drift. It was a wake-up call to arouse them from their spiritual stupor. God's words were written for all of God's people for all time. The cycle was a continuing pattern.

Is 2 Chronicles 7:14 Only for Israel?

Of the many volumes written on revival, only a few authors concentrate on the Old Testament. One such author is Dr. Walter Kaiser, one of the most highly regarded orthodox (evangelical), Old Testament scholars, and the former president of Gordon Conwell Theological Seminary. I am still amazed by his grasp of the Old Testament and his textual dexterity and ability when I remember a doctoral course he taught. He would quote a text in Hebrew, translate it, and explain it.

In his book, *Quest for Renewal: Personal Revival in the Old Testament,* Kaiser defines revival and then establishes the need for it. He moves immediately to what God told King Solomon when He appeared to him at night. "Almost everyone," he writes, "will agree that the greatest text on the subject [of revival] is 2 chronicles 7:14." [42]

Some think 2 Chronicles 7:14 is only for Israel, for the Old Covenant people of God, not the New Covenant Church of Jesus Christ, saying, "Don't go to 2 Chronicles 7:14 if you want to find instructions for revival in our times." It's true that the New Testament calls us to obedience and back to our first love. Revelation, chapters 2 and 3, provide good examples. Yet, excellent scholarship builds a strong case that God's words to Solomon and Israel are for all of God's *people* throughout all time. It's specific to Israel, but it's what the Church must do if she wants to see a firestorm of the Holy Spirit sweep across the nation.

In the text God addresses *"my people."* This is our first clue that it is God's instructions for His people throughout all time. Dr. Kaiser, explains it:

> First of all, the phrase "If my people" is immediately glossed, or explained, by the little exegetical, or appositional, clause "who are called by my name," a clause so distinctive to both Testaments that its meaning could

never be confused or mistaken. What God or man named, he owned and protected, whether that included cities (2 Samuel 12:28, Jeremiah 25:29, Daniel 9:18–19), the Temple (1 Kings 8:43, Jeremiah 7:10, 11, 14, 30; 32:34; 34:15), or men and women (Isaiah 4:1; Jeremiah 14:9; 15:16). When Israel walked by faith, Moses promised that "all peoples of the earth shall see that you are called by the name of the Lord" (Deuteronomy 28:10). In the same way, James noted how God had "visited the Gentiles to take out of them a people for his name" (Acts 15:14). Most convincing of all is the appearance of the phrase in Joel 2:32, "All who call on the name of the Lord will be saved." Those who did not believe were "like those who [were] not called by my name" (Isaiah 63:19). The fact that Peter used this expression on the day of Pentecost to inaugurate the age of the Spirit, the New Covenant, and the Church, is not altogether accidental. Therefore, although this promise was originally given to Israel, it is also most assuredly intended for us. [43]

The same principle is used in applying the New Covenant to the Church. Kaiser teaches that it was first addressed to the house of Israel and Judah (Jer. 31:31). However, he adds, we are ministers of the New Covenant (2 Cor. 3:6) and drink the blood of the New Covenant in the Lord's Supper (Matt. 26:28; 1 Cor. 11:25). "The climactic fulfillment of the New Covenant will not come until the Deliverer comes to Zion and He banishes ungodliness from Jacob in that day of the restoration of Israel to her Lord and her land (Romans 11:25–27)." [44] Kaiser's final argument comes from two New Testament scriptures. Romans 15:4 tells us, "Everything that was written in the past was written to teach us, so that through endurance and the encouragement of the Scriptures we might have hope." First Corinthians 10:11 adds, "These things happened to them as examples and were written down as warnings for us, on whom the fulfillment of the ages has come."

The Old Testament scholar explained that 2 Chronicles 7:14 formed the outline for the book of 2 Chronicles and set the agenda for the material selected from the lives of five key Davidic kings of Judah. One of the steps given in 2 Chroniclers 7:14 was strategic for each king. Kaiser said that the pattern formed an *inclusio* with the first and last king sharing the same step. An *inclusio* in the Hebrew Bible was a literary device that created a frame by placing similar material at the beginning and the end of a section, word, phrase, or even a larger portion of the text. (For a complete definition and explanation, see www.wikipedia.org/wiki/inclusio.) Nearly half of 2 Chronicles was dedicated to the leadership of these five kings and the revivals they led.

1. "*Humble yourselves*": Rehoboam in chapters 11–12.
2. "Seek my face": Asa in chapters 14–16
3. "Pray": Jehoshaphat in chapters 17–20
4. "Turn from your wicked way": Hezekiah in chapters 29–32
5. "*Humble yourselves*": Josiah in chapters 34–35 (5)

As he concluded his discussion of 2 Chronicles 7:14, Kaiser addressed the need for revival in the Church. He wrote:

> Therefore, today's believers must begin by following God's program for revival as set forth in 2 Chronicles 7:14, or our land will lie fallow and overgrown. If we follow the instructions of this revival text, the floodgates of heaven will open, and both we and our culture will be the surprised recipients of the blessing of God. When will revival come? No finer answer can be given than our paradigmatic verse from 2 Chronicles 7:14, which laid out the program for each of the revivals that span

almost half of the chapters of that great book …[While] we affirm that the work is most decidedly and uniquely the special prerogative of our Lord…we must prepare for that revival by following the four verbs…humility. . . prayer…spiritual hunger(seeking God's face)…confession and repentance [45].

The Characteristics of Old Testament Revival

Several authors identify Old Testament revival in terms of features, keys, or characteristics. Dr. Walter Kaiser lists ten. The features are:

1. Get rid of idols;
2. Confess sin;
3. Serve the Lord alone;
4. Let God be God;
5. Seek the Lord;
6. Pray to the Lord;
7. Turn back to the Lord;
8. Humble oneself before the Lord;
9. Renew the work of God; and
10. Rejoice in the Lord. [46]

Compare Wilbur M. Smith's "characteristics" of Old Testament revivals listed in his classic book, *The Glorious Revival Under King Hezekiah.*

1. Each revival occurred in a time of deep moral darkness and national depression.
2. Each revival began in the heart of one consecrated servant of God, who became the energizing power behind the revival, the agent God used to quicken and lead the nation back to faith in and obedience to God.

3. Each revival rested upon the Word of God, and most of the revivals were the result of a return to the Word of God and of preaching and of proclaiming the law of God with power.

4. All of the revivals were marked by a return to the worship of Jehovah.

5. Each revival, except the last two, witnessed a destruction of idols. These exceptions—the revival under Zerubbabel with Haggai and Zechariah in Ezra 5–6, and the revival under Nehemiah with Ezra, Nehemiah 8:9 and 12:44–47, occurred after the exile, when no idols were found in Judah.

6. Separation from sin was noted in each revival, with the exception of the revival under Asa. However, we can assume it was also true then because of the context of the revival and the behavior of God's people.

7. Every revival included a return to the offering of blood sacrifices.

8. Almost all of the revivals resulted in an experience of exuberant joy and gladness among people of God. The only two where this was not recorded were the revival in the house of Jacob, and the revival during the reign of Josiah (where it can be assumed from the context and behavior of God's people).

9. Each revival was followed by a period of great prosperity. [47]

TABLE 1 LISTS OF OLD TESTAMENT REVIVALS

Wilbur M. Smith Walter C. Kaiser
1. Jacob—Genesis 35:1–15 1. Jacob—Genesis 35:1–15
2. Asa—2 Chronicles 15:1–15* **10. (2. Moses—Exodus. 32–33)**
3. Jehoash—2 Kings 11–12 **11.(3. Samuel—1 Samuel. 7:1–13)**
2 Chronicles 23–24 **12.(4. Elijah—1 Kings 18)**
4. Hezekiah—2 Kings 18:4–7; 5Asa—2 Chronicles 14–16
2 Chronicles 29–31 6Jehoshaphat—2 Chronicles 20
5. Josiah—2 Kings 22–23; 7Hezekiah—2 Chr. 30:1–9
2 Chronicles 34–35 8Josiah—2 Chr. 34–35

6. Zerubbabel, Haggai 9. Zerubbabel—Haggai 1; Zech. 1:1–6
Zechariah, Ezra 5–6 10Nehemiah—Nehemiah 8
7. Nehemiah Ezra—Nehemiah 8:9; 12:44–47
8. Jonah in Nineveh
9. Jehoshaphat—2 Chr. 17:6–9 (*Revivals added to Smith's list to total twelve)

Humility, prayer, spiritual hunger (seeking God's face), confession and repentance, the four steps of revival in 2 Chronicles 7:14, are woven throughout the above lists. Take note! Write it down! If you want revival, follow the instructions! Revival comes in obedience to 2 Chronicles 7:14. History demonstrates that when God's people, Israel, and the Church have humbled themselves and begun to pray, God has responded. Out of these beginnings, passion and hunger for God began to grow and confession and repentance have followed.

If the Church of Jesus Christ wants to see historic revival sweep through her cities and nations with a mighty rushing wind and the firestorm of Pentecost, it will happen like it has in the past. Writers will report that a mighty move of God is sweeping through the land. The Church will be lining up with the pattern of history: obeying and praying, and God will be responding as promised.

Brian Edwards adds important characteristics of revival in his book, *Revival! A People Saturated With God.* While he agrees that the role of prayer is central, he explains that prayer, repentance, worship, and evangelization are heightened and intensified in revival. [48] Edwards says that from his study, two significant things can be missed. First, revival is "spontaneous and unpredictable." (Note that I have included "spontaneous" in my definition of revival in chapter 3.) Revival comes suddenly at a time of God's choosing. God moves in revival when His people set the stage by seeking Him in prayer, but the timing is up to Him. Second, Edwards says that

God's people become generous and redemptive as demonstrated in 2 Chronicles 31:4–5.

Out of dark and difficult times, as God's people humble themselves, repent and seek Him desperately, God affirms His willingness to heal and restore His people. "But Zion said, 'The LORD has forsaken me, the Lord has forgotten me.' Can a mother forget the baby at her breast and have no compassion on the child she has borne? Though she may forget, I will not forget you! See, I have engraved you on the palms of my hands; your walls are ever before me" (Isa. 49:14–16).

Although some authors emphasize different characteristics of revival, any list of characteristics must include prayer. I believe it is the primary catalyst that begins revival. That is why I have included chapter seven. Revival depends on passionate prayer and repentance—a significant spark that lights revival flame.

Elana Lynse, quoted earlier, identifies the role of prayer in the Old Testament. Prayer, she said, is at the core of 2 Chronicles 7:14. It was central in releasing great revival leaders like Moses (Exod. 2:23–25) and Samuel. Samuel's life and ministry flowed from the faithful prayers of Hanna (1 Sam. 2:1–8). It was at the heart of Nehemiah's leadership and ministry, and the result of his prayer (Neh. 1:6–9). It was a movement of God that produced the rebuilding of the wall of Jerusalem and ultimately a new nation in the book of Nehemiah. Lynse did not stop with these leaders. She explained that the intercessory prayer of other great leaders in Israel's history must include Abraham (Gen. 18:16–33), Moses (Deut. 9:25–29), Solomon (2 Chron. 6:12–42), Asa (2 Chron. 14:1–15:19), Hezekiah (2 Kgs. 19:1–19), Daniel (Dan. 9:1–19), and Ezra (Ezra 9:1–15). [49]

Read through 2 Chronicles, but wear your seat belt. It is an up-and-down ride of obedience and blessing, of falling into sin and disaster, and then revival. One thrills with the stories of godly leaders who are deeply committed to God and to serving His kingdom. The nation enjoys the covenant blessings of God and prospers as they live in obedience to Him. Then a godless king comes to power. He leads the nation into sin, and the pattern of disaster—God's covenant curses, or the natural consequences of their sin—is the news of the day.

Solomon began well, but then, down he went. Asa was a great king, but he, like others, drifted into sin in the end. Hezekiah stood out among the kings like a diamond that reflected the glory of God. Toward the end of his reign, he became proud. He repented and was honored in death. So went the story of Old Testament revival.

How did exiled Nehemiah respond when he heard about the tragic conditions of his homeland? "When I heard these words I sat down and wept, and mourned for days; fasting and praying before the God of heaven" (Neh. 1:4 NRS). Wallis affirmed, "Revivals have always flowed out of praying, but not of the cold, formal and tearless variety." [50] As we have affirmed the pattern of history, we can cry out: "Oh, that God's people today would begin to pray and seek His face—His presence!"

Before we look at New Testament and post-biblical revivals, the list of Old Testament characteristics will begin to shape them for all of revival history:

1. Revival occurred in times of personal or national crisis and great spiritual need, and in times of deep moral darkness and spiritual decline among God's people, Israel.
2. Revival began in the heart of a servant of God who became the agent God used to lead his people back to faith in Him and obedience to Him.
3. Prayer was central to revival. Leaders called out to God in prayer, passionately seeking His face in repentance, and confessing personal and national sins.
4. Revival rested upon the proclamation of God's Law and Israel's return to their covenant commitments.

5. Revival in the Old Testament reflected the work of God the Father to awaken His people, Israel, to a restored relationship with him, to obey Him and serve His purpose.
6. Revival was marked by a return to the worship of God.
7. Revival led to the destruction of idols or ungodly preoccupations and also to separation from personal and corporate sin.
8. Revival brought a return to the offering of blood sacrifices in the Old Testament.
9. Revival resulted in an experience of exuberant joy and gladness among God's people.
10. Revival was followed by a period of prosperity and social reform, Israel's covenant blessings.

This list can be refined by looking at revival in the New Testament and five selected post-biblical revivals. It will add consistency and affirm that there is a definite pattern of revival though all of history.

> *There is a threshold over which revival and transformation come. The Lord has come in answer to prayer. The result has been the salvation of many and church growth ...There are no cases of transformation that have happened by sheer programming, numbers of people involved, or human effort.* (George Otis)

Chapter 5

New Testament Firestorms

W HAT'S MORE EXCITING than reading the story of Jesus's life? If you want to know what God is like, read about Jesus; He is God in human flesh. But don't stop there. It's also exciting to read about the first-century Church and see how she turned her world upside down. From the dream-dashed disciples cowering in a locked room, to turning the Roman Empire on its ear a few centuries later, the Church was birthed in resurrection power and impact. The life, death, and resurrection of Jesus, the apex of human history, brought radical change to the lives of people as the Gospel spread like a prairie fire.

The Old Testament is the story of God preparing for His coming. Israel is the agent for accomplishing God's redemptive purpose and preparing the way. After Pentecost, the Church picks up God's redemptive mission. Unfortunately, the pattern of drift in the Old Testament is repeated throughout the history of the Church. In Revelation 2 and 3, the apostle John identifies drift in the early Church.

It is more challenging to trace the pattern of revival in the New Testament because the storms are different. However, they are revival nevertheless. The entire book of Acts is a firestorm and depicts the spread of the Gospel that burned its way through many cities and regions. What can compare with the firestorm of Pentecost (Acts

2) and the fire of God falling on the Gentiles in Acts 10? What can compare with the power of God falling on Saul as he walked along the road on a mission to persecute and kill followers of Jesus (Acts 22:4)? Knocked to the ground gasping, he cried, "Who are You, Lord?" This brilliant man, the persecutor of Christ-followers, later wrote much of the New Testament. God grabbed his attention, his heart, and his brilliant mind.

Let's look at revival in the New Testament. Can we isolate revivals from the birth of the Church and the spread of the Gospel? Malcom McDow and Alvin Reid answer this in their book, *Fire Fall: How God Has Shaped History through Revivals.* Is there anything more like fire fall or firestorms than the work of the Holy Spirit?

> The New Testament is the biblical account of one long spiritual awakening that had many revivals within the revival. Just as the First Great Awakening (1726–70) and the Second Great Awakening (1787–1843) in America were long revivals with many crests, the New Testament renewal, which was the first awakening in history that followed this pattern, experienced many revivals.
>
> The Church was birthed and expanded from the Upper Room to the outer borders of the Roman Empire, and even beyond. The revival started in 26 AD with John the Baptist in the Jordan region; intensified under Jesus; crested at Pentecost; spread to Samaria, Damascus, Cornelius' house, Antioch, Cyprus, Pisidia, Philippi, Thessalonica, Ephesus, and other places; and ended with John the Apostle on the Island of Patmos. During those seventy years the ministries of John the Baptist, Jesus, and the advent of the Holy Spirit at Pentecost exploded across the pages of history. The authorship of the twenty-seven books of the New Testament and many other

accomplishments occurred. Indeed, this renewal established the pattern for all subsequent biblical awakenings and is a magnificent example of the true meaning
of revival.

Jesus came in "the fullness of time" (Galatians 4:4, NRSV).
Before His coming, God was at work preparing the world
for His royal arrival. As a vital part of the preparation,
God united the Mediterranean world under one Roman
government and prepared the Jewish nation with a
Messianic hope. The New Testament revival occurred
within the Roman world, a Hellenistic culture, and a
Jewish context. [51]

The Church

The Church was birthed in a firestorm of the Holy Spirit at Pentecost.
How amazing it must have been in the upper room! Flames of fire
rested on the heads of those gathered in unity and prayer. The roar
of a mighty, "violent wind" (Acts 2:2) drew a crowd, just as people
run to see a burning building. That day people heard about Jesus
in their own language from those who could not naturally speak
it. Thousands came to faith and left the city to carry the fire to
the known world. When the Church was born, God's people were
clothed with the power of the Holy Spirit. Just as Jesus, the incarnation, walked this earth in human flesh, He continued to walk it
through His Church, the "body of Christ." The Church was Jesus
on earth again in human flesh, the second incarnation—the body
of Christ—directed by its Head. In unity, she loved as Jesus loved
and taught what He taught. He was alive again on earth.

The Church has fit this exciting description only at high points
of renewal. Only when revival has pulsated through her veins
has she looked like the early Church. Otherwise, in disunity and

disobedience, she has presented a crippled Christ, the body nearly severed from the Head. Troubled by sin and the same old drift into the surrounding culture, she has followed the pattern of the Old Testament and mirrored God's people, Israel. The Church has gone from vibrancy—new wine in new wineskins—to encrusted institutionalism, a form of godliness without the power of God and the fresh wind of the Holy Spirit blowing through her. She had a great beginning, but over and over, syncretism and universalism have watered down her dynamic faith to a tasteless brew of anything but living water. Her revivals have been periods of great joy and social reform. New wineskins have been able to handle the new wine.

Since Pentecost, the followers of Jesus have had a distinct advantage over God's people in the Old Testament. There, the Holy Spirit was given to individuals to accomplish specific callings or assignments. From Pentecost forward, the Holy Spirit came to reside in each believer. He gave spiritual gifts that are necessary for equipping them to be all God designed them to be. Through their communities, Jesus was alive again on earth, their gifts blended together to form the Body of Christ.

Jesus gave the Church the Great Commandment, to love God with all her heart, soul, mind, and strength (Matt. 22:37–40), just like Jesus loved the Father when He was here. This was always the top priority: to know Him, to seek His presence, to enjoy Him intimately, and to follow His leading. She was to love her neighbors as herself. Jesus modeled this passionately when He was on earth— love God and love people! Perhaps her greatest downfall has been to fail this mission. Jesus's intimacy with the Father set the pattern. Jesus showed us what to do; He discerned what the Father was doing and joined Him (John 5:19). The members of the body of Christ, the Church, were to be marked by love for everyone around them as they loved one another (Matt. 22:37–40).

Perhaps the second downfall of the Church has been that we have tended to do things our way or to follow the patterns that are attractive to our culture: a good business plan, good marketing, and wealthy influential community leaders, or the most popular and powerful people forming boards, rather than wise and godly elders.

The Great Commission in Matthew 28:19–20 and Acts 1:8, has always summarized the Church's assignment, to be God's redemptive agent in the world. In the pristine days of the Church, the Gospel spread rapidly. Peter's preaching rang clear with the central message of salvation through Jesus the Messiah. The Church was alive and functioning in great power. Acts 2:38–47 has provided a snapshot of powerful early preaching and the response of people:

> Repent and be baptized, every one of you, in the name of Jesus Christ for the forgiveness of your sins. And you will receive the gift of the Holy Spirit. The promise is for you and your children and for all who are far off—for all whom the Lord our God will call. With many other words he warned them; and he pleaded with them, "Save yourselves from this corrupt generation." Those who accepted his message were baptized, and about three thousand were added to their number that day. They devoted themselves to the apostles' teaching and to fellowship, to the breaking of bread and to prayer. Everyone was filled with awe, and many wonders and miraculous signs were done by the apostles. All the believers were together and had everything in common. Selling their possessions and goods, they gave to anyone as he had need. Every day they continued to meet together in the temple courts. They broke bread in their homes and ate together with glad and sincere hearts, praising God and enjoying the favor of all the people. And the Lord added to their number daily those who were being saved.

The Church has been the most dynamic and alive when she has been passionately sharing the Gospel and fulfilling the Great Commission. I have seen this firsthand when I served as campus pastor at a Christian university. When students were actively engaged in evangelism, locally or overseas, they demonstrated a much more vital faith and growing intimacy with Jesus than those who were not mobilized in mission. Having observed the Church across the nation over time, I see the same thing. The congregations that have been passionate about reaching people in their cities and beyond with the Gospel have been the most spiritually dynamic, alive, and growing, just like the Church in the first century.

The late Lyle Shaller, passionate about the Church and her growth, published the results of a significant study in 2002. He reported that 70 percent of churches in America were in "survival mode," 25 to 27 percent were in "growth mode," and 3 to 5 percent were in "kingdom building mode." Churches in survival mode asked, "How can we stop losing members and keep our doors open?" They were shrinking. Congregations in growth mode asked, "What programs and techniques can we implement that will attract new members?" They were growing. God's people who were in kingdom building mode asked, "How can we serve people and lead them to Christ?" They were exploding in members and ministry. [52]

John Dickerson, award winning journalist and pastor, as noted earlier, states that only 7 to 9 percent of the American population can be considered authentic followers of Jesus. He describes what we face as a Church, and interestingly, it's what the early church faced: "Living in a pagan and hypersexual culture may be new and frightening to us, but it was the norm for New Testament churches. Time and again, God repeats His strategy: live 'good' lives among pagans" (1 Pet. 2:15; 3:9–17; Titus 3:1, 8, 14; Rom. 12:21; Gal. 6:9–10; 2 Cor. 9:8; Heb. 10:24; Eph. 2: 8, 10; 1 Tim. 6:18; Matt. 5:16). [53]

Revival is restoring something to its original, or what has been lost. It's time to get back to first-century faith, to a revived, dynamic, world-changing movement of God.

The Characteristics of New Testament Revival

Revival is the same in both the Old and New Testaments. *It is a spontaneous spiritual awakening by God the Holy Spirit among His people. It comes in answer to their humble prayers as they passionately seek His face and repent for their sins. The awakening results in deepened intimacy with God, passion for Him, holy living, evangelism, and citywide or area-wide transformation, expressed through social reform.* The difficulty of understanding revival in the New Testament has been with its spontaneity. Did the Church, as she spread out over the Roman Empire, ever fall asleep spiritually? Were there times when she needed revival? Yes. Her need was recorded in Revelation 2 and 3.

Although few authors have attempted to list New Testament revivals, most writers have seen Pentecost as the greatest move of the Holy Spirit in history. Some have wondered if it was revival or just spiritual birth and growth. It certainly was the birth of the Church. Most have agreed that the disciples had placed their faith in Jesus as their Savior or Messiah before His death and resurrection. Was Pentecost a revival?

How do others view Pentecost? Arthur Wallis uses Pentecost, biblical and post-biblical, as the pattern of revival through all of redemptive history. In his book, *Rain from Heaven,* he reaches back to the prophet Habakkuk's prayer and vision in chapter 3. He says, "God came." He sees this in Isaiah's prayer for God's fire to fall from heaven in Isaiah 64:1–2. Revival is what happened at Pentecost and what happened in answer to Isaiah's prayer.

> Many other Old Testament prophets living in dark days found a ray of hope in the expectation of such a visitation. When we turn to the New Testament, such times are seen to be directly related to the pouring out of the Holy Spirit. As the birthday of the church, Pentecost was unique, but as a specimen outpouring of the Spirit, it was only unique in being the first ... We should not be surprised to find subsequent examples of this kind of visitation in the Acts record, notably that which took place in Caesarea, which Luke describes as a pouring out of the gift of the Holy Spirit (Acts 10:45). Similarly, Paul, who did not experience the outpouring at Pentecost or at Caesarea, uses the same expression when he reminds Titus of their own experience: "The Holy Spirit, which He poured out upon us generously ..." (Titus 3:5–6, NIV). [54]

Other authors have identified New Testament revivals. Stephen Olford included Pentecost in his book, *Heart-cry for Revival*. He included Pentecost (Acts 1:13–2:41). Following the pattern of preparation for the disciples in the upper room, he outlined how believers could be prepared for a visitation of the Holy Spirit. He called for unity among believers, unity in prayer, and prayer with expectancy, anchored in God's promise to move by the power of His Spirit. [55]

Other authors have contributed lists, like E. D. Head, the former president and professor of Evangelism of Southwestern Baptist Seminary. He listed the following New Testament revivals:

1. A revival in the streets: Matthew 21:1–17
2. A personal work revival: John 1:35–51
3. A woman's revival: John 4:28–42
4. A revival in a graveyard: John 11:30–45
5. A revival in a church: Acts 4:23–37

6. A revival in a carriage: Acts 8:26–40
7. An unlawful revival: Acts 10:23–48
8. A Sabbath Day revival: Acts 13:44–52
9. A revival by the riverside: Acts 16:9–15
10. A revival in a jail: Acts 16:23–34
11. A revival in Rome: Acts 28:30–31; Philippians 1:12–14 [56]

Head's list and helpful outlines could be used for a good teaching series, but some of the revivals do not quite fit the pattern of revival. For example, it is questionable to say that Jesus's triumphal entry into Jerusalem qualifies as a spiritual awakening. Matthew 21:10 says, "The whole city was stirred." There were miracles, the significant fulfillment of prophecy, and the cleansing of the temple. However, even though the crowds lay down clothing and branches as though to welcome a triumphant king, the text does not support the belief that the people were placing their faith in Jesus as Messiah. They want a king to overthrow Rome. When Jesus doesn't step up to their expectations, they soon began to shout, "Crucify Him." Other accounts on Head's list of revivals—such as the calling of John, Andrew, and Philip in John 1:35–51 miss the larger pattern or revival.

In contrast, a spontaneous move of God with a broad impact, the story of Peter's visit to a Gentile's home, is found in Acts 10:23–48. It isn't kosher to visit; it is "unclean." As Peter obeys God and breaks out of his traditional Jewish tradition, the Scripture records, "the Holy Spirit fell on all who heard the message" (vs. 44). The Gospel came to the Gentiles.

Acts 13:44–52, the account of Paul and Barnabas's ministry in Pisidia Antioch, describes what must have been a spontaneous visitation of the Spirit. "The whole city gathered" (vs. 44), and "the Word of the Lord spread through the whole region …The disciples were filled with joy and with the Holy Spirit" (vv. 49–52).

The following list fits the definition I have given for revival in both the Old Testament and the New Testament:

1. The revival under John the Baptist: Matthew 3:1–12
2. The revival at Pentecost: Acts 2:1–4, 14–47
3. The revival in the Church: Acts 4:23–37
4. The revival that grew out of fear: Acts 5:1–16
5. The revival that grew out of persecution: Acts 7:54–8:25
6. The revival with Cornelius and the Gentiles: Acts 10:23–48
7. The revival in Pisidia Antioch: Acts 13:44
8. The revival at Ephesus: Acts 19:1–20

The list below, adding the spontaneity of God's visitation, gives us the characteristics of biblical revival. Old and New Testament revivals share the following characteristics.

1. Revival occurred in a times of personal or national crisis and great spiritual need, and in times of deep moral darkness and spiritual decline among God's people Israel, or his Church.
2. Revival began in the heart(s) of one or more consecrated servants of God, who became the agents(s) God used of God to lead His people back to faith and obedience.
3. Prayer was central to revival. Leaders called out to God in prayer, passionately seeking His face in repentance and in the confession of their personal and national sins. They ignited prayer among God's people.
4. Revival rested upon the powerful proclamation—preaching and teaching—of the law of God and His Word. Many revivals were the result of a return to Scripture.
5. Revival in the Old Testament reflected the work of God the Father to awaken His people, Israel, to a restored relationship with Him, to obey Him, and serve his redemptive purpose. Revival in the New Testament and post-biblical history reflected

the work of the Holy Spirit in miracles and equipping people for ministry. It resulted in the spread of the Gospel and the growth of the Church.

6. Revival was marked by a return to the worship of God.
7. Revival led to repentance and the destruction of idols and ungodly preoccupations, and to turning away from personal and corporate sin.
8. Revival brought a return to the offering of blood sacrifices in the Old Testament and a concentration on the death, resurrection, and return of Jesus Christ in the New Testament—celebrated in the Lord's Supper.
9. Revival resulted in an experience of exuberant joy and gladness among the people of God.
10. Revival was followed by a period of blessing and area-wide transformation that produced spiritual, social, and economic reform.

These are the ten characteristics of revival in the Old and New Testaments. To the best of my understanding, this is biblical revival. When revival comes, it will follow this pattern. How can we set the stage for biblical revival? It is already set with the decline of the Church and the secularization of Western culture. The second characteristic, passionate prayer, is slowly emerging across the nation.

Obstacles to Transforming Revival

George Otis, Jr., the producer of videos on transformation or revival, was interviewed on February 8, 2005, by Mission America on a conference call. Otis had traveled the world to document moves of God in revival. I was on the call. During that interview, Otis said:

> There is a threshold over which revival and transformation comes. The Lord has come in answer to prayer. The result has been the salvation of many and Church growth

...There are no cases of transformation that have happened by sheer programming, numbers of people involved, or human effort. It happens by divine intervention. It comes in answer to prayer as in the prayer Jesus taught us, "Thy Kingdom come; Thy will be done on earth as it is in heaven." It is the Emmanuel Principle—God with us. God comes. Weeping and praying in sackcloth...returns God to His people, as in the Old Testament.

Otis said that widespread transformation is not occurring anywhere in the Western world, and he listed what he believed were the biggest obstacles:

1. We need to see a change in the way we do church in the West. It is obvious that we are falling short.
2. Where transformation has been scrutinized there is a common thread or simple formula: abandonment with expectation. In each community where transformation occurred, Christians wanted the presence of God to invade their area or church so much that they were willing to do anything to prepare the way for the Lord, and they believed He would come or respond (2 Chron. 7:14; Isa. 58).

As the phone interview continued, Otis said that most churches never experience abandonment. Instead, it is more like business as usual. They must come to the place of desperate hunger, willing to give up everything with great expectation for what God will do. A leader who was participating in the interview asked, "What is the role of theology?" Otis replied that there is a stream of theology, not major or widespread, that sees prayer and passion for revival as presumptuous. This perspective caused faith to dissipate or reduced it to a hope that somehow God in His sovereignty will choose to come in His way, in His time, and on His agenda. Another listener asked about the significance of leadership. George responded, "Huge." He observed a curious thing:

> The best leaders are found at the back of the line; ones God chooses. God reads hearts, not lips (1 Cor. 1:20–31). They may not have degrees or compelling gifts. It is like the Hebrides revival of 1949. Two ninety-year old women, housebound and mostly blind, began to pray for hours each day. Many people fast and pray, he said, but they are unwilling to conform to basic obedience… how we treat others, the unity of the church, and justice (Isa. 58). Sadly, he added, "There is a growing passion for God's presence, but it is lacking in pastoral leaders. They are distracted by external and internal pressures and by the American culture that has seeped into church, making pastors busy and compartmentalized.

Otis concluded saying that the flower of revival usually falls off within thirty-six months of the time it began to bloom. Why? Revival brought prosperity. Then came a plateau and throttling back. It was drift. To sustain revival, what birthed it must continue. [57]

After the hour-long conference call, I hung up the phone in tears. I was excited to have confirmation about how revival comes, but my heart was breaking with frustration because the Church was divided. She was like the English countryside, with nice hedges that keep people divided. We wanted God only within the hedges we grew. There have been exceptions. Some American churches have decided to suspend a lot of what they are doing to seek God for direction and how they can partner with other congregations to prepare a way for the Lord to bring revival.

Are the characteristics of revival in the Old and New Testaments the same as in the major revivals of post-biblical history? Was George Otis Jr. singing an age-old song? This is the subject of the next chapter, "Great Storms of Our Time, Part 1." The stories of these amazing moves of God raise new hopes that massive revival, a Third Great Awakening, could be just around the corner.

> *What's the condition of your city? What are her needs, and where can the unified Church step into her needs with help, hope, and the love of God?*
>
> (Bob Griffin)

Chapter 6

THE GREAT STORMS OF OUR TIME, PART I

W HEN WE SEE the increasing secularization of America and the limited impact of the Church, nothing is more encouraging than the stories of great revivals. Hope is born. Longing begins to stir, and passion for more of God is ignited. Perhaps America can once again be aflame with the fire of the Holy Spirit and moved by His mighty rushing wind in a firestorm of revival. Praying and waiting is a little like giving birth: labor pains, pushing, straining, and exhaustion. Long before labor and birthing, however, there is excitement, preparation, and anticipation.

Another picture helps me. Sometimes waiting for revival is like the heavy and exhausting waiting at the bedside of a close friend or family member as they fight for life. Time passes, and the loved one seems to get worse with little hope of recovery. Every effort is made to turn the tide, but nothing seems to make a difference. Then, miracle of miracles—suddenly, or within a few days—strength returns and health and vitality are restored. The celebration is great, and the story is told over and over again with excitement, thanksgiving, and praise to God. New life and health are like spring after a cold, harsh winter. Light breaks through dark and dire circumstances.

In the history of revival, spiritual and social life have declined to the place where God's people fear the demise of the Church, the judgment of God, and the crumbling of a once proud and strong society where biblical values were embraced. Some have been feeling this way about America, and a comparison has been made to the Roman Empire that declined from strength and greatness to non-existence.

As we look at Europe, and nations through which great moves of God once swept, we see that the Church is nearly non-existent. Wales, for example, is in great spiritual need today. In much of Europe, Christians form one or two percent of the population. The Church that once produced great theology, and even historic reformation, lies near death and certainly has little impact. Beautiful church buildings are now antique stores, tourist destinations, or mosques. There are some exciting exceptions, but they stand as monuments to past greatness, fallen far from the days of revival and the vibrant Christianity that followed.

I join many who are concerned that this describes America's future, apart from a great move of God. America is becoming untethered from her strong biblical moorings and the societal ethics of the Ten Commandments. "In God we trust" on our coins is at risk of being removed. Biblical marriage is under attack. Families continue to unravel. The percentage of stable nuclear families, with a husband and wife who keep their vows for life, are a minority. Abortion continues. The marketing of baby parts for research has been exposed. Pornography in America is an industry of billions of dollars a year. We need a move of God in our time. It's not about being angry about decline, but lovingly showing a broken culture God's abundant way (John 10:10; Eph. 4:15; John 3:17; Matt. 5:44).

The late Chuck Colson, in "Breakpoint," December 30, 2004, highlighted the tragedy of lost religious freedom in America:

> Pastor Richard Parker was ready to deliver the customary invocation prayer at the Warren County, Virginia, Board of Supervisors meeting. Just before he was to speak, the

county attorney alerted him that he could say "Lord" or "God," but not Jesus. Pastor Parker walked out, explaining that as a Christian pastor, he would not pray if he had to "exit Jesus." Literally hundreds of violations of religious freedom in the United States have been documented by the Liberty Legal Institute, a Texas-based group. On October 20, it presented the Senate Judiciary Subcommittee on the Constitution, Civil Rights and Property, a fifty-one-page report titled "Examples of Religious Hostility in the Public Square."

A Houston teacher trashed two students' Bibles, then marched them to the principal's office and threatened to report their parents to Child Protective Services for allowing them to bring Bibles to school. A ninth-grader got a zero on her research project because she chose Jesus as the topic; worse, her teacher refused to let her submit a substitute project. A St. Louis public school student was "caught" praying over his lunch. As punishment, he was lifted from his seat, reprimanded in front of classmates, and ordered never to pray in school again.

At a New Jersey Veteran's cemetery, an honor guard member was fired for telling a deceased veteran's family, "God bless you and your family." A Minnesota state employee was banned from parking in the state parking lot because his car had a sticker saying, "God is a loving and caring God" and "God defines marriage as a union between a man and a woman."

McKinney, Texas, "has no problem with people meeting in their homes for football watch parties, birthday parties, or even commercial gatherings to sell Tupperware."

> But when a few couples gathered in a pastor's home, they were told, "The city prohibits a church meeting in a home unless the home sits on at least two acres."

As I write in 2021, the secular drift appears to be accelerating. It is never too late for revival. With great hope, join me as I recount five of the great revivals of post-biblical history. (Do it again, Lord! Come Holy Spirit! May your fire fall again as at Pentecost.)

There are many revivals recorded in history, but the five I have chosen to study are the high points on the mountain range of revival history. Are the characteristics the same as the moves of God through the Scripture? Do they affirm 2 Chronicles 7:14 as the pattern? If so, the Church today can be confident that if she obeys God's Word, she will experience another outpouring of the Holy Spirit. By understanding the characteristics of revival that have been consistent throughout time, the Church can set the stage for another great historic move of God, perhaps the last one before Jesus returns for His Bride. His promises stand uncompromised in the Bible. History proves that God will keep them. With this assurance, we take a brief overview of five great firestorms of our time, to identify the ten characteristics of revival in each of them.

Five Firestorms

The First Great Awakening from 1726–1756, flamed up first in Europe and then spread to the American colonies. Puritanism had declined and faded away after the monarchy of England was restored in 1660. Godlessness, crime, and immorality followed, and deism—a form of godliness that was without power and very short on truth—arose and militated against Christian faith. A passionless brand of Christianity was prominent and defenseless.

The roots of revival came from Pietism which was led by two men, Phillip Spencer and August Francke. They birthed the

Moravian movement in 1457, and Count Nikolaus Ludwig Von Zinzendorf—a central figure in the movement—sparked the flames of revival through prayer. He began a twenty-four hour a day prayer gathering in his home in 1724 that birthed a movement that lasted for one hundred years. John Wesley had contact with the Moravians in 1738 and came to personal faith in Christ shortly thereafter. He became one of the greatest revivalists of history. Cairns told the story of the First Great Awakening this way.

> The American awakening occurred from 1726 to 1741 (His dating closes the revival earlier than other observers.) It emerged in the middle colonies among the Reformed and Presbyterian groups, in the New England Congregational churches, and in the South among the Baptists. In England, Wales, and Scotland, the Awakening was predominantly Calvinistic. In England, the awakened Christians formed a Methodist group which later broke into Moravians, Calvinistic Methodists under Lady Huntingdon, and Armenian Methodists under the Wesleys. Multiplied thousands of Christians were renewed and sinners brought to salvation. Faith in Christ was made practical in loving service to man. [58]

George Whitfield emerged from the First Awakening as one of the most famous preachers and revivalists of history. Unity of doctrine, itinerant preaching, spontaneous prayer, and the strong involvement of ordinary people were the characteristics of the revival.

The Second Great Awakening, from 1776 to 1810, was transatlantic. It was Protestant and Anglo-Saxon and included a Scandinavian slice under a revivalist by the name of Hauge. As in the First Great Awakening, conditions were terrible. In the Church, doctrinal division and politics produced a dull spiritual edge. Rationalism was the curse of the day and took over colleges, which interestingly were a common setting for the move of God's Spirit. The most common setting of the revival was the camp meeting. Charles Finney was one of the great preacher-leaders as well as the Methodist circuit riders, Devereux Jarratt, Peter Cartwright, and Isaac Backus. In a foreshadowing of the current prayer movements, Backus began concerts of prayer in New England. The revival profoundly touched Methodists, Presbyterians, and Baptists. Lay preachers were prominent as in the first Great Awakening and they became the promoters of social reform. Thousands came to Christ.

How will the next Great Awakening come? Could it be that the next Great Awakening across America will not come out of the religious establishment? Some have said it will be birthed among youth, and others believe it will spring up in the marketplace.

The Prayer Meeting Revival in New York City, 1857–1858, is the thrilling story of a sparsely attended prayer meeting that grew into a massive firestorm. At first it is like the small spark from a flint, but it ignites an explosion of revival across New York City and beyond to other major cities and around the world. It began in prayer meetings through the ministry of Jeremiah Lanphier in New York City and Phoebe and Walter Palmer in Canada.

Lanphier handed out inexpensive handbills inviting people to pray at noon. At first he thought no one would show up, but finally, several came. The little group that met in a small, second-story room in downtown New York multiplied to thousands who prayed together several days a week across the city. The times were tough spiritually, socially, and financially. Crime was pervasive, and banks were closing. Breadlines stretched for city blocks. The Church was impotent. Prayer was predominant in the revival and preaching, although important, played a secondary role. One million came to Christ, one million came back into the Church, and reports indicated that one million came to faith in Christ when the revival spread to Europe. Society was dramatically impacted.

Add the powerful impact of Phoebe Palmer to the role of Jeremiah Lanphier, and you have built a package of dynamite. She and her husband were powerful prayer warriors as much as they were revivalists. Thousands came to their meetings in both Canada and the United States; revival followed them.

Do we really want revival today? It is ours if we will pray. Prayer is at the center of revival. It is at the heart of the instructions for revival in 2 Chronicles 7:14. Small sparks of persistent prayer burst into a firestorm.

The Welsh Revival of 1904, like the preceding revivals, was born out of great social and spiritual need. In her book, *The Cure of All Ills,* Mary Stewart Relfe reported that Wales topped the world in need. It was "drunken and profane due to its struggling mining economy. The Church was largely ignored and the few believers distraught." [59] Evan Roberts was the most predominant leader in the revival, but others played important roles, too. They included Rosina Davies who was converted through the Salvation Army, and Jessie Penn-Lewis who set up the Welsh Keswick movement. Seth Joshua stood out as a key leader. Cairns summarized the results of the Welsh Revival:

> Prayer, praise in ecstatic singing, and testimony of lay converts with much emotion, was emphasized. Roberts was an exhorter rather than expositor ...The 1904 awakening was more subjective and often mystical in its expression of God's love, loyalty to Christ, the cross, the need for the Holy Spirit, and a love for souls. It did... have practical results in the short run. Confession of sin brought restitution of property and money. Gambling and the consumption of liquor dropped in many places.

> Swearing in the mines ended; the pit ponies even had to learn to respond to a new vocabulary of gentle words to replace the cursing of former days. [60]

The Azusa Street Revival, 1906–1909, launched the Pentecostal movement and denominations across America and the world. By 1980, there were fifty million who claimed to be Pentecostal and many other Charismatics were salted through more traditional denominations. Synan reported, "Central to the Azusa event was a teacher, Charles Parham; a preacher, William J. Seymour; a city, Los Angeles; a journalist, Frank Bartleman; and a building, the Azusa Street Mission." [61] He stated that "within a short time the Azusa Street Pentecost became a worldwide move of the Holy Spirit." [62] In fact, when introducing the eye witness account of Bartleman in 1980, he wrote that one million persons per year had accepted the premises of the Los Angeles Pentecost. In 1975, he reported that ten thousand Pentecostal Catholics met in Rome. In 1978, two thousand Anglicans met in Canterbury Cathedral in London for a similar meeting.

Riss reports that the results of the revival were nearly as great as the Protestant Reformation:

> The early Pentecostal Revival came as one of the greatest revivals of the modern period, perhaps almost as important in its effects as the Protestant Reformation of the sixteenth century. It brought into existence hundreds of ecclesiastical bodies and denominations worldwide, many of which quickly became some of the fastest growing religious organizations in the world. [63]

Today, this widening stream of Christianity includes some of the largest and fastest-growing congregations and denominations in the country. In mission circles, Pentecostals are known for having great impact for the Gospel around the world. In the 1990s brush fires of revival—such as in Pensacola, Florida, the Airport Fellowship in Toronto, Canada, in Smithton, Missouri, and the fourteen-year movement of revival across Argentina are Pentecostal or charismatic in nature.

With this brief overview, can we identify the characteristics of New and Old Testament revival in these firestorms of our time? I believe the answer is a confident, yes! As we look at each characteristic in these five great revivals, I'm sure revival hunger will grow for a powerful move of God in our day. *You may get lost in the details that substantiate the characteristics of revival.* If so, skim through them to pick up highlights. As we look at each characteristic, we will find ourselves in familiar territory. It will be a return to what we found in the Old and New Testaments.

The Ten Characteristics in the Firestorms of Our Time

The instructions for revival in 2 Chronicles 7:14 are in response to Solomon's questions in his temple dedication prayer. He asks God what He will do in times of trouble, the result of Israel's drift into the sin of the nations that surround them, defeated by an enemy because of sin, and no rain in their agrarian world, resulting in famine, plagues, blight or mildew, locusts or grasshoppers, disaster, and disease. God's answer is clear. If they humbled themselves, prayed, sought His face, repented, and turned from their sinful ways, God would hear from heaven and forgive them. He would heal their land. This is the climate out of which the *firestorms* of revival begin to heat up.

CHARACTERISTIC 1
Dark and Difficult Times: Storms Appear on the Radar

Revival occurred in times of personal or national crisis, and great spiritual need, and in times of moral darkness and spiritual decline among God's people, Israel, or His Church.

We rarely hear the morning or evening news without a weather forecast. Why do we care about the weather? It helps us with our planning: Can we travel? What shall we wear? Should we avoid excessive heat or a dangerous storm? Meteorologists often point to the Doppler radar to show the beginnings of a pattern, "We'll keep our eyes on this for you," they promise.

Revival radar, prior to every great firestorm of history, shows dark clouds of economic, spiritual, and social decline. It is ominous, but it's out of these circumstances that longings for much better times begin to grow. What is happening to us? Why are we so like the culture, sucked into a secular way of thinking and living? Why does God seem so far away? Why are things so bad? Why is sin so blatant? Why do we fail to make an impact? Why aren't we pushing back the encroachment of Satan? When did competition and empire building sneak into the Church to rob her of obedience to the critically important prayer of Jesus for unity in John 17:20–23? Is it why our city doesn't know the Father sent the Son? Why are we not obeying the command for unity in Ephesians 4:1–16 and in most of the apostle Paul's letters? The pattern is consistent. It is the first characteristic of revival.

The First Great Awakening

Authors McDow and Reid described the conditions before the First Great Awakening. There was great spiritual decline and liberalism.

Higher criticism and theological liberalism had emerged from the Enlightenment. Spiritual life had been squeezed out of Christian schools and the Church. [64] Darkness has often been the greatest just before dawn, as it was just before the First Great Awakening.

Deism was growing in popularity, and Christianity became encrusted with powerless tradition. Pastors were some of the most ritualistic, enslaved by tradition, dry in faith like a drought, and "more concerned with political unity than spiritual fervency. The result was a twin problem which brought the need of awakening to the forefront: deviant orthodoxy (a departure from historic Christian belief) and dead orthodoxy (correct belief devoid of corresponding Christian behavior)." [65]

The wealthy were addicted to a lifestyle of behavior that would have eventually produced as much chaos as in the French Revolution. "The worst vices prevailed, and were by many considered marks of good breeding; if any one condemned them, they were set down as a fool, and jeered at for their pains. Most rural laborers had no formal education, and it is scarcely surprising that they were vary widely sunk in depravity and animalism." [66] The consumption of alcohol in England rose from five and one half million gallons in a population of six million in 1735 to eleven million in 1751. Signs advertised the problem. "Drunk for one penny; dead drunk for two pence, and straw for nothing." [67] Crime was out of control, as in many cities of America today. To be out at night in certain areas would be to risk mugging or death. An attorney, by the name of Blackstone, reported that after hearing every clergyman of any note in London, not one sermon "had more Christianity in it than the works of Cicero." [68] Johnson quoted Archbishop Secker as saying, "An open and professed disregard to religion has become, through a variety of unhappy causes, the distinguishing character of the present age." [69]

The American colonies were not much different than Europe. People had courageously gone west for freedom, but it turned into license. "The French and Indian wars had fed all the fiercest passions of human nature...and relaxed all moral convictions and restraints. Every form of vice prevailed as never before in their history." [70]

The Second Great Awakening

Unfortunately, it was bad again before the Second Great Awakening. The source was different, however, because spiritual decline and apostasy grew out of a more intellectual climate. Doctrinal division and politics had soured the results of the First Great Awakening. A flood of rationalistic literature came from France and Great Britain.

The effect on US colleges was incredible. Students embraced rationalism and called themselves by the names of famous skeptics and infidels. Even Bible colleges became centers of skepticism. Christian students became such a minority on some campuses that they felt compelled to meet secretly. [71]

The French had helped the colonists fight for freedom, but they also brought with them "much of the spiritual and moral refuse of the Enlightenment to the New World. Skepticism, deism, even atheism, came through the writings of Voltaire, Rousseau, and David Hume," and they were promoted by people such as Thomas Paine, Ethan Allen, and others who opposed biblical Christianity.

The French and Indian War, 1754 to 1763, and the Revolutionary War, 1776 to 1783, distracted many from the fiery faith of the First Great Awakening. Many clergy left their congregations to report for military duty. Worship was neglected. The impact of the Enlightenment, the war efforts, and the drift from the Church produced tragic results. Putting it briefly, "promiscuity, profanity, gambling, and drunkenness increased." [72]

Warren Candler calls the days before the Second Great Awakening, a time "of great religious declension." He adds, "When it began, the state of both the nation and the Churches was gloomy by reason of faith decayed and hearts grown cold. Iniquity abounded and skepticism prevailed on all sides." Reflecting on the negative impact of the Enlightenment, he quotes a Bishop who remarked, "I can truly say that...in every educated young man in Virginia whom I met I expected to find a skeptic, if not an avowed unbeliever. [73]

The following entry from a General Assembly meeting of the Presbyterian Church in 1798, confirms the conditions before the Second Great Awakening.

> Formidable innovations and convulsions in Europe threaten destruction to morals and religion ...We perceive with pain and fearful apprehension a general dereliction of religious principles and practice among our fellow-citizens, a visible and prevailing impiety and contempt for the laws and institutions of religion, and an abounding infidelity, which, in many instances, tends to atheism itself. The profligacy and corruption of the public morals have advanced with a progress proportionate to our declension in religion. Profaneness, pride, luxury, injustice, intemperance, lewdness, and every species of debauchery and loose indulgence greatly abound. [74]

The Prayer Meeting Revival in New York City

Before the Prayer Meeting Revival in New York City, it was the "same old song, second verse, a whole lot louder and a whole lot worse!" J. Edwin Orr wrote.

> Religious life in the United States of America was in decline. There were many reasons for decline, political and social as well as religious. The conflict over slavery diverted attention from spiritual pursuits to debate and argue over this wrenching concern. Attacking the Church was a widespread teaching that Christ was going

to return in 1843 or 1844. William Miller and others were spreading this idea. When it didn't happen, there was a general loss of faith in spiritual things. Public confidence was shaken. Some even responded by becoming bitter infidels while others embraced a cynical materialism. It was so widespread that churches were ridiculed and Church growth could not keep pace with decline in attendance. [75]

Prosperity affected Christianity negatively. The accumulation of wealth was a national priority. Warren Candler wrote, "As gains grew, godliness declined. Men forgot God in pursuit of gold." [76]

The passion for the accumulation of available and inexpensive land on the frontier complicated the situation. Opportunities for land were abundant for those who could take a little risk. They joined many who caught the excitement of moving to the new edge of opportunity as the frontier stretched west. It all fell apart with a financial crash, the third in American history. Panic followed prosperity. Banks failed, factories were shut down, and at one time, thirty thousand men were unemployed in New York City alone. Hunger and despair characterized the city. [77]

The issue of slavery was growing into a national crisis in the 1840s and 1850s. It birthed the Civil War. The Missouri Compromise of 1850, the Fugitive Slave Law, the Kansas-Nebraska Act, abolitionist agitation, and the march of slavery in the South and West became the birth pangs.

It wasn't just slavery that troubled the nation. Heavy Irish and German immigration in the same period introduced the European idea of how to live on Sunday. After a morning service, it was just like every other day in the week. The Economic Panic of 1857, reaching a crisis level on October 14, made people more aware of the impotence of material goods and toys. Corruption during the

Grant administration put a sour taste in the mouths of many, and a call began to arise for morality. [78]

The Welsh Revival of 1904

The Welsh Revival of 1904 followed the same pattern of spiritual, moral, and social decline. Great revival had swept Wales in 1859, and some reports indicated that as many as one hundred thousand people came to faith in Christ. [79] Unfortunately, by 1904, the country was in great decline again. Henry Johnson included a quote from the journal of Evan Roberts as he wrote the story of the Welsh revival, "For a long, long time I was much troubled in my soul and my heart by thinking over the failure of Christianity. Oh! It seemed a failure; and I prayed and prayed." [80]

An article by Dean David Howell, just before he died in 1902, was one of the tools God used to call the nation to prayer. In the article, Howell described the conditions of the day. Preaching he said was "able, scholarly, interesting, and instructive...but little unction and anointing." Biblical concepts like conviction, conversion, repentance, adoption, and sin became foreign ideas. He concluded, "The principal need of my country and dear nation at present is still spiritual revival through a special outpouring of the Holy Spirit." [81]

A Chicago newspaper characterized the national spirit of Wales as "dull depression and gloomy doubt." The report stated that the time was ripe for a great religious revival. The efforts of many, it reported, were unable to "stem the flood of evil or stop the growth of pleasure-seeking and mammon worship. A generation had risen that had not seen the arm of God working as it had done in 1859 in Ireland." [82] Wales was in bad spiritual and social shape.

The Azusa Street Revival

Close on the heels of the 1904 Welsh revival came Azusa Street, 1906 through 1909. Frank Bartleman wrote an eyewitness account in his book, *Azusa Street: The Roots of Modern-day Pentecost*. Introducing the book, Vinson Synan described Los Angeles, California, as "a city of some 228,000, which was growing at a rate of 15 percent a year …[Many strange] religions and a multiplicity of denominations occupied the religious attentions of the city. Los Angeles was a melting pot with large numbers of Hispanics, Chinese, Russians, Greeks, Japanese, Koreans, and Anglo-Americans." [83] Expressing the need for revival, one of Bartleman's journal entries stated, "The Holiness people are loaded down to the water's edge with a spirit of prejudice and pharisaism…sectarian prejudice, a party spirit, and pessimism." [84] In an entry dated July 1905, he wrote, "The present warlike attitude and distress…makes us wonder if the judgment to follow may not even plunge us into the tribulation." Another journal entry said, "Unbelief of every form has come in upon us like a flood. But lo, our God comes also." [85]

Mary Stewart Relfe described the spiritual and social scene in America around the turn of the century, just prior to revival:

> Spiritual decadence pervaded society in the late 1890's. Corruption, immorality, drunkenness, cults, gambling and agnosticism rose in proportion to the Church's ineptness. By the turn of the century, the glory had departed, the saints had defected, the salt had lost its savor, the world had lost its light, and deep moral darkness prevailed. [86]

Relfe quoted a statement from a publication called "The Western Christian Advocate," printed in 1902.

Again, there is the outcry of a public aghast at a seeming "tidal-wave of immorality" breaking over the land. On every hand political corruption is rife. Divorce and lax marriage relations, fornication and adultery, scandalize us. In great cities, like New York and Chicago, murders, suicides, and "hold-ups" crowd on each other's heels. The newspapers every morning are a record of a carnival of crime. [87]

From an article written in 1904, Relfe quotes its expression of concern and hope, "Revival is needed. Revival is possible. Revival will set back the strong tide of sin and corruption that is sweeping away the life of the nation." [88]

McDow and Reid wrote that reconstruction, the spread of the nation westward, industrialization, technical advances like the automobile, telephone, and electric light, as well as immigration and urbanization, seriously affected the nation. "Spiritual life ebbed... trends that would strangle the spiritual life of the nation." Some of these trends were the rise of higher criticism, the promotion of a social gospel, and the incipient decay of conviction brought on by liberalism. [89] The stage was set again for a move of God.

The first characteristic of revival in the Scripture and the setting of 2 Chronicles 7:14 line up in all five major post-biblical revivals. Could it be that Jesus's words in Mark 7:9 apply today as secularism and sensuality characterize America? "You have a fine way of setting aside the commands of God in order to observe your own traditions." When the nations decline into secular, economic, and spiritual chaos, the stage is set for revival if the Church will arise in humble prayer to seek God's face.

CHARACTERISTIC 2
Leadership: Servants of God Step Out of the Crowd

**Revival began in the heart(s) of one or more conse-
crated servants of God, who became the agent(s) God
used to lead God's people back to faith and obedience.**

Have you ever noticed that in random groups, sooner or later,
someone emerges to give leadership, frustrated with chaos or confusion or sensing that no one is in charge? In a similar way, out of
the difficult times of the first characteristic, God's ordained leaders
begin to step out to give leadership, particularly to call God's people
to prayer. Often it is not the wise, influential, or noble. It is the
foolish, weak, lowly, despised, but in Christ (1 Cor. 1:26–31). They
are some of the most well-known heroes of faith. Many writers and
many volumes capture their stories, yet much more is yet to be told.
Think about the volumes it would take to tell the personal story of
each one, their birth, God's shaping in their lives, their spiritual
birth, their weakness, God's calling, His unique equipping, and their
effectiveness. In response to the prayers, preaching, and leadership
of these giants of faith, thousands come to faith in Christ. Cities
and nations are transformed.

The First Great Awakening—1726

The First Great Awakening between 1726 and 1756 had many
leaders who called God's people to prayer and repentance. They
lit the match of revival. In the British Isles, the well-known Wesley
brothers—Charles and John—along with George Whitfield, ignited
the move of God's Spirit. In Wales, Howell Harris and others were
God's influential leaders. In the American colonies, it was men
like Jonathan Edwards and lesser known leaders like Gilbert and
William Tennent, Bellamy, Griswold, Wheelick, Robinson, and

Blair. In 1740, the great revival preacher, George Whitfield, came to America. His preaching had as great an impact in the colonies as it did in Europe. These men were the most visible and notable, but others were influential as well, through more localized or behind the scenes. They set the stage for the movement of God. Earle Cairns believed that the leaders of Pietism laid a solid foundation for revival in Germany. Spencer and Franckell, leaders of Pietism, along with Zinzendorf of the Moravians, were a product of Pietism.

In the British Isles, primarily Wales, Jones, Harris, and Rowland were the key leaders. Cambuslang and Kilsyth were leaders in Scotland. Arminian Perfectionists like the Wesleys, and Calvinists like Whitfield and Lady Huntingdon came out of England. Influential clergy were Venn, Walker, Berridge, Grimshaw, Romaine, and Fletcher. In the American colonies, Southern Presbyterians Morris and Davies, and Frelinghuysen and the Tennents in the middle colonies, were great leaders. Stearns, a Baptist, and Presbyterians Morris and Davies were also great revival leaders. In New England, Jonathan Edwards, a Congregationalist, and Backus, a Baptist, gave leadership to the move of God's Spirit. [90]

Humanity had raced forward at unprecedented speed with the Reformation and Renaissance. The Enlightenment followed. No longer was the earth considered by many to be the center of the universe. Rationalism, deism, and empiricism had a significant impact on Western society. It wasn't so much a sprint toward heresy and rebellion against God and the Bible, but it stole from the Church her wonder and awe of God, the sense of His majesty. Spirituality took a nosedive, not of radical and sudden rejection of faith and belief in the Bible, but "because of the drip, drip, drip of culture, pushing the conviction of a transcendent God further to the periphery." [91]

The Puritan movement took a strong stand against this drift. The leaders of the movement included Laurence Humphrey, president of Magdalen College, Oxford, Thomas Cartwright, a professor of theology at Cambridge, Thomas Wilcox, a London pastor, William

Travers, a Cambridge professor, and John Bunyan, the well-known author. Many others stood strong against the drift in the Church of England, and their leadership shaped the early stages of revival.

The Second Great Awakening—1776

Evangelical Protestant churches, on the defensive against deism and rational religion through the Revolutionary era, recovered their confidence during the Second Great Awakening. They were the primary revival force in the country. During the later stages of the awakening, hundreds of thousands of new converts became full members of Protestant churches, many of them convinced that the kingdom of God was at hand. [92] Camp meetings, college revivals, and great interest in foreign missions were characteristics of this second great move of God.

Who stepped out of the crowd to pray, to preach, and to call the Church back to God? The best-known leader of the revival was Charles Finney, but there were others. Preachers called down God's fire at camp meetings. At the turn of the century, like harvesters moving across fields of ripe grain, itinerants like Asahel Nettleton saw great crops of new believers. Many professing Christians returned to biblical "first love" and renewed their Christian faith. On the college scene, movements were led by students at Hampden-Sydney College in Virginia. Daniel Baker, a Hampden-Sydney student, spoke at Yale and "became the impetus of revival," spreading the flame. At Yale, Timothy Dwight, the son of Jonathan Edwards, became president. His preaching and teaching were a powerful force in turning the students to Christ from "deplorable" behavior and secularism. [93]

The Hay Stack Revival, at Williams College Massachusetts, was well known as a part of the Second Great Awakening. Student Samuel Mills led a by-weekly prayer meeting where revival broke out at a prayer time one rainy day. Students found shelter by a large haystack. This was the day that Mills proposed a mission to India, a vision that was later fulfilled when Adoniram Judson, Samuel Mott, Luther Rice, Gordon Hall, and Samuel Newell went to India as missionaries. [94]

John Erskine of Scotland was another great leader who lived during the First Great Awakening. His writing launched a Concert of Prayer movement and with it, fanned the revival that swept across England. Jonathan Edward's treatise, *A Humble Attempt in Extraordinary Prayer for the Revival of Religion and the Advancement of Christ's Kingdom to Promote Explicit Agreement and Visible Union of God's People,* was written in 1747 after the crest of the First Great Awakening. It provided fuel for the Second Great Awakening. It was based on Erskine's work. It was sent to John Ryland and Andrew Fuller, two Baptist leaders. Baptists Isaac Backus and Stephen Gano, and as many as twenty other pastors in New England, distributed a circular letter in 1794 calling for prayer for an awakening. All denominations supported the call, and revival fires were fanned.

Francis Asbury was used to spark revival in Western camp meetings in Kentucky. On the American frontier, James McGready, was one of the primary leaders, along with Lyman Beecher, James Caughey, and Jacob Knapp. Charles Finney's ministry (1792–1847) took place toward the end of the Second Great Awakening. [95]

The Prayer Meeting Revival of New York City

Some believe that the Prayer Meeting Revival in New York City, 1857–1858, was an extension of the Second Great Awakening. Jeremiah Lanphier (sometimes spelled Lamphier) was the best-known leader. Having retired from business at age forty-eight, he felt called to the inner city of New York to do mission work. He began with distributing gospel tracts. Passionate about revival and a man of prayer, he published and distributed handbills calling for a noontime prayer meeting. Conditions in the city and nation were terrible. Banks were closing, thousands were out of work, and crime ravaged New York and many other cities. The Church was weak against the pervasive strength of the darkness.

Lanphier was no stranger to revival. He came to faith in Christ at the Broadway Tabernacle under the preaching of Charles Finney who led revival toward the end of the second Great Awakening. In this setting, a passion for prayer and revival was birthed in Lanphier's soul. He had lived in difficult times. He had seen people begin to call out to God in prayer. He knew its power. Only three came to his first prayer meeting—late at that. The following week, there were six. Soon it became a daily event, and within six months, one thousand were meeting at noon for prayer in New York City. [96]

The meetings grew into the thousands, as reported by the *New York Times*. A reported ten thousand came to Christ in New York City alone. The movement spread to Texas and then to the Ohio valley. One hundred thousand came to Christ by May 1858. In Boston, Chicago, Pittsburgh, Cincinnati, and other cities across the country, prayer meetings were drawing thousands to Christ. "The Methodists and Baptists in the South gained a total of about two hundred thousand and one hundred thousand respectively in a three-year period." [97]

R. A. Torrey reported that prayer meetings were soon held every hour of the day and night in New York City, and not only in churches, but also in theaters and other public places. Horace Greeley, the newspaper giant, sent a reporter to check out what was happening. He could only visit twelve meetings, but counted 6,100 people. Mary Stewart Relfe wrote, "Tens of thousands of New Yorkers were praying around the clock, seven days a week. The fire spread from New York to Philadelphia, and to other cities, and then swept the entire country." One million were drawn to Christ in the Church and about the same number outside the Church. [98]

Phoebe Palmer was one of the most influential leaders in the Prayer Meeting revival and one of the first prominent female preachers in America. Relfe believed that it was Palmer's fervent prayers and ministry that laid a significant part of the foundation. "For years she had been cloistered away in her prayer closet." [99] Phoebe Palmer was as influential in America as Catherine Booth was in England. Both women were great intercessors, used mightily by God. Relfe wrote:

> In the decade of the 1850's, Phoebe's physician-husband, Dr. Walter Palmer, decided to retire from his medical practice and accompany her as an evangelistic team. By the close of 1857, these anointed meetings had so impacted the churches in the eastern states that in December, the Presbyterians called for a Convention on Prayer and Revival in New York, and much of it was spent on their knees. Baptists and Methodists in New York set aside a day a week to pray for revival in their churches for revival. By New Year's Day 1858, pastors all over the East were preaching on prayer, revival and holiness with a social conscience. [100]

In Ontario, Canada, in October 1857, twenty-one came to Christ as Savior the first night of Palmer's meetings. Soon forty people were coming to faith every day. One hundred came to Christ on the last day of the meetings. The Camp Meetings at which the Palmers preached saw five to six thousand in attendance. Reports in papers stated that revival was spreading across Canada. [101]

Following on the heels of the prayer meeting movement, revival spread to the Confederate Army with estimates of conversions as high as one hundred fifty thousand. Revival flames were fanned through letters from home, Bible distribution, and godly officers and chaplains. Woven through this period were great itinerant preachers, including the best known, D. L. Moody. Children were not excluded from this revival. Under the ministries of Sam Jones and Edward Hammond, many children came to Christ.

The Welsh Revival of 1904

The key leader of the Welsh Revival of 1904 was Evan Roberts, a miner's son. God called him much like he called Samuel in the Old Testament. In the spring of 1904, Roberts was awakened many times during the night with a sense of God's presence. God was calling him to preach. In a meeting in September 1904, history records that Seth Roberts, a contemporary of Evan Roberts, was crying out to God, saying, "Lord, bend us." Evan Roberts picked up on this passionate cry and his plea became, "Lord, bend me." Roberts did not complete his education. He left school to go home to Loughor, and began to meet with young people. It was among the youth that revival broke out and spread as Roberts traveled and spoke. By the end of 1905, one hundred thousand were converted. [102]

Roberts was not the only leader. Another was Rosina Daves who came to faith in Christ through the ministry of the Salvation Army. Many conversions were recorded in her meetings, 250 in 1905. Seth Joshua, a Welsh Presbyterian, converted in 1872, was another influential revival preacher. Other leaders included Jessie Penn-Lewis and J. J. Welsh, who led Keswick conferences. The Keswick movement has been credited for stopping the rapid spiritual decline of the time. In one Keswick meeting, a young Welsh girl stood to her feet to declare, "If no one else will, then I must say that I do love the Lord Jesus Christ with all my heart." It was this simple testimony that sparked revival in the group. [103]

Dean David Howell, another significant leader, wrote an article that spread across the nation. In it, he described the appalling conditions he observed in the Church and called for "a spiritual revival through a special outpouring of the Holy Spirit." W. S. Jones, the pastor of a Welsh Baptist congregation in Scranton, Pennsylvania, experienced a personal transformation in his own life, and he returned to Wales with a passion to see revival among clergy. [104]

Leadership is God's way of developing and reshaping His people. They rise out of the pre-revival soil like spring crocuses pushing through the snow and ice of winter. They call God's people to prayer and repentance. The bloom of hope is birthed, and dreams begin to take shape for a mighty move of God to revive the Church and reform society.

The Azusa Street Revival

The Azusa Street Revival of 1906, like the other four revivals, can be credited to chosen people, called and empowered by God to lead the Church back to her "first love" and biblical mission. Richard Riss writes about the larger story of the Pentecostal movement that was birthed at Azusa Street:

> The early Pentecostal Revival came as one of the greatest revivals of the modern period, perhaps almost as important in its effects as the Protestant Reformation of the sixteenth century. It brought into existence hundreds of ecclesiastical bodies and denominations worldwide, many of which quickly became some of the fastest growing religious organizations in the world. The Pentecostal Revival started at Azusa Street in Los Angeles in a dilapidated building that once served as a Methodist church. Continuous meetings were held...every day for a period of three years...becoming known throughout the world as the focal point of the Pentecostal outpouring of God's Spirit. [105]

William Seymore, an African American Holiness preacher, was the leader God used to spark the Azusa Street revival. He was a disciple of Charles Parham, whose ministry was known for the Baptism of the Holy Spirit, authenticated by speaking in tongues. There had been several localized revival movements in Parham's ministry. Seymore caught the fire, and the mantle from his mentor fell across his shoulders.

The Azusa Street movement began in cottage prayer meetings led by Seymore. It was in the home of Richard and Ruth Asberry "that the Spirit of God fell on April 9, 1906, after many months of concerted prayer." [106] It was a firestorm!

Prior to the outpouring, Frank Bartleman, a young holiness preacher and emerging writer, had distributed tracts and preached on the streets of Los Angeles and in holiness missions. He had a deep passion, not only for revival, but also to meet the needs of the poor. Bartleman was one of many who had heard F. B. Meyer tell about the Welsh revival when he came to Los Angeles. Meyer had met with Evan Roberts, the spark plug of the Welsh outpouring and carried the revival torch from Wales by often describing the events of what happened there. The stories burned like fire within Bartleman, who longed for a similar move of God in America, especially in Los Angeles. [107]

Bartleman and Seymore were the key leaders of the Azusa Street Revival, as F.B. Meyer carried the spark from Wales. It was obvious, again, that out of dark and difficult times, God raised up leaders to pray, to call the Church to prayer, and to preach conviction that sparks repentance across the Church, the second characteristic of revival. The first two characteristics have been similar to the revival in Scripture.

CHARACTERISTIC 3
Prayer: Fanning the Flame from Spark to Fire

Prayer was central to revival. Leaders called out to God in prayer, passionately seeking His face in repentance,

and in the confession of their personal and national sins. They ignited prayer among God's people.

Nothing is more central to revival than prayer. There has never been a revival without it. It's characteristic 3. Brian Edwards says it well:

> "You cannot read far into the story of a revival without discovering that not only is prayer part of the inevitable result of an outpouring of the Spirit, but from a human standpoint, it is also the single most significant cause." [108]

It is time for God's people to pray; really pray. Jesus said, "My house will be called a house of prayer for all nations," not a den of robbers (Mark 11:17). What is Jesus thinking about today's Church? Is the Church across America a house of prayer?

Many things characterize the Church, from contemporary worship to a vast diversity of programs for a variety of needs. There are only a few major congregations that have a reputation for making prayer central. The Brooklyn Tabernacle in New York City is one of them.

I believe that prayer is not only how revival comes, but it is also how God gets His work done. It is no wonder that prayer is at the pinnacle of 2 Chronicles 7:14. It is no surprise that the enemy comes to steal this strategic weapon and to encumber the Church with its traditions and activities. Encrusted ecclesiology hinders the life and flow of the Holy Spirit and keeps the Church bound to her old wineskins.

Matthew Henry wrote, "When God intends great mercy [for His people] the first thing he does is to set them a-prayin." John Wesley said, "God does nothing but in answer to prayer." Arthur Pierson captures the importance of prayer in one sentence. "There has been not one great spiritual awakening in any land which has not begun in a union of prayer." [109]

The First Great Awakening

As with the first two characteristics of revival, prayer was central to post-biblical revivals. The roots of the First Great Awakening were planted in Germany through the amazing life and ministry of Count Nikolaus Ludwig Van Zinzendorf, a Moravian. In 1724 he established a community of believers called the "Herrnhut" (The Lord's Watch). Within that community, prayer became central to their life and passion. It has been difficult to comprehend the duration and passion of their prayer meetings. The community prayed for 100 years, 24 hours a day! "In this, even children wept with power before God." [110]

John Wesley met a group of Moravians on a ship taking him to America. Wesley had little assurance of his salvation and was impressed with the faith and assurance of the Moravians during periods of danger at sea. Obviously they had an Anchor in the storm. It was an unlikely paradox that this meeting took place, except in answer to prayer and God's design. It was this encounter that began Wesley's passionate search for what was missing in his relationship with God. He wanted the kind of faith that gave peace in difficult situations. It was in prayer and through the study of Luther's *Preface to Romans* that he came to the assurance of salvation through faith in Christ as his Savior. In unique style, he described it this way. "I did trust Christ, Christ alone for salvation; and an assurance was given me that He had taken away my sins, even mine, and saved me from the law of sin and death." [111]

John Wesley became one of the greatest revival preachers of history, and he was God's instrument of revival in the First Great Awakening. Who could have guessed it would be the impact of godly Moravians on a ship in the middle of the ocean? The influence of the Moravians was immense. They were prayer warriors. Think about the influence they had, not only on John Wesley, but on his friends of the Holy Club at Oxford University. Among them was not only the Wesleys, but George Whitfield. Listen to the exciting account of the Holy Club as told by Wesley Duewel.

> In the early 1730's the Wesley brothers gathered several student friends into John's room at Lincoln College, Oxford University, to earnestly seek to be holy. Membership ran ten to fifteen, and never more than twenty-five.

> On New Year's Day, 1739, John and Charles Wesley, George Whitfield, and four other members of the Holy Club, plus about sixty other like-minded people, held a love feast in London at Fetter's Lane. "About three in the morning, as we were continuing instant in prayer, the power of God came mightily upon us, inasmuch that many cried out for exceeding joy, and many fell to the ground (overcome by the power of God). As soon as we recovered a little from that awe and amazement at the presence of His Majesty, we broke out with one voice, "We praise Thee, O God; we acknowledge thee to be the Lord." This event has been called the Methodist Pentecost.

> Five nights later, eight of these 'Methodists' prayed and discussed 'till the early morning hours and left with the conviction that God was about to do great things.' Another night that week a group of them met and spent the whole night in prayer.

> The next weekend, January 14, 1739, Whitfield was ordained. He spent the day before his ordination in prayer and fasting, praying on into the evening. Sunday morning he arose early to pray. "When I went up to the altar, I could think of nothing but Samuel's standing as a

little child before the Lord …When the bishop laid hands upon my head my heart was melted down, and I offered my whole spirit, soul, and body to the service of God's sanctuary!" [112]

Whitfield was converted in a time of despair and discouragement after he dropped out of the Holy Club. God met him profoundly in his misery and confusion as he searched for truth and a personal encounter with God. God has rarely used people significantly until they have come to a place of deep breaking. The risks of pride have been too great. Adulators have destroyed the work of God in leaders as much as criticizers. Popularity, power, and prestige have tended to corrupt leadership, unless deep breaking occurred. Whitfield preached to as many as thirty thousand at one time with amazing, life-changing results. Some reported that he gave eighteen thousand sermons. He worked and preached tirelessly, but his secret was time alone with God in prayer. He usually rose at 4:00 a.m. and sometimes spent whole nights in devotional reading. [113]

McDow and Reid affirm the impact of prayer on the First Great Awakening, "By the turn of the eighteenth century…most believed that only united, earnest prayer could bring a divine outpouring. The Prayer became the emphasis of preachers, rather than calling people to change their behavior. 'Revival of religion' became the phrase used in the 1720's. Ministers began calling people to seek God's face in prayer, in order that He would lead the people into revival." [114]

God has answered throughout history, just like He promised, when only two or three have met together consistently in His name. In times when there seemed to be little change, encouragement has come from the promise of God. "Be strong and courageous, for your work will be rewarded" (2 Chron. 15:7, NLT). Johnson recounts sparks created by the flint of prayer scattered across London:

In London, although the darkness was widespread, gleams of light shone here and there, in the towns, and in country places. Spiritual religion was not left without witness. A few men and women were praying, waiting, and watching for the coming of the power of God to banish darkness, and breathe new life into the heart of the nation ...Day and night the prayer went up from the faithful disciples of Christ as they witnessed the degradation, the wickedness, the brutality, and the spiritual lifelessness of their countrymen. [115]

The Second Great Awakening

Before the Second Great Awakening, "wickedness in general reached such a crescendo that men of the cloth were despairing about the future of Christendom. Into these conditions came Isaac Backus, a man of prayer. Known as much for his praying as for his exhorting, he had an encounter with the Holy Spirit which drew him to the conclusion: There's only one power on earth that commands the power of heaven—prayer." [116]

Backus wrote a paper, "Pleas for Prayer for Revival of Religion" that was patterned after a British Prayer Plan. It was delivered to clergy of all denominations. He pleaded for churches to open for prayer all day the first Monday of every month. They were to pray for revival. Bishop Francis Asbury adopted the plan for all Methodists. Baptists, Presbyterians, Congregationalists, Reformed, and Moravians approved it. America was moved to prayer through a network of organized prayer meetings. What was the impact? "This united prayer effort, instigated by one lone man, brought... heaven down. In 1798 revival fires began to burn again in New England." [117]

On the frontier of America, James McGready, a staid Presbyterian pastor, heard about the movement of God's Spirit. Revival fire began to ignite in his soul. A journal entry read, "In addition to praying all day the first Monday of each month, I insisted my people also spend each Saturday at sunset to Sunday at sunrise in prayer for Revival. The depth of seeking God's face and repentance were amazing. The winter of 1799 was one of weeping and mourning with the people of God." [118]

At one point, McGready called the Church of South-Central Kentucky to a four-day observance of the Lord's Supper. Revival broke out, and people met God in dramatic ways. A similar meeting was held in Cane Ridge in Bourbon County with the same results. Three months later, another area-wide communion was held. This time it was called a camp meeting. Twenty thousand came and thousands were converted. [119]

Prayer and the Second Awakening were "joined at the hip." In 1747, John Erskine of Scotland published an article just after the crest of the First Great Awakening to encourage God's people to gather in prayer, seeking Him for an "outpouring of the Holy Spirit." Jonathan Edwards's treatise, *A Humble Attempt to Promote Explicit Agreement and Visible Union of God's People in Extraordinary Prayer for the Revival of Religion and the Advancement of Christ's Kingdom,* was based on Erskine's article. "In 1784 Erskine sent Baptist leaders John Ryland and Andrew Fuller the treatise. Thus began what was soon a concert of prayer' throughout England. Soon reports of revival...spread across the nation." [120]

The first sparks of revival in the Second Awakening began on college campuses. Prayer and study meetings spread, and waves of revival soon swept campuses into the growing tide of awakening. At Hampden-Sydney College in Virginia, a group of four students met to pray, study, and worship. Fearing the wrath and mockery of fellow students, they met in the woods away from the campus. John Brown, the college president, had come to faith in Christ during the First Great Awakening. He knew the power of prayer. Revival swept through the campus several times over three decades.

The Hay Stack revival at Williams College in Massachusetts was well known. Students found shelter under a haystack during a rainstorm. The passionate prayer of students sparked a firestorm like that of a haystack going up in flames. [121]

It was prayer that sparked revival at Yale. In the fall of 1796, only one freshman, one junior, and eight seniors professed faith in Christ. President Dwight, with scholarship and passionate faith in Christ, taught students biblical truth, and deism was demolished at the school. Story after story recorded the work of the Holy Spirit as revival spread across college campuses as a result of Dwight's influence. [122]

The Prayer Meeting Revival of New York City

The Prayer Meeting Revival of 1857 was a thrilling story of a sparsely attended prayer meeting that grew into a massive firestorm. At first it was like the small spark from a flint, but it ignited an explosion that shot revival across New York City and beyond to other major cities and around the world. It began when Jeremiah Lanphier handed out inexpensive handbills inviting people to pray at noon. At first he thought no one would show up, but finally, several came. The little group that met in a small second story room in downtown New York multiplied to thousands who prayed together seven days a week across the city.

Add the powerful impact of Phoebe Palmer to the role of Jeremiah Lanphier, and you had built package of dynamite. She and her husband were powerful prayer warriors and revivalists. Thousands came to their meetings in both Canada and the United States; revival followed them.

Do we really want revival today? It is ours if we will humble ourselves and pray. Prayer is the heart of revival. It is at the heart of the instructions for revival in 2 Chronicles 7:14. When the Church is passionate about fervent, effectual prayer, she can declare, "Revival is on the way."

The Welsh Revival of 1904 and Azusa Street of 1906

What was the role of prayer in the Welsh and Azusa Street Revivals? It was the same story, the story of prayer. Both of these revivals were a part of the Pentecostal revival that began as early as 1900. Some believe Charles R. Parham lit the spark of the Azusa Street Revival. He took his first church—a Methodist Episcopal Church in Kansas—when he was only nineteen. It wasn't long, however, before he left the church to become a nondenominational evangelist. In 1900 he opened a Bible school with only one textbook, the Bible. Unique to the school was "continuous prayer...maintained in the tower." [123]

Prayer and Bible teaching laid a solid foundation for the revival that followed at Azusa Street. In 1905, J. W. Seymour attended Parham's school in Texas and was in his class. He was the man who held a cottage prayer meeting on Azusa Street in Los Angeles, California, the setting at which the fire of God erupted. As the fire spread through similar meetings, the movement became known for what some have called "Pentecostal distinctives." The meetings included prayers for healing, the experience of the Baptism of the Holy Spirit, and speaking in tongues.

It was not only at Azusa Street where passionate prayer was taking center stage. From the same period of time, the people of Moody Bible Church were passionately praying in Chicago. It wasn't part of the Pentecostal movement, but it certainly was part of the prayer fuel that sparked revival across the nation. Two thousand members were added to the church in a period of eight years. Imagine what it must have been like to visit Moody Church.

In January 1898, at the conclusion of an entire week of prayer at the Church, Pastor R. J. Torrey and the teachers and leaders of Moody Bible Institute, began a weekly prayer gathering every Saturday evening, and continued these meetings for three years. A passionate remnant stayed until 2:00 a.m. or longer. During this time, Torrey was "impressed in one meeting to ask God to use him to lead a worldwide revival." [124]

God answered Torrey. It was like the calling of Saul and Barnabas. The Church was worshiping and fasting when God said, "Set apart for me Barnabas and Saul for the work to which I have called them" (Acts 13:2). That is what happened at Moody, and it was an example of what happens when God's people commit themselves to prayer—global awakening. For example, in 1902, Torrey spoke for large gatherings in Australia and New Zealand. The revival followed a Saturday morning prayer meeting of pastors and laymen. It extended from 1890 to 1901. Torrey was known generally as a great preacher, educator, author, and evangelist, but his skills were refined in prayer.

As a result of the Azusa Street Revival, by 1960 ten million people throughout the world held Pentecostal views—2.3 million in the United States alone. [125] By 1980, there were fifty million classical Pentecostals in churches and missions in practically every nation of the world. Untold numbers of charismatics, in every denomination, have traced part of their spiritual heritage to Azusa Street. [126]

Frank Bartleman, who served with great passion, wrote a personal account of the movement of God at Azusa Street. Brief sketches from history have demonstrated the influence of this humble man. Listen as he told the story. The language was unique, the story, exciting:

> About the first of May a powerful revival broke out in the Lake Avenue M. E. Church in Pasadena. The young men who had been dug out in the meetings in Peniel Mission...attended this church. They had gotten under the burden for a revival there. In fact we had been

praying for a sweeping revival for Pasadena...then we began to pray for an outpouring of the Spirit for Los Angeles and the whole of Southern California. The Spirit is breathing prayer through us for a mighty, general outpouring. Great things are coming. We are asking largely, that our joy may be full. God is moving. We are praying for the churches and their pastors. The Lord will visit those willing to yield to Him. And the same is true today of the Pentecostal people. Their ultimate failure or success for God will be realized just at this point. [127]

Other snapshots of prayer have come from Bartleman's firsthand account. A congregation was waiting for a speaker who had just returned from the revival in Wales. He wrote, "I started the service...on the church steps ...We had a season of prayer ...The evening was a steady sweep of victory." [128] Later, at the beginning of cottage meetings, he recorded, "I kept going day and night...exhorting continually to prayer ...I started a little cottage prayer meeting where we could have more liberty to pray ...We had the devil to fight ...The priests were alive unto God...through much preparation and prayer ...Brother Seymour generally sat behind two empty shoeboxes, one on top of the other. He usually kept his head inside the top one during the meeting." [129]

God tells us what to do if we want to see a move of God in our time—passionately pray. It's time for a firestorm of the Holy Spirit to sweep across America and the world. It's time for the Third Great Awakening.

A haunting question has stood in the shadows of revival history. Why haven't great revivals lasted longer? It has been the pattern of drift. God's people, alive with passion for Him and for serving His purposes, have become comfortable and apathetic. It's what has happened to many marriages. After several years, "first love" faded into ordinary routines. It's what has happened with a personal relationship to God. Times of disciplined Bible reading and prayer faded away.

Sooner or later, Christian life and ministry are reduced to, "just go to church" instead of "go into the world." They must be twin passions. Along with these subtle changes, Satan successfully draws God's people into the culture that surrounds them. As an angel of light, he introduces a lot of good busyness to replace biblical basics. The light of the Gospel and the dynamic witness of authentic Christians becomes nearly nonexistent in the marketplace.

Maxie Dunnam told a great story. "Three Miles from the Coffee." A cowboy was camping out on the prairie. When it was time to cook breakfast, he decided to light the grass and hold his skillet over the flame. But the wind came up, so he kept moving his skillet to keep it over the flame. All seemed to be going well, but when his eggs were cooked, he was three miles from his coffee. [130]

I fear this is a picture of personal and Church drift. We keep moving with the winds of cultural change until one day, we find ourselves miles from basic Christianity.

Central to this drift is the neglect of passionate, disciplined prayer—the key to revival and one of the keys to sustaining it. Communication is the secret of intimacy with others. Your closest friends are those with whom you communicate the most and with whom you share the most deeply. Communication is the secret of intimacy with God. Prayer at its best is a profound two-way communication with God.

Having considered this third characteristic of revival, I want to pause to look more deeply at the discipline of prayer. It's the way to personally and corporately maintain revival and vital Christian faith.

Chapter 7

PRAYER: FANNING THE FLAMES OF CONVERSATIONAL INTIMACY WITH GOD

It must never be forgotten that Almighty God rules this world...just as He rules the Church, through prayer. In dealing with mankind, nothing is more important to God than prayer ...It is only by prayer that God can help people. He who does not pray, therefore, robs himself of God's help and places God where He cannot help ...God's purposes and plans are conditioned on prayer. His will and His glory are bound up in praying ...The days of God's splendor and renown have always been the great days of prayer. (E. M. Bounds) [131]

To say prayers in a decent, delicate way is not heavy work. But to pray really, to pray 'til hell feels the ponderous stroke, to pray 'til the iron gates of difficulty are opened, 'til the mountains of obstacles are removed, 'til the mists are exhaled and the clouds are lifted, and the sunshine of a cloudless day brightens—this is hard work, but it is God's work and man's best labor. (E. M. Bounds) [132]

Tomorrow I plan to work, work, work, from early until late. In fact, I have so much to do that I shall spend the first three hours in prayer. (Martin Luther) [133]

We can do nothing without prayer. All things can be done by importunate prayer. It surmounts or removes all obstacles, overcomes every resisting force and gains its ends in the face of invincible hindrances. (E. M. Bounds) [134]

Today's believers must begin by following God's program for revival as set forth in 2 Chronicles 7:14. If we follow the instructions of this revival text, the floodgates of heaven will open, and both we and our culture will be the surprised recipients of the blessing of God. (Dr. Walter Kaiser) [135]

Prayer is more fundamental in the spiritual life than is speaking a word and indeed is the indispensable foundation for doing so. (Dallas Willard) [136]

"The one constant element in all spiritual revivals is prevailing, extraordinary prayer. (Timothy and Kathy Keller) [137]

HAVE YOU HEARD about the unique ways of the bull moose? Nationals from Northern Canada recount stories of their strange behavior during mating season. The eighteen hundred pound bulls, with massive racks and proud spirits, are tense and irritable during this time as they gather a herd of cows around themselves. Their passions run deep. You get the picture; don't mess with their cows or their territory. The freight trains that thunder through the area are irritants, a serious invasion of privacy. As the stories go, these bulls are known to lower their heads and charge the engines of the trains. A grinding clash of antlers, flesh, and steel follows, and—the moose loses.

What does this have to do with prayer? It seems that God's people sometimes try to do God's work like a bull moose during mating season. Lower your head, grab your impressive experience and degrees, and charge! Pick up the pace! Gather a herd, protect it, and beat out any competition that comes close, no matter what it is.

But that's not how the manual on the Church tells us to build God's kingdom. The ways of man and moose do not work. God's ways are higher than our ways, and His thoughts higher than our thoughts (Isa. 55:8). It's very much like Isaiah 30:15–18, "But you would have none of it. You said, 'No,'...yet the Lord longs to be gracious to you." If we would quit charging freight trains and do God's work God's way, the Church could be vibrant and revived. If God's people would stay with the designer's manual, the Bible, they would grow in intimacy with Him and in effective service for Him. The pattern of drift would be broken; their excitement and passion would not wash out. It would certainly be wise to find a different approach to distractions and irritations.

I have told Connie, "I feel like I am running full speed into concrete walls." This comment has usually followed the frustration of making another effort to unify the area-wide Church and break down the walls of denominational, gender, and racial division. Or it may have followed another passionate plea for the area Church to gather for prayer and worship. Again and again, Connie and I have had to agree, "Let's keep going, but let's be faithful in prayer, and depend on the Holy Spirit to do what needs to be done. Let's continue to call God's people together, but let's make sure we are enjoying this life and calling."

"Unless the Lord builds a house, the work of the builders is unless. Unless the Lord protects a city, guarding it with sentries will do no good. It is useless for you to work so hard from early morning until late at night, anxiously working for food to eat; for God gives rest to his loved ones" (Ps. 127:1–2, NLT). Here's the bottom line. We must do God's work God's way. When we do, His work gets done in His time, and we do not burn out doing it. The kingdom of God thrives, and God's people flourish as they live the abundant life. I believe that prayer is how God gets His work done, and that prayer is the key to revival and how revival is sustained. It is the top priority for the Church, the secret of growing intimacy with God and the catalyst for unleashing the power of God. The older I become, the more I realize that intimacy with God through conversation in prayer is one of life's greatest treasures. When doing God's work His way, the work is done in His time, and with His power and ability. The kingdom of God thrives and His people thrive. It is the "abundant life" (KJV), or "life to the full" (NIV) (John 10:10).

The western Church is declining. We know that God told King Solomon what to do in times of decline and difficulty—2 Chronicles 7:14. We know that prayer is at the apex of this text and has always been the high point of knowing and serving God. We know that Jesus taught us, "My house shall be a house of prayer for all nations" (Isa. 56:7; Luke 19:46). We know that Paul the apostle taught us, "By [God's] mighty power at work within us, He is able to accomplish infinitely more than we would ever dare to ask or hope" (Eph. 3:20, NLT).

Sometimes God's ways have not made sense. Would you have chosen a teenager to kill a giant nine feet tall and deliver a nation? God did (1 Samuel 17). The soldiers in Israel's army were cowering under the threats of Goliath. The entire nation was held hostage by his threats. The king was afraid. He couldn't find anyone to take on the giant.

God sent a teenage shepherd to face Goliath when he was visiting his brothers with food from home. With one rock from a creek, young David hit the giant in the forehead, knocked him out, and used Goliath's own sword to cut off his head. God's ways have rarely been our ways. It has not been productive to try accomplishing His purposes with great human ingenuity and ideas. His ways have only begun to make sense when we have seen the incredible results.

Would you have chosen a man who said he couldn't talk to confront one of the most powerful rulers in the world and lead Israel out of slavery and across a desert? God did! Would you have chosen a man who killed someone in anger and then ran? God did! Even then, this man, Moses, asked God to get someone else. "O Lord," Moses said, "I have never been eloquent, neither in the past nor since you have spoken to your servant. I am slow of speech and tongue" (Exod. 4:10). How could Moses have talked to the king of Egypt and asked him to release the Israeli slaves?

God chose him. He was raised and educated in the palace, more than likely groomed to be the next Pharaoh. He spent forty years on the backside of the desert, herding sheep. This was the most menial, low-class job an Egyptian could do. Moses had become a broken, humble person. Don't miss it. He was living in the very desert through which he would later lead God's people.

Have you thought about God's brilliant military strategy for taking the city of Jericho? God told Israel to march around the city walls once a day for six days and then march around seven times on the seventh day. When they finished, the priests were to blow their trumpets, and all the people were to give a loud shout. The group of escaped slaves, nomads who had wandered in the desert, obeyed in faith, and the massive walls fell down. The nomads won. *God won.*

Would you have used a boy's lunch, five loaves and two fish, to feed five thousand hungry people? The crowd had been following Jesus and listening to His teaching. Jesus's disciples were rather stunned when He told them to prepare lunch. Where was the wholesale food store? Where would they get enough money to pay for it? Yet, everyone was fed, and there was plenty left for the twelve faithless followers.

God's ways are not our ways, and His thoughts are not our thoughts (Isa. 55:8–9). We will see that prayer is central to serving God—seeking His face, receiving His direction, and following Him in obedience. It is the way God will bring revival and city transformation.

God uses people who are available to Him, those who will listen to His still, small voice and are broken, humble, and obedient. "How gracious he will be when you cry for help. As soon as he hears, he will answer (even though there is adversity and affliction—troubles). Your ears will hear...a voice behind you, saying, 'This is the way; walk in it'" (Isa. 30:19–21). If prayer is the key to accomplishing God's purposes, we must pray. The dynamic work of prayer builds intimacy with God and trains us to hear Him. Hearing His still, small voice allows us to learn the next step in accomplishing His purpose. Prayer is how we do God's work. Don't pick up the pace. Don't lower your head and charge.

You may say, "I try to pray. I drift off to sleep, or my mind wanders off in all directions." Some may add, "Church prayer meetings are boring. I like action. Prayer is an exercise in futility." I believe the answer to this is discipline. There are very few valuable endeavors in life that do not take hard work, practice, and discipline. We must, with tenacity and creativity, keep learning and growing in prayer until it becomes as natural as talking with a good friend. The disciples of Jesus learned the power of prayer by watching Him speak to His Father day after day.

Luke 11:28 declares, "Blessed...are those who hear the word of God and obey it." Vance Havner writes, "In the course of history, Christianity periodically clutters up with its own projects and paraphernalia." [138] He is speaking about the priority of prayer.

If we are going to experience "Firestorms of Revival," a historic move of God in our time, it will be the result of following God's instructions in 2 Chronicles 7:14.

The Impact of Prayer

Revival has always been inextricably linked to prayer. Brian Edwards, in his classic book, *Revival*, affirmed it:

> You cannot read far into the story of revival without discovering that not only is prayer a part of the inevitable result of an outpouring of the Spirit, but from a human standpoint, it is also the single most significant cause. [139]

Listen to the words of 1 Peter 4:7: "The end of all things is near." What are we to do? "Be alert and of sober mind so that you may pray" (NIV). As we get closer to the end of time as we know it, we are commanded to pray. No one knows the time of our Lord's return for His Church, but signs seem to indicate that it could be near. It is certainly closer than it has ever been (1 Thess. 5:1–11). It's time to pray.

Prayer is not only at the apex of the instructions for revival in 2 Chronicles 7:14, it is the secret of knowing God intimately and conversationally. Deuteronomy 4:7 tells us, "What other nation is so great as to have their gods near them the way the LORD our God is *near us whenever we pray to him*?" Psalm 145:18 says, "The Lord is *near* to all who call on him." James 4:8 counsels, "Come *near* to God, and he will come *near* to you." "The Lord *confides* in those who fear [revere] him" (Ps. 25:14). The closest of friends confide in each other. We are promised, "You will hear a still small voice behind you saying, 'This is the way. Walk in it'" (Isa. 30:21). Jesus said that His sheep "listen to his voice. He calls his own sheep by name and leads them ...His sheep follow Him because they know his voice" (John 10:3–4).

The only way I know how to draw close to God is by reading His Word and through conversation with Him, talking and listening. It's the same with anyone we love. We have to spend quality time talking and listening. God gave us two ears and one mouth. We need to use them proportionately. God lives within us—always there and available. Everyone's approach will be different, but we all need to jump in and learn as we grow spiritually and prayerfully. (See appendix III for "Some Tips on Prayer.")

An excellent source on hearing God is Dallas Willard's book, *Hearing God: Developing a Conversational Relationship with God*, InterVarsity Press, 1999. Allow me offer a gentle caution. We must always get confirmation from wise godly friends or leaders when we believe we have heard God's still, small voice directing us to make a major change, and especially when we think it's a message for another person or group.

Prayer is the catalyst for unleashing God's power and answers. "Now to him who is able to do immeasurably more than all we ask or imagine, according to his power that is at work within us" (Eph. 3:20). John 16:24 combines asking and receiving, "Until now you have not asked for anything in my name. Ask and you will receive, and your joy will be complete."

The more Connie and I have prayed, the more incredible the results have been. We have seen many answers to prayer. In the introduction, I shared the story of how God called us to our current ministry. I mentioned our concern about raising financial support. Looking back, God has been faithful to provide for us abundantly. For example, shortly after we launched our faith ministry, we faced a day when we had eighteen hundred dollars of bills in envelopes, nicely stacked on the desk, and waiting to be mailed. We didn't have enough money to cover the checks. We were praying for income. I attended a meeting at a nearby church on the morning of the need. After the meeting concluded with prayer, the pastor of the church turned to me and asked, "Do you need money?" The Lord just told me to write you a check."

Smiling and fighting back tears, I simply said, "Yes; bills are waiting to be paid." He went to his study, and when he returned he handed me a check for one thousand dollars. As I returned home from the meeting, and pulled into our driveway, another car pulled up behind me. A retired doctor greeted us. He had served on the mission board that Connie had led when she was the missions director. He came in for a brief chat and then handed us an envelope with five hundred dollars in it. "I just had the sense that you night need this," He said. It was turning out to be a wonderful day. Not much later, the mail came. It included the remaining amount we needed to mail the bills on time.

The Priority of Prayer in the Scripture

Is prayer really as important as I have presented it? Does it release the power of God? Can it spark and sustain revival? A careful reading of the Bible proves that prayer is to be a top priority in the life and ministry of the Church and in the lives of God's people.

Jesus said, "If you remain in me (intentionally focus on practicing my presence), and my words (the Word of God), remain in you, ask whatever you wish, and it will be given you" (John 15:7). The apostle James reminded his readers, "You do not have, because you do not ask God" (4:2).

Luke 18:1 says, "[We] should always pray and not give up." First Thessalonians 5:17 adds, "Pray continually." I like to think of this as a conversational relationship with God, step-by-step, day-by-day. It's what Brother Lawrence, the monk assigned to washing dishes in a monastery, urged. The title of his book, *The Practice of the Presence of God*, says it well. [140] Consider the great leader, the apostle Paul, as he instructs his understudy, Timothy:

> I urge, then, *first of all*, that requests, prayers, intercession and thanksgiving be made for everyone—for kings and all those in authority, that we may live peaceful and quiet lives in all godliness and holiness. This is good, and

pleases God our Savior, who wants all men to be saved and to come to a knowledge of the truth. I want men [and women] everywhere to lift up holy hands in prayer, without anger or disputing. (1 Tim. 2:1–4)

What did Jesus say about prayer and His Church? "My house will be called *a house of prayer*" (Matt. 21:13). Jesus was angry—tipping over tables and driving moneychangers out of the temple. The place had become a lot of things, but it was no longer a house of prayer.

Acts 2:42 describes the activity or the priorities of the early Church. "They devoted themselves to the apostles' teaching and to fellowship, to the breaking of bread and *to prayer*. Today, many congregations do well at teaching and fellowship, some serve their communities well, but few are known for prayer.

In Acts 13:2, the church was worshiping and fasting. That's when the Holy Spirit said, "Set apart for me Barnabas and Saul for the work to which I have called them." With *fasting and prayer*, they laid hands on them and sent them out. These two men turned the known world upside down with the Good News of Jesus. Prayer gave the Church strategic direction. In Acts 14:23, there was a similar pattern. "Paul and Barnabas appointed elders in each church and, with prayer and fasting, committed them to the Lord." This was the first century model for appointing church leadership.

Romans 12:10–12 (NKJV) says, "Be kindly affectionate to one another with brotherly love, in honor giving preference to one another; not lagging in diligence, fervent in spirit, serving the Lord; rejoicing in hope, patient in tribulation, *continuing steadfastly in prayer*."

It is time to get back to basics, to the importance and priority of prayer. Is our lack of prayer the reason we are living in a post-Christian era? Could it be the reason many burned out pastors are leaving the ministry, and why many churches are closing their doors? Could it be that we have been "doing Church" our way? It's what concerned Isaiah as he spoke to God's people:

> This is what the Sovereign LORD, the Holy One of Israel, says: "In repentance and rest is your salvation, in quietness and trust is your strength, but you would have none of it. You said, No, we will flee on horses." Therefore you will flee! You said, "We will ride off on swift horses." Therefore your pursuers will be swift! A thousand will flee at the threat of one; at the threat of five you will all flee away till you are left like a flagstaff on a mountain, like a banner on a hill. How gracious he will be when you **cry for help**. As soon as he hears, he will answer you …Your ears will hear a voice behind you saying, "This is the way; walk in it." (Isa. 30:15–18)

Consider the concern of Samuel. He is responsible to lead God's people as their prophet, judge, and deliverer. In 1 Samuel 12:23, in his address to Israel, he tells them, "As for me, far be it from me that I should sin against the Lord by *failing to pray for you*." Each of us have a radius of people and responsibilities, areas of influence that call us to prayer. On a broader level, we need to pray for our cities and nation, and certainly for revival, a move of God in our time.

Congregations must learn how to make prayer gatherings some of the most God-focused, exciting, and energized meetings of the church. For example, worship and praise must be woven together with prayer. Praying individually, in small groups, and with leaders praying for areas of their concern all provide creative diversity in a prayer gathering.

Acts 1 presents a powerful picture of pristine Christianity. Before the Church is born, before the Holy Spirit came at Pentecost, before thousands came to faith in Christ on the streets of Jerusalem, the followers of Jesus were *obediently praying in an upper room* and waiting for what the Lord promised. They were following His instructions when they were clothed with the promised power of the Holy Spirit. It was the birth of the Church. A mighty rushing wind swept through the room and through the city. People visiting Jerusalem for the feast of Pentecost were drawn to the scene. They heard the gospel in their own languages. One hundred twenty people from the upper room spoke in languages they had not learned.

In Acts 12:1–5, the Church faced a crisis. The self-serving Herod had killed the apostle James. Because this pleased those who opposed Christ's followers, Herod decided to arrest Peter, too. He had Him seized and thrown into prison. Verse five says, "The church was *earnestly praying* to God for him." An angel appeared in the prison, and light filled the cell. When the angel awakened Peter, his chains fell off. The angel told him to get dressed, then walked them through the prison gate right past the guards. Peter himself walked out onto the street in freedom and made his way to the prayer meeting.

Romans 12:2 tells us, "*Be...faithful in prayer.*"

King David, the model King of Israel, received the most honorable epitaph anyone could have: "A man after God's own heart." Why? His life was centered in prayer, praise, and worship. To read the Psalms is like reading David's personal journal. He was an adulterer and murderer, but he repented and mourned over his sin.

Do you remember the story of Mt. Carmel and the prophets of Baal in 1 Kings 18? Elijah was an ordinary man like you and me. He prayed for a drought, and it didn't rain for three and a half years. After three years, God told Elijah to visit King Ahab with a plan to end the drought. God's prophet had a plan to prove who was God. The prophets of Baal and God's prophet, Elijah, would pray for fire to consume a large altar constructed for the contest. The prophets of Baal prayed passionately, even cutting themselves. When Elijah prayed, God's fire consumed the altar, even the rocks and the water that had drenched it.

After the contest, it was time for Elijah to pray for rain, proving again that Israel's God was God. He told Ahab to get ready, then he bowed his head between his knees and began to pray. It was the familiar human-divine partnership. God promised, and Elijah prayed. *He waited and prayed—prayed and waited.* Then a small cloud, the size of a man's hand, appeared. The answer was on the way, an abundance of rain. The drought was over. Elijah's prayers were answered. Prayer brought fire from heaven, destroyed pagan prophets, honored God, and returned rain to the land.

In 2 Chronicles 20, Judah and her godly king, Jehoshaphat, were under the threat of an imminent attack by a "vast" army. A coalition was coming to attack them and were not far away. Many great kings would have mounted their steeds, called up the army, and faced the onslaught—but not this king. He had followed and served the one who could win battles. He knew he was powerless before the advancing army. Jehoshaphat called the nation to fast and pray. He personally bowed in prayer to lead them, his face to the ground.

God answered: "Do not be afraid or discouraged because of this vast army. For the battle is not yours, but God's" (2 Chron. 20:15). There was great victory that day. Amazingly, the instructions called for singers to lead the army into battle, praising God as they went. There was a great victory that day led by a great leader who fasted and prayed.

When the apostle Paul teaches us about the armor of God, he emphasizes the priority of prayer. He introduces the teaching when he writes:

> Be strong in the Lord and in His mighty power. Put on the full armor of God, so that you can take your stand against the devil's schemes. For our struggle is not against flesh and blood, but against the rulers, against the authorities, against the powers of this dark world and against the spiritual forces of evil in the heavenly realms.

Therefore put on the full armor of God, so that when the day of evil comes, you may be able to stand your ground, and after you have done everything, to stand. (Eph. 6:10–20)

From a Roman prison with guards decked out in their military gear, Paul observed and drew a picture of the spiritual armor of God: the belt of truth, the breastplate of righteousness, feet fitted with the readiness that comes from the gospel of peace, the shield of faith, the helmet of salvation, and the sword of the Spirit, the word of God. Paul added strategic war wisdom:

And pray in the Spirit on all occasions with all kinds of prayers and requests. With this in mind, be alert and always keep on praying for all the Lord's people. Pray also for me, that whenever I speak, words may be given me so that I will fearlessly make known the mystery of the gospel, for which I am an ambassador in chains. Pray that I may declare it fearlessly, as I should. (Eph. 6:14–17)

Having your armor on without prayer is like launching a battleship in a mud puddle. It's a gun without a bullet. It's a computer without a hard drive. It's a smart phone without the internet. Prayer is strategic to winning the battles of each day and the wars of life. Putting on this armor is not a quick, "I put on the full armor of God," when running out the door in the morning. It's praying though these great truths. An example of praying though the armor might be:

Holy Spirit, You who remind me of Truth, give me great skill with the *sword* today, Your Word. Bring it to mind at strategic times. Grow my faith, my *shield* that will protect me from all I will face today. I want to do battle like you did, Jesus, when you were confronted by the half-truths

of Satan in the wilderness. You quoted scripture. Help
me to stand firm with the *belt of truth* buckled around my
waist, integrity, and with the *breastplate* of righteousness
in place—aware of the gift of your imputed righteousness. I put *on my feet* the readiness to walk out the gospel
of peace. I put on the *helmet* of salvation, covering my
mind to remember who and whose I am.

Where was the Church born? It was born in a *prayer meeting*
and on the streets of a great city. Where will the church catch fire
again? It will begin in a *prayer meeting*! Revival will be the result of
passionate prayer and repentance. God's people will be doing their
part; God will be doing His. The Church will be embracing the priority of prayer in the Scripture.

Prayer and the Promises of God

Ephesians 3:20 teaches us that God promises to do "immeasurably
more than all we ask or imagine." We need to dream; we need to
ask. Jeremiah 32:17 gives a no-limits description of God's power:
"Ah, Sovereign Lord, you have made the heavens and the earth by
your great power and outstretched arm. Nothing is too hard for you."
As a loving Father, God will not allow us to ride our bikes on the
freeway at rush hour. He knows best. His love is incomprehensible,
and His timing is always precise. It doesn't seem like it sometimes,
but when we look back, it's amazing to trace God's plans. We can
trust His heart of love and wisdom.

God wants us to ask, and He tells us to ask. As noted above, Jesus
says, "Until now you have not asked for anything in my name. Ask
and you will receive, and your joy will be complete" (John 16:24).
Our God is the God of the impossible. Luke 18:27 says. "What is
impossible with men is possible with God." He tells us: "Call to me
and I will answer you and tell you great and mighty things you do

not know" (Jer. 33:3). God loves to give us the desires of our hearts as we delight in Him (Ps. 37:4). The psalmist also tells us, "No good thing will he withhold from those whose walk is blameless" (Ps. 84:11). Keep in mind the prayer wisdom of Jesus. Facing hideous torture and crucifixion in the garden of Gethsemane, He prays, "Yet not my will, but yours be done" (Luke 22:42). He feels free to ask the Father if He can escape the horrors of taking on the sin of everyone for all time, even though it is the purpose for which He came. I can't imagine the horrific battle Jesus fights in that garden as He prays to His Father. The capillaries of His skin break under the intense spiritual and emotional pressure as He sweats blood. However, when it is over, He is equipped to do what He came to do—what He chose to do. In the end, the battle was won in prayer, for the joy set before Him He endures the mocking, the hideous torture, and the cross.

Will we need to sweat blood in spiritual warfare? Probably not, but if so, if we do it in prayer, we will experience victory. Jesus has always been our best example of passionate prayer in all the circumstances of life, especially in the most difficult ones.

Review some of God's amazing promises. Let your faith be strengthened. Dream big. Romans 10:17 tells us, "Faith comes by hearing the message, and the message is heard through the word of Christ." Some of these texts are "Griffin paraphrases." I have italicized some phrases.

> Don't worry about anything; instead, *pray about everything*. Tell God what you need, and thank him for all he has done. If you do this, you will experience God's peace, which is far more wonderful than the human mind can understand (Phil. 4:6–7, NLT). [Prayer and peace go hand in hand. Prayer is the antidote to the poison of anxiety.]

So let us come boldly to the throne of our gracious God. There we will receive his mercy, and we will find grace to help us when we need it (Heb. 4:16, NLT).

Confess your sins to each other and pray for each other so that you may be healed. *The earnest prayer of a righteous person has great power and wonderful results* (James 5:16, NLT).

Keep on asking, and you will be given what you ask for. Keep on looking, and you will find. Keep on knocking, and the door will be opened. For everyone who asks, receives. Everyone who seeks, finds. And the door is opened to everyone who knocks. You parents—if your children ask for a loaf of bread, do you give them a stone instead? Or if they ask for a fish, do you give them a snake? Of course not! If you sinful people know how to give good gifts to your children, how much more will your heavenly Father give good gifts to those who *ask* Him (Matt. 7:7–11, NLT).

The Lord...delights in the prayers of the upright. The Lord is far from the wicked, but He hears the prayers of the righteous (Prov. 15:8, 29, NLT).

At that time you won't need to ask me for anything. The truth is, you can go directly to the Father and ask Him, and he will grant your request because you use my name. You haven't done this before. Ask, using my name, and you will receive, and you will have abundant joy (John 16:23–24, NLT).

You didn't choose me. I chose you. I appointed you to go and produce fruit that will last, so that the Father *will give you whatever you ask for, using my name* (John 15:16, NLT).

The Lord longs to be gracious to you; he rises to show you compassion. For the Lord is a God of Justice. Blessed are all who wait for him! O people of Zion...you will weep no more. How gracious he will be when you cry for help! As soon as he hears, he will answer you. Although the Lord gives you the bread of adversity and the water of affliction, your teachers will be hidden no more; with your own eyes you will see them. Whether you turn to the right or to the left, your ears will hear a voice behind you, saying, "This is the way; walk in it" (Isa. 30:18–21).

Jesus replied, "I tell you the truth, if you have faith and do not doubt, not only can you do what was done to the fig tree, but also you can say to this mountain, 'Go throw yourself into the sea,' and it will be done. 'If you believe, you will receive whatever you ask for in prayer'" (Matt. 21:21–22).

Take delight in the Lord, and he will give you your heart's desires (Ps. 37:4, NLT).

For the eyes of the Lord are on the righteous and *his ears are attentive to their prayer* (1 Pet. 3:12).

James teaches us that "the prayer of a righteous [person] is powerful and effective" (5:16). Why does God ask us to pray? He certainly doesn't need us, although it's exciting to be a part of what He is doing. The only logical answer is that *God has chosen to work through His people as they pray.* He chooses us to be in partnership with Him. *Without God, we can't; without us, God won't.*

The challenge of understanding the interaction of our part and God's part is an area of "creative tension." In the Western world, most of us reason in Roman or Greek ways, with everything lined up in a logical and orderly way. We have a hard time seeing how two seemingly opposite things can be true at the same time. In Hebrew thought, however, this is common. There is a general understanding that people will never understand God and His ways. Mystery and faith in God are at play.

It's like the creative tension between God's sovereignty and our responsibility. Both are true at the same time. Both God's sovereignty and our responsibility make sense. If we move too far toward the responsibility side, we can easily crumble under the load. On the other hand, if we move too far toward the sovereignty side, we have a tendency to become apathetic. We feel our efforts do not matter or change things. The Bible helps us understand that these are areas where faith is required. The apostle Paul says:

> For we know in part and we prophesy *in part*, but when perfection comes, the imperfect disappears ...Now we see but a poor reflection as in a mirror, *then* [in heaven, in God's presence] we shall see face to face. Now I know in part; then I shall know fully, even as I am fully known. (1 Cor. 13:9–10, 12)

God chooses us to be a part of what He is doing. Our prayers can bring revival and healing transformation to a city or a nation. Satan's strongholds can be brought down. His agenda can be cancelled and his plans thwarted. It is all God's power, but we have a necessary and strategic part to play. E.M. Bounds puts it this way: "The possibilities of prayer are found in its allying itself with the purposes of God, for God's purposes and man's praying are the combination of all potent and omnipotent." [141]

Psalm 27:14 tells us, "Wait for the Lord; be strong and take heart and wait for the Lord." Prayer and waiting on the Lord go together. God's timing is flawless. *The "wait" work of prayer produces the necessary spiritual muscle to handle God's answers humbly.* It builds faith muscle and strength to handle awesome assignments and great victories without pride. Waiting for God's answers is the difficult part of faith. We must understand in our quick-paced, fast-food, texting, door delivery, Western world that God is not into microwaving, but into marinating.

Is it really true that God promises to answer prayer? In John 14:14, Jesus tells us, "You may ask me for anything in my name, and I will do it." The apostle John affirms it. "This is the confidence we have in approaching God: that if we ask anything according to his will, he hears us. And if we know that he hears us—whatever we ask—we know that we have what we asked of him" (1 John 5:14–15). Our Lord may answer yes, no, wait, or I have a better idea. Sometimes I sense He is saying make a choice; all options are OK.

The Pattern of Prayer in the Life of Jesus

When I study prayer, I am drawn to the pattern of prayer in the life of Jesus. We are His apprentices, doing His work His way. Consider Hebrews 5:7: "During the days of Jesus's life on earth, he offered up prayers and petitions with loud cries and tears to the One who could save him from death, and he was heard because of his reverent submission."

From the beginning of Jesus's ministry, He set the example for prayer. After He was baptized, He spent forty days in the Judean wilderness, alone with the Father in fasting and prayer. Following those grueling weeks, He went head to head, or mind to mind, with

Satan who hit Him with subtle half-truths and grand ideas. He won every battle by speaking the Word of God to Satan.

From this ministry launch, Jesus is often praying. In Mark 1:35, after a long and busy day of ministry and people, Jesus is up early the next morning before dawn—to pray. I love this text. For most of my life the early morning has been my best time to have uninterrupted conversational intimacy with the Father. If you are not a morning person, this could be daunting. However, you can be encouraged by Matthew 14:22–23. Jesus also prays late at night.

Prayer was woven into the events of Jesus's life and ministry. In Matthew 14:13, He went off to be alone with the Father after hearing that John the Baptist had been beheaded. Verse 19 tells us that He prayed before He fed the five thousand (or 10 to 15 thousand or more with women and children). In Luke 6:12, when Jesus was facing threats against His life, and just before He chose His twelve disciples, Jesus "spent all night praying."

Luke 11:1 says, "One day Jesus was praying in a certain place. When he finished, one of his disciples said to him, "Lord, teach us to pray." Jesus gave them, and us, a model prayer—the Lord's Prayer. Why did the disciples ask Jesus to teach them to pray? If I had been following Jesus day after day, I would have asked Him how to raise the dead, heal withered hands, or make fish sandwiches for thousands. The only thing that makes sense is that the disciples were connecting the dots between His miracles, His prayer life, and His intimacy with the Father.

The eternal Son of God who came to us in human flesh was like us, a person of prayer. Luke 5:16 summarized his passion for prayer: "But Jesus *often* withdrew to lonely places and prayed."

What is Jesus doing now? According to Hebrews 7:25, He "lives to intercede for [us]." He is joined by the Holy Spirit who "intercedes for us with groans that words cannot express" (Rom. 8:26). This is a mystery as we ponder the Trinity (God is one in essence, but in three persons), but still, the importance of prayer is not a mystery. If we are in hot pursuit of Jesus, really wanting to follow and be like Him—committed apprentices—we will be talking with Him often, conversationally intimate.

Intimacy with God the Father comes before productivity for Him. In John 5:19–24, Jesus says, "I tell you, the Son can do nothing by himself; He can do only what he sees his Father doing." We need guidance from our Father, too. Prayer is not something to be added to our other duties. Prayer and intimacy with God are to be the center of our lives. Prayer integrates and shapes all of life. It is the way God accomplishes His work through us. Prayer is how we do God's work God's way. We get to be a part of what He is doing.

I shudder sometimes when I read what Jesus said to the religious leaders and establishment of His day. "Why do you break the command of God for the sake of your tradition? You nullify the word of God for the sake of your traditions" (Matt. 15:3, 6). I pause to ponder, would he be saying something like this to us, the Church of our time? On the other hand, can you imagine the impact of the Church united in prayer in cities or regions across the world? Paul the apostle urges unity in His letters to cities, city-wide or regional churches (Rom. 12:1–16; 15:5; 1 Cor. 1:10–14 Gal. 3:26–29; Eph. 2:11–22, and especially 4:1–16; Phil. 1:27, and especially 2:1–11; Col. 3:12–17; 1 Thess. 3:12; 4:9; 5:11–15). Picture the largest arena in your city packed with the regional Church worshipping and praying in unity!

Prayer and God's Power

We may have some wonderful gifts—spiritual gifts to grace others (the Greek word for gifts comes from the same root word as grace)—and natural abilities, but without the power of the Holy Spirit flowing through them, they are not spiritually effective. God's power is more than enough for anything God may ask us to do or be. *Prayer is the catalyst for unleashing the power of God through our lives and ministries.*

Who is "able to do immeasurably more than all we ask or imagine, according to His power that is at work within us...throughout all generations, for ever and ever?" God is! (Eph. 3:20) Imagine it—beyond all we can ask, think or imagine. What are your dreams and passions?

In Ephesians 1:19, Paul prays that we would know God's incomparably great power, *the same power* that raised Jesus from the dead and seated Him in the heavenly realms at the right hand of the Father—resurrection power! We are seated with Jesus at this place of honor, power, and authority. It is in the intangible world of spiritual reality. He is above all rule and authority, power and dominion, in this age, and in the age to come (Eph. 2:6)! We are told to "ask and receive,"—to see God's power at work so that our joy might be full (John 16:24; Matt. 7:8, 11:24). We must never forget, God's power is in Jesus's name and the authority He has given us in His Word. It's not our power. It's dangerous to become enamored with a sense of being powerful. "Pride goes before a fall" (Prov. 16:18).

First Corinthians 3:7 reminds us of our limits when it says, "So neither he who plants nor he who waters is anything, but only God, who makes things grow." Ephesians 6:10 adds that we are to "be strong in the Lord and in his mighty power," not our own. Hosea 10:13 warns about the terrible result of trying to do God's work with our power or strength. It says that God's people planned wickedness, reaped evil, and ate the fruit of deception because they depended on their own strength. A few chapters later (14:8–9), God speaks through the prophet to say, "Your fruitfulness comes from me. Who is wise? He will realize these things."

In my years of serving the Lord and having a passion to see our city transformed, I lean into Psalm 127:1: "Unless the Lord builds the house, its builders labor in vain. Unless the Lord *watches over the city,* the watchmen stand guard in vain." Let's find like-minded followers of Jesus who will pray for the city-wide Church and for revival.

Think about this, when the exiles returned to Jerusalem to rebuild the temple, some complained that the work was insignificant. God's spokesman, Zechariah, told Zerubbabel these powerful words in the extremely challenging work of rebuilding:

> This is the word of the Lord to Zerubbabel: [It's] "not by might nor by power, but by my Spirit," says the Lord Almighty. "What are you, mighty mountain? Before Zerubbabel you will become level ground. Then he will bring out the capstone to shouts of 'God bless it! God bless it!'"

> Zerubbabel is the one who laid the foundation of this Temple, and he will complete it. Then you will know that the Lord of Heaven's Armies has sent me. Do not despise these small beginnings, for the Lord rejoices to see the work begin, to see the plumb line in Zerubbabel's hand. (Zech. 4:6–10, NLT)

God's power in the hands of His people accomplishes great things. Take heart! Keep praying.-First Thessalonians 5:24 says, "The one who calls you is faithful, and *he will do it.*" Remember King, Jehoshaphat, when a coalition of armies was about to attack him his people? He called for a national time of fasting and prayer. As they were standing in prayer, God told them the battle was not theirs, but His. They were to stand, wait, and see what He would do (2 Chron. 20:15, 17).

First Corinthians 4:20 says, "The kingdom of God is not a matter of talk but of power." If prayer takes its rightful place in the regional Churches of America, I believe God will respond in great power. We will see another Great Awakening, a historic move of God.

We are at war against a very skillful enemy (Eph. 6:12). Satan is the god of this world system, but "The earth is the Lord's, and everything in it, the world, and all who live in it" (Ps. 24:1; 1 Cor. 10:25–26). We must never forget that "our struggle is not against flesh and blood, but against the rulers, against the authorities, against the powers of this dark world and against the spiritual forces of evil in the heavenly realms" (Eph. 6:12). Satan has power, but our Lord is all powerful, omnipotent. Satan is tethered to a long rope. He is only allowed to go so far. Another friend says that Satan is like a pesky gnat with a big mouth.

Satan is subtle and very good at what he does—stealing, killing, destroying, and especially deceiving. He's an angel of light. He's the master of deception, a liar of the first order. It is important to understand we personally have very little power to fight him. The apostle Paul gives us a key that will unlock the secret of victory in spiritual warfare.

> For though we live in the world, we do not wage war as the world does. The weapons we fight with are not the weapons of the world. On the contrary, they have divine power to demolish strongholds. We demolish arguments [Satan is a liar, a deceiver] and every pretension that sets itself up against the knowledge of God, and *we take captive every thought to make it obedient to Christ.* (2 Cor. 10:3–5)

Someone once commented that our nothingness gives God a chance to fill us with His something-ness, and blow the devil away. It made sense. We have been given God's divine power, and His working through us can demolish Satan's fortresses large or small, over cities or quietly tucked away in our souls.

The more strategic our warfare praying is, like praying down historic regional enemy strongholds, the wiser it is to pray with a committed group of prayer warriors.

Proverbs 21:30–31 tells us, "There is no wisdom, no insight, and no plan that can succeed against the Lord. The horse is made ready for the day of battle, but victory rests with the Lord." As we obey and follow Jesus, do His work His way, we have the opportunity to see great things accomplished by God's power and ability. Listen to the words of Isaiah: All that we have accomplished you have done for us (Isa. 26:12). Those who hope in me will not be disappointed (Isa. 49:23). He gives strength to the weary and increases the power of the weak (Isa. 40:29).

What Isaiah teaches us is reinforced by 2 Peter 1:3. "His divine power has given us everything we need for a godly life through our knowledge of him who called us by his own glory and goodness." Earlier, Peter wrote, "If anyone serves, he should do it with the strength God provides" (1 Pet. 4:11). A contemporary Christian music group takes the name, "Jars of Clay." They understand the truth of 2 Corinthians 4:7 where Paul the apostle talks about his preaching: "But we have this treasure [the Gospel] in jars of clay to show that this all surpassing power is from God and not from us."

God chooses to use people like us. We are all broken to one degree or another. God encourages me many times with the truth of 1 Corinthians 1:26–31. I remember it with an acrostic: God does not use **WIN—ners**, the **W**ise, **I**nfluential, and **N**oble. He uses the **foolish WILD**—the **W**eak, **I**n Christ, **L**owly, and **D**espised. Paul knew the power of this firsthand. It was Paul who obtained permission to imprison the followers of Christ before He encountered Jesus on the road to Damascus. Paul reminds us, as he reminded the believers in the pagan city of Corinth. Read Paul's encouragement:

Brothers, think of what you were when you were called. Not many of you were *wise* by human standards; not

127

many were *influential*; not many were of *noble* birth. But God chose the *foolish* things of the world to shame the wise; God chose the *weak* things of the world to shame the strong. He chose the *lowly* things of this world and the despised things—and the things that are not—to nullify the things that are, so that no one may boast before him. It is because of him that you are in Christ Jesus, who has become for us wisdom from God—that is, our righteousness, holiness and redemption. Therefore, as it is written: "Let him who boasts boast in the Lord." (1 Cor. 1:26–31)

We get to be a part of what God is doing. Psalm 37 says, "Commit your way to the Lord; trust in him, and he will do this: He will make your righteous reward shine like the dawn, your vindication like the noonday sun. Be still before the LORD and wait patiently for him."

In John 15:5, Jesus said, "I am the vine, you are the branches. If a man remains in me, and I in him, he will bear much fruit; *apart from me you can do nothing.*" Is it any wonder that Jesus told the disciples in Luke 24:49, "Stay in the city until you have been clothed with power from on high." As his followers obeyed these instructions, God sent the firestorm of Pentecost, and the Church was born. Over 3,000 came to faith in Jesus from all over the known world. It was God's power through His unified people in prayer that since then has always brought revival.

Oswald Chambers has often been quoted saying: "Prayer does not fit us for the greater work; prayer is the greater work. The measure of the worth of our public activity for God is the private profound communion we have with God." [142] Dr. Martin Lloyd Jones once said, "Prayer is the highest activity of the human soul, and therefore it is at the same time the ultimate test of a man's true spiritual condition. Everything we do in the Christian life is easier than prayer." [143] E.M. Bounds declared, "Prayer is our most formidable weapon, the thing which makes all else we do efficient." [144]

What "we do," we do with and for our Lord as we talk and listen to Him along life's way. *Intimacy with God comes before productivity for God.*

One of my all-time favorite stories has come from Washington State and her logging industry. As a boy, I lived in Port Angeles, Washington. It boasted several large paper pulp and lumber mills. Huge logging trucks frequented our highways. Long before the days of chainsaws and the heavy equipment that harvest lumber now, logging crews looked for men who were skilled with a double-bladed ax. Wherever the logging industry flourished, a man's man was a lumberjack.

As the story goes, a young man had often dreamed of working in the woods. After graduating from high school, he decided to drive up to a logging camp where a crew was felling trees for a lumber mill. He had purchased a "professional" double-bladed ax as soon as his dad—or should I say his mother—would let him. He had honed his tree-felling skills as carefully as he had learned to keep his ax as sharp as a razor's edge.

When he found the job foreman, he asked if he could come to work, at least for the summer. The big burly veteran of the woods looked down his nose at him and said, "Son, we only hire men on this job, men who can handle the big trees." No matter how much the kid begged, the boss wasn't about to let the boy work with the crew in the woods. Finally, after producing his double-edged ax, the young man, in desperation, asked if he could just show him what he could do, then he would leave.

It was about lunchtime, so the foreman gathered some of the men around a large Douglas fir tree to see what the boy could do. Of course, it was partly in humor, a little comic relief from the hard work of the day. With amazing skill and with his razor sharp ax, the boy shaped a back cut. Rounding the tree, he skillfully finessed the front cut. The tree fell perfectly. He skinned off the branches in short order, then stood, sweat pouring down his face and back, and waited for a response. What had he proved to the big boys?

They were amazed. With some cheers and some "way to go kid" compliments, they recognized that a prima donna of the woods stood before them. The young man had convinced not only the foreman, but the crew, that he had what it took to join them. The summer in the woods began with great hope for the strong young buck.

Trouble was just around the corner. As the first few days on the job passed, the young hero worked slower and slower. After giving the boy a warning, the foreman called the wanna-be woodsman into his trailer. "Here's your pay, kid," he said. "You're slowing the crew down. You can't keep up."

With pleas of despair, the young guy begged to stay on. It was then that the seasoned foreman leaned back in his rickety old chair to ponder what was happening. Finally, scratching his head, he asked, "Son, did you forget to sharpen your ax?"

The response was immediate and defensive. "Yes," he said. "I was afraid to take the time. I didn't want to hold up the crew." With a deep sigh, the foreman said to him, "Son, that's exactly what you did. You must sharpen your ax every morning, and several times during the day. Get back out in the woods. Keep your ax sharp, and you will do fine." [145]

Prayer keeps the ax of ministry and passion for revival sharp. *Take time to pray.* Satan is masterful at thwarting the forward progress of God's kingdom because our prayer axes are dull. It's time to pray—in the morning, at night, in between, and in special unified gatherings of prayer in upper rooms and large arenas. We must keep our axes razor sharp. (In Appendix II, I have included some tips on prayer to help us do this.)

As Dutch Sheets wrote, "We can run our churches and ministries from the boardroom or the prayer room. The first produces the works of man, the other births a move of God." [146]

When God's people become untethered from truth, they begin to float purposelessly on their whims or speculation. They are easily drawn into the culture or philosophies that surround them. It is the pattern of history. (Bob Griffin)

Chapter 8

GREAT STORMS OF OUR TIME, PART 2

WHEN I WAS a boy, we heated our farmhouse with a large wood-burning stove in our living room and cooked our food on an iron wood-burning stove in the kitchen. Sometimes, it was necessary to stir a neglected fire, and I remember getting dizzy as I tried to blow sparks back into flame. Although we didn't have a bellows on our farm, I later learned that the power of a few pumps with a bellows was all that was needed to produce a new flame from the embers of a fading fire.

Bellows might connote the old idea of "blowing hot air," but this is not true of the fourth characteristic of revival—the powerful preaching and teaching of the Bible. It blows renewed spiritual life and passion into God's people. It brings conviction of sin and repentance. The truth sets people free (John 8:32; Heb. 4:12). It burns off impurities—the old dross of cultural drift—and calls God's people to the pure gold of holiness that reflects Jesus.

God's truth is alive and powerful. It penetrates deeply into the soul like a double-edged sword. It discerns what is on the inside. It brings conviction of sin and renewed spiritual life. It's no wonder that the preaching and teaching of the Word of God takes center stage in revival. Consider the following declaration of the apostle Paul:

All Scripture is inspired by God and is useful to teach us what is true and to make us realize what is wrong in our lives. It straightens us out, and teaches us to do what is right. It is God's way of preparing us in every way, fully equipped for every good thing God wants us to do. (2 Tim. 3:15, NLT)

This is the power of the fourth characteristic of revival.

CHARACTERISTIC 4
Biblical Preaching, the Bellows to Fan the Flame

Revival rested upon the powerful proclamation— preaching and teaching—of the law of God and His Word. Many of the revivals were the result of a return to the Scripture.

God raises up great preachers, evangelists, and teachers to lead revival. Some call God's people to prayer and repentance while others set the stage for prayer and revival. When these leaders are anchored to biblical truth, the Word of God shapes the movements they spark. God's truth must guide revival to keep it in balance under the direction of the Holy Spirit. Although revival can be like the flame of a newly lit fire, it can become something other than a move of God. In fact, without a passion for God's truth or biblical teaching, and for humility, prayer, and the leading of the Holy Spirit, revival can flame out, just like kindling and paper without dry wood.

At first glance, some have wondered if the Word of God really did play a major role in the Prayer Meeting, Welsh, and Azusa Street revivals. In the first case, prayer seemed to stand alone without preaching. In the second, it could appear that Evan Roberts didn't give adequate attention to the Scripture. Some have even said that the revival was brief for that reason. Some have questioned the significant role of preaching or teaching in the Azusa Street Revival. However, if we take a broad view, preaching and teaching were central to all three.

Look at the role preaching has played in post-biblical revivals. *The First and Second Great Awakenings* were known by the effective preachers whose stories we have already told and by the powerful preaching that wove its way through the warp and woof of revival tapestry. The strong presentation of Scripture brought the "living and active" impact of God's Word in evangelism and drew the fire of conviction from heaven (Heb. 4:12, NIV). Thousands responded by streaming forward at invitations to receive Christ as Savior. Believers were convicted of sin that so easily entangled them (Heb. 12:1, NIV).

What was the role of the Scripture in *the Prayer Meeting Revival of New York City*? J. Edwin Orr, one of the greatest revival historians, saw the New York City revival as a part of a much wider movement of God's Spirit. He wrote:

> Finney became the literary mouthpiece of revivalism, and his works were soon spread all over the world, bearing fruit to this day ...Finney lived to see the greatest religious revival of all time, the Great Revival...in 1857 [that] swept through the United States, Northern Ireland, Scotland, Wales, England, South Africa, Scandinavia, Switzerland, and many other evangelical countries, adding millions to the professing Church. [147]

Revival meetings that swept the country were initiated by prayer. However, as the Holy Spirit began to work among God's people, preaching and teaching either ran alongside the prayer movements or followed closely on their heels. Orr wrote: "Although prayer-meetings were the greatest vehicle of blessing in the Awakening of 1858, preaching was by no means as neglected or discarded as some writers insist …There was truly a great revival of the ministry of preaching." Noon prayer meetings were dominant in the New York City revival, but Orr confirmed, "The interest… was immediately captured and used by the evening preaching services. The…awakening was a revival of preaching. [148] The ministry of D. L. Moody began during the first part of the Awakening, and, as Orr reported, he became a powerful force in Britain as well as America. [149]

Although prayer was the central characteristic in the Prayer Meeting Revival, thousands returned to church and therefore to biblical instruction. How many returned to the Church? Orr stated that there were thirty million in the United States in 1858. When all statistical figuring was complete, there were one million converted to Christ within twenty-four months of the first outbreak. [150] Summarizing the larger sweep of the revival, he said that approximately two million converts were added to the various churches. "The quality of the conversions was excellent and abiding." [151]

What was the role of preaching and teaching in *the Welsh revival of 1904*? The revival was associated with Evan Roberts, and it was generally true that Roberts was an "an exhorter rather than an expositor, and he neglected preaching and teaching the Bible." Others played important roles. Rosina Davies was known for singing and preaching the Word of God. Jessie Penn-Lewis led Bible classes and set up the Welsh Keswick movement in 1903, a great movement centered on teaching the Bible. Seth Joshua, a Welsh Presbyterian, was an effective evangelist and held Bible conferences to teach believers about a deeper life in Christ. Joseph Jenkins, the pastor of a congregation in New Quay, had a passion to stop spiritual decline. [152]

Local revivals happened independent of Roberts's ministry. Preaching was much more central to them. For example, special meetings were held in Llanerchymedd. These were preaching services. The first night, sixty-seven received Christ, and on the second night, one hundred eleven came to Christ. The preacher spoke on the Holiness of God [153] Dr. Relfe reported:

> Though loudly scorned by some staid ministers for being a "youthful see" [Evan Roberts], within five months 100,000 Welsh had been added to church rolls, and many more nominal church-goers had been soundly converted. The Chapels in Wales were crowded day and night for about two years...the need for additional chairs...in the aisles for another twenty years. A survey indicated that 80% of those born again during the revival of Wales, five years later, were still steadfast Christians. [154]

Revival draws people back to a deep love for God and then to the nurture of His Word. As thousands come to faith in Christ, they are nurtured through the Scripture. Evan Roberts is an example of one deeply impacted by the Scripture. One observer states that he was not an orator or even widely read except for the Bible. It is clear that he knew it from cover to cover—probably through to the maps. When Roberts was working in a coal mine, his Bible was close at hand on a ledge or beam, ready for any pause or break where he could read it. [155]

Bible sales mushroomed during the Welsh revival, and there was a decline in the purchase of other literature. People were purchasing Bibles in large quantities, especially pocket Testaments which were snatched up by young men. One bookstore owner had his supply of Bibles in "dead stock" before the revival, but soon he had to pull them out to sell. He ran out of Bibles as revival came. Some who had never owned a Bible "carried one off as a hoarded treasure." [156]

In *the Azusa Street Revival*, teaching became very important. The Pentecostal experiences, the Baptism of the Holy Spirit, prophecy, and speaking in tongues that were new to most people had to be explained biblically. Parham had established Bible schools for teaching the Word, and the revival leader, Seymour, was a product of one of these schools. The Azusa Street meetings grew out of cottage meetings where Bible study and prayer were central.

The Word of God has been central to every revival along with a renewed passion for prayer, or it followed a prayer movement. As revival came, so did the teaching and study of the Word of God.

When God's people become untethered from truth, they float purposelessly on their whims or speculation. They are easily drawn into the culture or philosophies that surround them. It is the pattern of history, but the truth sets people free. A careful reading and a basic understanding of the Word of God nourishes the abundant life, the life that God intends for them (John 10:10).

One of life's most important questions is, "What does the Bible say?" One of life's most important decisions is the choice to do what it says. The Bible answers a basic question, "How shall we live?" The Word of God is the manual on life, given to us by the Engineer of the universe. It is alive and active like yeast in dough. It discerns and corrects the thoughts and attitudes that breeze through our minds (Heb. 4). This is why I have chosen to include the next chapter on God's Word. Being nurtured or fed by the Word of God must be balanced by obediently exercising its truth.

> *Sink the Bible to the bottom of the sea, and man's obligation to God would be unchanged. He would have the same path to tread, only his map and his guide would be gone; he would have the same voyage to make, only his compass and chart would be overboard. The Bible is God's chart for you to steer by, to keep you from the bottom of the sea, and to show you where the harbor is, and how to reach it without running on the rocks.* **(Henry Ward Beecher)**

Chapter 9

STRATEGIC FUEL: THE WORD OF GOD

One of France's greatest thinkers, Voltaire, once said that in 100 years the Bible would be a forgotten book, found only in museums. When the 100 years were up, Voltaire's home was occupied by the Geneva Bible Society.

MOST AMERICANS REMEMBER the date, September 11, 2001 (9/11). For those old enough to have understood what was happening, it sends flashbacks—if not chills—across their memories. On that terrible day, religious terrorists penetrated the security of our nation and inflicted devastation and death. Militant Muslims, commandeering two commercial planes, attacked the Twin Towers in New York City. One moment, the towers stood as the proud symbols of America's financial strength, international economic superiority, and architectural creativity. In a brief moment of time, they became a pile of rubble and bodies, symbolizing the vulnerability of a nation that thought her security was impenetrable.

A third plane hit the Pentagon, the headquarters of the nation's military. A fourth plane was probably targeting the White House. A penetrating question swept through our minds. How could this have been possible? We were the most powerful military power in the world.

America's pride and security were reduced to a pile of debris. A cross was placed on top of it. Churches were opened, and prayer became popular again. For two months, it looked like America was turning back to God. For a brief time, "In God we trust," the motto printed on American coins, had become true again. In the grief and horror that followed the attack, the Bible was quoted and embraced, as millions found comfort in God and His truth. The liberal press and the American Civil Liberties Union were silent.

If you are a follower of Jesus, you face a terrorist every day, Satan, the god of this world. He goes about to steal, kill, and destroy (1 Pet. 5:8; John 10:10). You are at war. No follower of Jesus is exempt. Each day you face potential attacks and deception from this enemy and his hierarchy of principalities, powers, and rulers in dark and wicked high places. He is sometimes a roaring lion, but when he roars, it is only to strike fear in people, to intimidate them. Satan's strategy is to deceive, like those who deceptively used our airlines to wreak death and destruction in our land. Deception is Satan's heart language.

Our battle is psychological and emotional. It is cultural and cross-cultural. It is spiritual. Our eyes and ears are inundated with enemy rhetoric from secular media and Satan's cunning half-truths.

Our nation, once considered Christian, has become post-Christian. Over the years and slowly, but subtly, she has become untethered from what once was a biblical consensus on values. The god of this world has been an angel of light from the time of his fall. His subtlety has been magnetic, like his redefining tolerance to steal biblical truth. Tolerance used to mean that people would try to convert each other to their faith or point of view and live civilly together in society. Now it has become intolerant to share that Jesus is the way, the truth, and the life, and that no one comes to the Father except through Him (John 14:6). It has become unacceptable to share well-established biblical values on marriage. For many, it has become like a time long ago. "In those days Israel had no king; everyone did what was right in their own eyes" (Judg. 17:6).

The war in which we are engaged began eons ago. Satan, with ego in hand, tried to take over God's throne and was kicked out of heaven. With him went a host of lesser spirits—demons and a hierarchy of leaders. A battle raged in the Garden of Eden after man was created. Satan subtlety drew Adam and Eve to sin, and they had to leave beautiful, pristine Eden, God's artistic natural masterpiece and perfect environment.

Adam and Eve had been warned, and were separated from God, the holy and righteous one. God's righteousness required Him to keep His Word, even as He loved them unconditionally, with incomprehensible love, as He does you and me. Sin had to have a payday. Nature fell with the terrible consequences of hard labor and pain in childbirth, and life was characterized by sweat, blood, and tears.

Spiritual war continued throughout Israel's history. In chapter 3, we learned how Israel was called to be a vibrant community of faith, a witness to all the nations around them. She was to tell the story about the love and grace of one true God. After many centuries, suffering time and again from the disease of drift, she was declared to be "a prostitute people" (See Ezek. 16:15). She worshipped and served other gods and went through the pattern of revival many times until God's patience ran out, and God sent them into Babylonian captivity.

Warfare became more intense when Jesus was born. King Herod, whimsically evil and under the influence of Satan, tried to win a decisive, once-for-all victory by wiping out the Messiah. Herod missed his target and destroyed many other young innocent lives. Furious fighting raged as Jesus began His public ministry. He went head-to-head with Satan in the Judean wilderness after he fasted and prayed for forty days. Jesus won the battle. His victory was decisive as he fasted and prayed and quoted Scripture in response to each of Satan's efforts to deceive Him. Satan finally departed in defeat but continued to look for a more opportune time (Luke 4:14).

The enemy found an avenue of attack through the religious leadership of the day as they rejected their Messiah. At Gethsemane, Jesus fought His final battle to submit to the bitter cup of the cross. He endured hideous torture and abuse at the hands of religious and civic leaders. Jesus went confidently to Golgotha, the place of the skull. Satan thought he had won the final victory when Jesus gave up His life, but Satan was wrong. It was all part of God's plan to provide redemption through the resurrection of Jesus from the grave. Sin's debt was paid. Death died that day. Glory to God!

Satan had laid out the worst he had in his awful arsenal. The celebration had more than likely begun among the hateful hordes of hell, when three days after Jesus's death, word came that He was alive.

It was the pinnacle of redemptive history. War had been waged, and Jesus had won. Satan, death, and hell were defeated for all time. Satan was disarmed (Col. 2:15) and condemned to hell with all his evil cohorts and waits until the time of his total defeat, confined to the lake of fire. However, for now, God has allowed Satan to operate within a limited sphere of influence—tethered, as it were, to a long rope—until Jesus returns for His Church.

Jesus's death provided eternal life for all who believe in Him. He made eternity with God possible, a new home in heaven, abundant life until then, and the opportunity to serve the righteous and redemptive kingdom of God.

We are still engaged in a war for the souls of mankind. We are fighting a defeated enemy, and we have the assurance of Christ's unconditional and incomprehensible love, His presence, and His powerful help through all life's battles. We tend to forget this and soon find ourselves living in defeat. If we resist Satan and his demons, they have to flee from us (James 4:7). We have God-given strategic weapons for defeating Satan (Eph. 6), but here is a warning for us. If we forget we are at war, we could be defeated by inattentive apathy (v. 12). With this historic battle raging, is it any wonder that the problem of drift has plagued God's people through time?

It's God's truth that sets people free (John 8:32). The Word of God is powerful. It is no wonder that the fourth characteristic of revival is a return to the Word of God, with its teaching and preaching. "The word of God is living and active, sharper than any double-edged sword; it penetrates even to dividing soul and spirit, joints and marrow; it judges the thoughts and attitudes of the heart" (Heb. 4:12).

Prayer and the Word of God are the two primary strategic weapons in the war that we are fighting. They are the keys to sustain spiritual vitality.

Before I discuss the remaining characteristics of revival, I want to suggest a victory strategy. I believe it is very important if we are going to see revival sweep our nation and the world before Jesus returns.

GOOD NEWS

Spiritual warfare rages around us each day. Recognizing this, and understanding our need for fighting equipment, we turn our attention to 2 Peter 1:3–4: "His divine power has given us everything we need for a godly life through our knowledge of him who called us by his own glory and goodness. Through these he has given us his very great and precious promises, so that through them you may participate in the divine nature, having escaped the corruption in the world caused by evil desires." This is good news as we face the enemy day by day. If we try to win battles with our own wisdom and strategies, we lose. The apostle Paul warns us, "Though we live in the world, we do not wage war as the world does. The weapons we fight with are not the weapons of the world. On the contrary, they have divine power to demolish strongholds (2 Cor. 10:3–4), a central strategy of enemy influence.

We are warned about choices that open the door to Satan's influence in our lives—enemy encampments in our souls. "In your anger do not sin. Do not let the sun go down while you are still angry. Do not give the devil a foothold" (Eph. 4:26–27). Notice that the battlefront is our minds (our conscious and subconscious mind, our emotions, and our will). Anger is the example in this text, but I believe it is just one example of potential areas of Satan's influence. Another area of influence is through generational sins passed down to us from our families. (More about this later.)

In 2 Corinthians, Paul tells us how to fight off Satan's footholds. "We demolish arguments and every pretension that sets itself up against the knowledge of God." Here's the secret: "We take captive every thought to make it obedient to Christ" (2 Cor. 10:5). "Take captive" is an aggressive intentional phrase. While we would probably recognize a bold-faced lie, most of what Satan whispers are half-truths.

We must replace Satan's lies with biblical truth. It is what Jesus did when He went head-to-head with Satan in the wilderness. Jesus resisted him with truth and Satan left. With each half-truth, Jesus came back with truth. We can do what He did.

The one who defeated Satan indwells us. "Greater is He who is in us than the one who is in the world" (1 John 4:4). He has taken up residence in our spirits. Paul tells us that before being redeemed we were "dead in trespasses and sins." Now we are in heavenly places, the intangible spiritual world, and seated at the right hand of Jesus. He is the head over all principalities and powers. We are in Him, like a fish is in the sea, drawing all it needs from the water (Eph. 2:6–7, 10, 13; 1 Cor. 1:30; 15:22).

We have incredible resources. When we speak in Jesus's name, Satan must listen. Resisting him, he must flee. In Ephesians 1, Paul tells us that God's resurrection power is available to us who believe.

Paul tells the Galatian believers that sin's power over them is broken. The same is true for all believers. It is for freedom that Christ sets us free (Gal. 5:1), and Paul cautions us to keep standing strong in our freedom.

The war zone is sitting on our shoulders. It's how we think about things, our perspective. God may allow situations for our growth that we do not understand. In those times, we must keep God's truth and love central to our thinking and attitudes. The apostle Paul is helpful. In Ephesians 4:22-24 he writes, "You were taught, with regard to your former way of life, to *put off* your old self, which is being corrupted by its deceitful desires; to be made new *in the attitude of your minds;* and to *put on* the new self, created to be like God in true righteousness and holiness."

We not only have war wisdom; we have strategic weapons. The power we have available in Christ is incomparably great (Eph. 1:17). Sin's power over us is broken (Gal. 5:1). Jesus sets us free. He assures us that whatever we bind on earth will be bound in heaven, or in heavenly realms, the intangible world (Matt. 18:18–19). In Job 1:10 a hedge of protection is mentioned. Do we have it for dangerous times, or all the time? It's not clear. Angels serve us. They pick us up lest we dash our foot against a stone. They guard us (Ps. 91:9–12). The angel of the Lord encamps about those who honor God, and they are present to deliver them (Ps. 34:7). This may be our hedge of protection. There are over 300 references to angels in the Bible. "When the enemy comes in like a flood, the Lord will raise up a standard against him" (Isa. 59:19, KJV; see also, NKJV).

Several years ago, I was in charge of the intercessory prayer team for a major outreach held in our city. It was at a park in what we called the "war zone," an area of a high crime and great need. A large quantity of food was distributed and many social services were provided. The Gospel was presented by local pastors every half-hour. The day before the big event, a group of intercessors gathered with me to commit the park to the Lord and to ask for God's protection from any enemy efforts to distract from the outreach. We asked God to post angels at each corner.

On the day of the outreach, things were going very well. Hundreds from the local housing projects and neighborhoods gathered. Many were coming to faith in Christ. The intercessors were on duty with me, praying the entire day. Midmorning, we were standing in a circle praying under a large oak tree when an older man walked down the street, entered the park, and joined the circle. At one point, he interrupted saying, "You may think I am crazy, but as I walked up to the park a few minutes ago, I saw four massive angels, each with long swords raised, standing at the four corners of the park. I just wanted to let you know." What he described was what we had requested.

There is power in the blood of Jesus. It is somewhat a mystery, but we must apply this truth in faith to the best of our understanding. I believe it is strategic in the battle against Satan and his kingdom. Remember the story of the Exodus of Israel from Egypt? The last plague is the death of the Egyptian first-born boys. A death angel was released to kill them. For protection, God's people were told to kill a lamb and place the blood at the top and sides of their doorways. This is a picture of the Cross on which, in time, the eternal Lamb of God, Jesus—slain before the foundation of the world—would die to save us from sin, Satan, death, and hell.

In the book of Revelation, chapter 12, the saints are gathering around the throne of God. The report is that they have defeated Satan by the blood of the Lamb, Jesus. In the dedication of the Temple in the Old Testament (Exod. 45:18; 29:19ff), and in the anointing of the priest's garments, a lamb was killed and its blood was sprinkled strategically on them. How is this practical today? When we picture these Old Testament events, we can by faith apply the blood of Jesus, to ourselves, body, soul, and spirit, and to our dwellings. Our faith is enriched by understanding the power of the blood of the Lamb, Jesus, pictured centuries ago throughout Israel's sacrificial system.

In Colossians 2:15, we are given more strategic weaponry. We are told that Jesus disarmed the powers and authorities, made a spectacle of them, and triumphed over them by the cross. Satan and his cohorts are disarmed and toothless. It's *truth for the trenches of spiritual warfare*. We have all the armor and strategic weaponry we need.

BAD NEWS

In spite of the Good News, we must face some bad news: *we can lose the battle.* The main power Satan and his demons have is deception. When Satan can get God's people to believe His lies, they are defeated. He is skilled at making accusations against them "night and day" (Rev. 12:10). If we are not managing our minds and emotions, we can be deceived, and the enemy can establish strongholds, or areas of influence, within our souls. However, Satan can never touch our spirits because they are the dwelling place of the Holy Spirit. We belong to Him.

Picture a target with three rings and a red bull's eye in the center. For the purpose of this picture, the bull's eye represents our spirit. That's where the Holy Spirit resides. The Christian can never be demon possessed, only demonized—that's bad enough. The next ring pictures our soul. This is the area of our mind, our conscious and subconscious mind, our emotions, and our will. This is where Satan can influence us with some demonic deception. It's the example in Ephesians 4 that warns us not to let the sun go down on our anger or we could give the devil a foothold. Unprocessed anger is only one area of potential influence. Other areas of unconfessed sins could be troublesome as well. The third and final ring is our body, the house in which we live.

We looked at Galatians 5:1, Paul's instructions. He taught us to keep standing firm, to not be subject again to *a yoke of slavery*. Paul was writing about the Old Covenant law. Since Jesus came, we live and thrive under the New Covenant of grace, love, and mercy. Legalism, our best efforts—and failures to keep up—will defeat us, or at least cause us to struggle or fail spiritually (2 Cor. 3:6). Many people try hard to live biblically and fail. But it's not about trying, it is about trusting God's love, mercy, and grace. If we confess our sins, God is faithful and just to forgive us and cleanse us from all sin (1 John 1:9). The Christian life is not about arriving at perfection, it's about laying the past aside and pressing on to the wonderful calling of God, the apostle Paul's testimony Philippians 3:1–17. It's the *definition of maturity* under the New Covenant: "All of us, then, who are *mature* should take such a view of things" (verse 15). It's not about arriving, but being on the way, pressing on toward God's high calling. It's done in the power of the Holy Spirit. It's a life of growth in Christ in the context of His lavish love. As mentioned earlier, it is also about identifying strongholds and getting rid of them.

There is another level where we can live in greater freedom. It is identifying generational sins and curses passed on to us. We can renounce them in Jesus's name, and break them along with any and all perpetuating demonic activity. Texts like Exodus 34:6–8 describe God's love to a thousand generations, but they also describe the sins of the fathers which are passed on to the third and fourth generation. (Also see Exod. 20:6; Deut. 5:9–10) For example, children who have been abused, often grow up to be abusers. Promiscuity, divorce, violent behavior, alcoholism, or drug abuse seem to be passed on from one generation to another unless interrupted by God's mercy and love. These issues can be identified by carefully reviewing one's life story and praying with discerning intercessors to break their influence.

Every believer would be wise to be intentional about getting rid of generational sins or curses that have made life difficult, especially for those who have been engaged in sexual sin. Sexual bonds must be broken and renounced in Jesus's name. Patterns of addiction, abusive talk or behavior, divorce, fear, anger, and depression, for example, could indicate generational strongholds or curses. Jesus wants His people free and thriving in Him. A very helpful tool for these purposes is Dr. Neil Anderson's book, *The Bondage Breaker*, listed in the bibliography. This material is proving to be very helpful for people who desire to grow into a much deeper level of freedom in Christ. It is a wonderful beginning place. (See appendix IV)

Sin's power over us is broken, but we can be subject again to its power and invasion. Satan has no right of ownership or authority over us. He is defeated. However, he is bound and determined to keep us from understanding the truth. He knows he can block our effectiveness as individuals by deceiving us. Paul warns the believers in Corinth about this. In 2 Corinthians 11:3–4, he expresses his concern. "I am afraid that just as Eve was *deceived* by the serpent's cunning, your *minds* may somehow be led astray from your sincere and pure devotion of Christ." Paul is concerned about the Thessalonians, too. "I sent to find out about your faith. I was afraid that in some way the tempter might have tempted you and our efforts might have been useless" (1 Thess. 3:5).

It's not a few raging demoniacs that cause the Church to be nominal and ineffective. It is the more subtle deceptive work of Satan in the lives of believers and in the Church.

> *Spiritual warfare is not necessarily a power encounter, but it is always a truth encounter. That is why John 8:32 is so important. If you obey me, Jesus says, then truly you are my disciples and "you will know the truth and the truth will set you free."*

If people claim to be disciples or apprentices of Jesus but make no effort to be like Him or to know His Word, there is a disconnect somewhere. As a pastoral counselor, I meet professing Christians whose lives are a difficult struggle. Some who come for help are angry with God because they don't think He has kept His Word. After listening to their stories, I discover that they have lived lives of quiet and sometimes overt disobedience. Here is a truth you can stake your life on. *God's love is unconditional and incomprehensible, but the blessings of God depend on growing obedience,* or living life God's way. He knows us and knows how we can thrive. It's not legalism, but living out the freedom provided by God's truth to live a life of growing obedience. Believers need to be in hot pursuit of following Jesus, laying aside the past and *pressing on* to all God has for them—the abundant life—His lavish love, gracious gifts, then growing to live in conversational closeness to Him (John 10:10). God is the Engineer of life and living. We must grow to know the manual, the Word of God, and press ahead to what Paul calls the mark of God's high calling. Isaiah 32:17 says, "The fruit of righteousness will be <u>peace</u>; the effect of righteousness will be *quietness and confidence forever.*" God's *perfect love*, when embraced, casts away fear (1 John 4:18).

We know that Satan is the father of lies (John 8:44). He deceives the whole world and leads it astray. He accuses believers night and day. When we sin, he accuses us of being phonies, hypocritical, or something worse. If we are not careful and alert, we can be easily tempted to believe Satan's condemnation, rather than embracing God's wonderful truth: the love and the grace of 1 John 1:9. "If we confess our sins, He is faithful and just to forgive us our sins and to cleanse us from all unrighteousness." We need to agree with God that we have sinned. That is the definition of confession. Once we have, we must lay it down, and grow on.

The entire world is under the influence of Satan (1 John 5:19). He goes about to steal, kill and destroy. In contrast, Jesus comes to give us abundant life or life to the full (John 10:10). We need to lock on to this truth when the enemy tells us the unbelieving world or culture has it much better. It's a lie. There is enjoyment in sin for a short time, but the end result is terrible. Look around at the brokenness in the world, even among professing Christians (Prov. 10:23; 21:17; 2 Tim. 3:4).

In the Old Testament, King Saul had great potential, but he flagrantly disobeyed God, and it cost him the throne. King David succeeded him. He was called "a man after God's own heart." He sinned too, but repentance and brokenness restored him. The rich blessing of God has been promised to those who "hunger and thirst after righteousness" (Matt. 5:6). King David was known for that.

We must out-truth Satan. Many find it personally helpful to pray biblical truth into their souls and behavior, like praying the apostolic prayers in Ephesians 1 and 3, and Philippians 1, and to confess their way through Galatians 5—the fruit of the Spirit—even as they worship God who is the epitome of these character qualities. Truth is the liberating agent from Satan's subtle deception.

We can misunderstand the promise of an abundant life in John 10:10, by thinking that if we receive Christ as Savior, we live free from warfare or problems. The Christian life is abundant, and God does have a wonderful plan for us (Jer. 29:11), the best life possible. He promises to meet our needs (not necessarily our wants) as He sees them. We who have followed Jesus for a long time can see that life is absolutely abundant and blessed, but we know that at other times, it's very difficult. We can confess that the most difficult times have produced the most faith and growth. The apostle Peter tells us that we are like gold that is being refined by fire. The more pure the gold, the more perfect the reflection of Jesus in our lives. Abundant life, you say? In John 16:33, we have some growth-producing wisdom. "I have told you these things, so that in me you may have peace. In this world you will have trouble. But take heart! I have overcome the world." Trouble is a biblical promise.

One of my favorite statements from C. S. Lewis captures life for me. It is helpful to me as I ponder the purpose of life. It holds a prominent place in my soul, and it is prominently displayed in my study. "I believe in Christianity as I believe the sun has risen. Not just because I see it, but by it, I see everything else." [157]

I understand the Christian life better when I remember that I am at war and that the last battle has already been won. It helps me when I remember that I fight a defeated enemy. Jesus in me is greater than the enemy with whom I battle each day, "he who is in the world" (1 John 4:4). When I am exhausted, I really appreciate the counsel of Jesus to His disciples, and to me, when He says, "Come with me by yourselves to a quiet place and get some rest" (Mark 6:31). It helps to remember that this life is brief, and that I am heading home to glory for all eternity. I get to be a part of what God is doing. I have a Good Shepherd (Ps. 23; John 10).

VERY GOOD NEWS

Now let me share some good news with you. Listen to the powerful and progressive logic of the Bible. We can know the *truth* and the *truth* will set us free. Jesus is the way, the *truth* and the life (John 8:32; 14:6). The Holy Spirit guides us into all *truth*, and He lives inside us (16:13). Jesus's prayer for us is that we will be set apart, sanctified through the *truth*. God's Word is *truth*. The *truth* keeps us strong against the enemy of our souls until we are taken out of this world (John 17:15, 17). We have all the resources we need through the Word of God, God's resurrection power within us, and through the spiritual armor God provides for our daily battle (Eph. 6). There is wonderful biblical truth on which we can focus our minds and with which we can take captive every thought (2 Cor. 10:4). When we do, we know God's peace. The apostle Paul counsels us to manage our minds well. "Finally, brothers, whatever is true, whatever is noble, whatever is right, whatever is pure, whatever is lovely, whatever is admirable—if anything is excellent or praiseworthy—*think about such things*. Whatever you have learned or received or heard from me, or seen in me—*put it into practice*. And the God of peace will be with you" (Phil. 4:8–9).

We cannot expose Satan's lies by our reasoning, *but by God's revelation*! Faith does not create reality. Faith responds to reality. Faith is choosing to believe God's revealed truth and being set free. In the armor of God, there is only one offensive weapon. It is the sword of the Spirit, *the Word of God*. The rest of the armor is defensive. Paul tells the Romans that what was written in the past was written to teach us. Why? Through endurance and the encouragement of the Scriptures, we have hope (Rom. 15:4). This sword is an amazing strategic weapon! The Psalmist celebrates and describes it. It's perfect, reviving the soul. It's trustworthy. It makes simple folks wise. It enlightens the heart. Its commands are radiant, and they give light to the eyes. This sword is more valuable than pure gold. It can warn us, and by using it wisely, there is great reward (Ps. 19:7–8). It would take an entire book to unpack the incredible truths of Psalm 119, 176 verses devoted to the sword, the Word of God. For example, by the Word of God a young man (and older man) can keep their way pure (vs. 9). In verse 11, it says that if we hide the Word of God in our hearts (souls), it keeps us from sin.

Knowing that the Bible says a lot about managing the mind, I made a list (See appendix VII). Remember, the war zone sits on our shoulders. Martin Luther penned a great hymn: "A Mighty Fortress Is Our God." Luther knew the power of the Word. It was the truth of the Word of God that changed his theology and birthed the Protestant Reformation and changed the course of history. He wrote, "Still our ancient foe doth seek to work us woe, his craft and power are great, and armed with cruel hate, on earth is not his equal. Did we in our own strength confide, our striving would be losing ...We tremble not at him. His rage we can endure. *One little Word will fell him*." Sing it, Martin!

The entire Bible, the Greek word *logos* is translated "word." *Rhema* is also translated "word" and is a small portion. Biblically it pictures a small dagger for close in fighting. It is a good idea to find biblical texts, *rhemas* that speak to our greatest challenges and needs. It's helpful to write them out on pocket-sized cards or in our smart phones for quick reference or memorization. God's truth sets us free. We must never forget that "faith comes by hearing and hearing by the Word of God" (Rom. 10:17). (Some of my helpful verses are listed in appendix VII).

When reading through the Gospels, have you noticed how much Jesus was steeped in the Scripture? At the moment of His greatest temptation, he quoted the Word of God. When he introduced His ministry, He quoted Isaiah's prophesy about himself. At His trial, he quoted the Scripture, and when He was hanging on the cross, He quoted the Word of God from Psalm 22.

The teaching and application of the Word of God is central to revival. It sustains and grows God's people in discipleship, understanding, and intimacy with Him. It keeps our "first love" fresh and vital. "Holiness" in the Bible means being totally God's person in every way. Sanctification is the process of growing in holiness or becoming more and more like Jesus.

Chapter 10

GREAT STORMS OF OUR TIME, PART THREE

M Y LIFETIME HAS seen the use of some four-letter words become cursing. However, some powerfully positive four-letter words have always had great significance, like true, live, love, and care. Another four-letter word has been woven through the Bible and has been historically life-giving, the way to enjoy all of God's good gifts. It has required one to stand strong against the secular cultural tide and has been the source of God's promised covenant blessings.

This powerful little word is *obey*. God's love is incomprehensible and immense, beyond measure, but if we want to enjoy all God has for us, there is no other way than to obey. It's the truth of a great hymn. "Trust and obey, for there's no other way, to be happy in Jesus, but to trust and obey."

The fifth characteristic of revival is a return to first love: intimacy with God and a deep growing commitment to holiness and obedience. Think about it as growing to be more like Jesus day by day. As the fire of revival burns, Christian leaders teach and equip believers to passionately follow Jesus and to know His Word. This fifth characteristic stokes the fire of faith. God's people are motivated and mobilized to serve Him. They move out to love others and to change their world.

CHARACTERISTIC 5
Equipping the Saints, Stoking the Fire

Revival in the Old Testament reflected the work of God the Father to awaken His people Israel to a restored relationship with him, to obey Him, and serve His redemptive purposes. Revival in the New Testament, and post biblical history, reflected the work of the Holy Spirit and miracles, and in the equipping of people for ministry. It resulted in the spread of the gospel and the growth of the Church.

This characteristic describes a newly revived Church that is motivated and mobilized in ministry to draw thousands to faith in Christ as Savior. It's this fresh, excited, passionate Church that brings radical social change. In all five of the post-biblical revivals, the Church grows in great numbers. Church buildings, once serving a modest gathering of faithful saints, are full to overflowing. Out of this electrified spiritual environment, many are called into vocational ministry and/or missionary work at home and abroad.

One of the exciting results of the First Great Awakening was the creation of new approaches to evangelism. Itinerant preachers were common. Even those in more localized ministries often took a leave of absence to travel and speak. The Church came "out of the box," out of her four walls, and into the streets. Incredible social impact resulted. Many schools and orphanages were birthed. The moral climate of the colonies was changed. Jonathan Edwards left behind a fervent piety to be modeled alongside excellence in intellectual pursuits. [158] Mary Relfe, in her unique style, told the story.

> Multitudes of new Christian Protestants addressed social sins with such compassion and mercy, that enemies of the state were unable to incite unrest among the poor and

needy. The Christian conscience permeated society after this Great Revival as yeast does dough. Education was Bible-oriented again ...Believers, as in prior years, began caring for the elderly in their homes, and an intense sympathy was created for the poor. Genuine national prosperity followed. It was called the Industrial Revolution. [159]

Pratney described one of the concerns of the preacher/scholar, Jonathan Edwards. He was troubled by some of the emotional extremes in meetings, concerned that they were merely expressions of the flesh. Edwards wanted concrete results, not just emotion. In genuine results, Edwards warned, there must first be demonstrated an "aversion to judging other professing Christians...a very great sense of the importance of moral social duties and how great a part religion lay in them ...There was such a new sense and conviction of this beyond what had been before that it seemed to be as if it were a clear discovery was made to the soul." [160]

Henry Johnson described what was happening in the United Kingdom. God called and equipped gifted revivalists for the hour.

They awakened thousands of nominal Christians to realize the true meaning of the Divine revelation in Jesus Christ. They induced thousands of persons to read and study the Bible, which had been regarded by multitudes as a mere fetish, by other large numbers as a book intended only for parsons, and which to a majority of the rural population was practically unknown. They were the means of raising up bands of lay-preachers, on fire with love and zeal, for disseminating the Gospel among the poor and the laboring classes of towns and villages ...They were the means of the conversion of hundreds of ministers, in the established Church and in the nonconformist Church, from neglect, coldness, and dead works, to serve with heart and soul the living God. Then, when the conscience of the churches had been illumined, and it grasped its immense responsibility, and realized the world-embracing evangel of the cross, there came into existence agencies for the spread of the Truth—Missionary, Bible, and Tract Societies, and Sunday Schools. The social and political results are manifest to all who have studied history. [161]

Candler reports that there were more than fifty thousand who came to faith in Christ as a result of the First Great Awakening. Then he asks, "If the sons of Levi were thus without God, what must have been the condition of the unofficial membership of the churches?" Decrying the spiritual state of not only the clergy, but most of the people in churches, he reports, "The Great Awakening changed all that." [162]

Candler affirmed the beginning of many new ministries and the advancement of education. Colleges like Dartmouth and Princeton were born. A new spirit between England and the American colonies was created and a..."moral revolution of the most beneficent sort." [163]

It is amazing to see what happens in the Church and society when God's people are revived and mobilized out of their religious, cultural, and traditional ruts. (Someone described a rut as a casket with both ends kicked out.) The Second Great Awakening is an example. Snapshots of the results include what Candler writes about the revival at Yale. "In 1802, a revival at Yale College, shook the institution to its center, and it seemed for a time that the whole mass of students would press into the kingdom, and nearly all the converts entered the ministry." [164]

One of the most significant movements of God's Spirit was at Cane Ridge in 1801. Twenty thousand people attended a six-day camp meeting. Pratney said the results of this meeting on the frontier spread revival like a prairie fire. "The Presbyterians and Methodists immediately caught fire, and then the flame broke out among the Baptists in Carroll County on the Ohio River." Leaders like Peter Cartwright, Charles Finney, and the Methodist circuit riders emerged from the revival. Baptist revivalism was birthed in this movement; the camp meetings spread all over eastern America. The wild frontier was tamed. Gambling, cursing, and vice were transformed into genuine Christianity. "It was God's great hour. Revival stopped skepticism in its tracks and returned the helm of the country to the godly ...The revivalists linked conversion and spiritual growth directly to the alteration of society." [165]

Relfe described the results of the Second Great Awakening on the American frontier in a similar way. "It turned drunkards, horse thieves, gamblers, cock fighters, and murderers into evangelists." Many who were converted east of the frontier moved west. They took the frontier for Christ. The missionary movement grew and spread. The roots of the abolition of slavery and the roots of popular education were both products of the awakening. More than six hundred colleges were founded and "the Church began influencing the world once more." [166]

These results continued for many years according to McDow and Reid. They reported phenomenal Church growth. For example, Presbyterians grew four times larger than before the move of God. Stretching out the dates of the awakening to 1850, Methodists grew to over 1,200,000. The American Bible Society was born; many Christian magazines were birthed. The American Tract Society was born, and the American Sunday School Union was created to support the growing Sunday school movement. The YMCA, a Christian ministry to nurture young believers, was birthed. Many other agencies sprang up across America. Historian Lacy concluded that the revival actually saved the nation from French infidelity, crass materialism, rapacious greed, godlessness, and violence on American frontiers. [167]

The Church of Jesus Christ became alive and mobilized in ministry as a result of the Second Great Awakening; the equipping of God's people for ministry was evident. The Church flourished, and as it did, society was changed. America had returned to her biblical, God centered roots.

The result of the New York City Prayer Meeting Revival, of 1857, was similar. It spread nationwide and eventually, worldwide, mirroring the impact of the First and Second Great Awakenings. J. Edwin Orr wrote, "It became world-wide and lasted fifty years, something that could not be said of any other movement in America except the Great Awakening of the eighteenth century." [168] He estimated that at least one million people came to Christ in America, and when it jumped the Atlantic, about the same number came to Christ. Orr has been quoted as saying that there were one million Christians in America who, having drifted away from the Church, returned to be active again. [169] Candler reports the same mushrooming results. It began, he says, "the era of lay work in American Christianity." [170]

J. Edwin Orr referred to others who documented results. One said that it was "a great training school for laymen" and brought to the world great leaders like D. L. Moody. One of the most encouraging results of the New York City revival was unity. "With scarcely an exception, the churches were working as one man." (Oh God, do it again!) Even more amazing were reports related to doctrinal and denominational differences. "Arminians and Calvinists ignored their differences...doctrinal controversies were left alone ...The world knew again that God the Father had sent Jesus, His Son." [171] Orr wrote, "At last the world was able to say, 'Behold, how these Christians love one another.'" [172] They were answering the prayer of Jesus for unity in John 17:20–23.

Some writers believe that the Civil War postponed missionary advance in America. After the war, a great missionary movement broke out and spread God's people across the world. In England, Orr wrote, "Free from war, the oppressed at home were liberated ...Many Christian organizations and the creation of new ones brought a flood of blessing down the old channels and broke through obstacles to form new rivers of Christian enterprise. An author from the British Isles stated, "Humanitarian activity was the characteristic form in which their religious piety expressed itself." [173]

The Welsh Revival of 1904 demonstrated the fifth characteristic. George T.B. Davis, in his book, *When the Fire Fell,* gave a firsthand report from Wales. "Evidences of great renewing and the mobilization of the Church were reflected in a rash of Bible sales unseen for eighteen years. Others simply report faith and fervor and...forsaking sin." [174]

William Stead, one of the most powerful men of London, the editor of the "Pall Mall Gazette," visited the Welsh revival. Not known to be a Christian or even religious, he was asked if the results would be lasting. He replied:

> Nothing lasts forever in this mutable world ...But if the
> analogy of all previous revivals holds good, this religious
> awakening will be influencing for good the lives of numberless men and women who will be living and toiling
> and carrying on the work of this God's world of ours
> long after you and I have been gathered to our fathers. [175]

The move of God at Azusa Street launched the Pentecostal/Charismatic movement. Remember, as of 1980, there were fifty million classical Pentecostals in uncounted churches and missions in practically every nation of the world. There were charismatics in many of the Christian denominations, many who could trace at least part of their spiritual heritage to the Azusa Street meeting. [176] It is widely accepted that the Pentecostal or Charismatic believers have made an amazing impact around the world through their missionary outreach. Many of the largest and fastest growing churches in the world are charismatic. Although they have not been without controversy, the Charismatic/Pentecostal movement has been a spark to ignite passion and emotion across the Church. It has brought balance to the more cognitive, unemotional part of the Church.

CHARACTERISTIC 6
The Church Aflame, Back to Worship

Revival was marked by a return to the worship of God.

Nothing characterizes revival more than worship. As people see their sin in the light of God's holiness and respond in repentance, they are deeply moved to praise and worship. It is a return to spiritual passion and its expression—deep gratitude for God's grace and mercy. It is the awakening of "first love" (Rev. 2:4). It is like the people of God who fall on their faces at the dedication of Solomon's temple, watching the firestorm of God consume the sacrifices and His glory filling the house. In revival, hearts and emotions explode with praise. Hands are lifted in adoration, and feet dance with excitement. This is the sixth characteristic of biblical and post-biblical revival. The five post-biblical revivals are great examples of worship, and three of them stand at the center of this characteristic. They are the Welsh Revival, sometimes criticized for a lack of content and preaching, the Prayer Meeting Revival, known for less preaching than others, and the Azusa Street revival.

Many of the worship hymns that are sung today in traditional congregations, were written during the five revivals that span the history of the Church from 1726 through the early twentieth century. The great hymns written by the Wesley brothers, Charles being the primary songwriter, have endured through time. The Methodist movement was at the center of the *First Great Awakening,* and others have said it laid the foundation for the Second Great Awakening. The Wesleys bridged both. Writing about the First Great Awakening, Jonathan Edwards is known to have said that the worship was a deep longing for two things, to be more perfect in humility and more perfect in adoration.

> The flesh and the heart seem often to cry out, lying low before God and adoring Him with greater love and humility ...The person felt a great delight in singing praises to God and Jesus Christ, and longing that this present life may be as it were one continued song of praise to God. There was a longing as one person expressed it, "to sit and sing this life away." [177]

Sovereignly orchestrated by the Spirit of God, new songs of praise captured the hearts of His people and turned their souls to singing songs of love and worship. Isaac Watts created much of this great music. Edwards wrote, "Revival under Whitfield and Wesley gave a boost to hymn-writing ...Singing was so central to the Methodist movement that John Wesley wrote, 'Rules for Methodist Singers.' Charles wrote more than 6,000 hymns." [178]

In his description of both the First and Second Awakenings, Pratney said, "God restored facets of His awesome nature and super-natural power, allowing Him due worship in spirit and truth." [179]

In the *New York City Prayer Meeting Revival*, worship often took the form of testimonies. People stood to praise and thank God for answering prayers for the conversion of their friends and family and for the changes God had made in their lives.

The *Azusa Street* revival created a major paradigm shift in worship that has continued. Even the most traditional and formal churches, have included contemporary worship in at least one of their services. Some have blended the former rich hymnody with contemporary Christian music. Hymnals have been disappearing as words to songs are projected on screens or walls. Grand organs have become rare as praise and worship bands have taken center stage.

Under the preaching of Evan Roberts in the *Welsh revival*, the services were described as "go-as-you-please for two hours or more ...People prayed and sang, gave testimony; exhorted as the Spirit moved them ...They sang with unusual elevation of heart and voice. People were spontaneously drawn to worship ...Public praises were then greatly enlivened." [180] Brian Edwards devoted an entire chapter to worship as a primary characteristic of revival.

> So when the Spirit came to Wales, there were frequent outbursts of praising at the preaching services. Sometimes the preachers were interrupted and not able to continue because the praising was so great. On the other hand, a little before this, in Dundee, an awful and breathless stillness pervaded the assembly, "each hearer bent forward in the posture of rapt attention." [181]

There is rarely great passion for God without great expressions of adoration, worship, and praise. In revival, it spills out of hearts too full to contain it and springs heavenward, right on time, like Old Faithful in Yellowstone National Park. Passionate relationships between lovers results in heartfelt expressions such as love songs, poetry, and romantic creativity. This is what happens when God's people return to their first love for Him.

CHARACTERISTIC 7
The Confession of Sin, Personal and Corporate Clean-up

Revival led to repentance and the destruction of idols and ungodly preoccupations, and to turning away from personal and corporate sin.

When the *firestorms* of the Holy Spirit sweep across the Church, His refining fire purifies His people. Time-robbing cultural pre-occupations are replaced with balanced priorities and a passion for personal holiness and kingdom service. Spiritual growth and living biblically are priorities. Understanding the Word of God and walking it out in life take on new importance. The fruit of the Holy Spirit is the measure of maturity. All this is the seventh characteristic of revival.

As worship becomes the expression of revival, repentance and a return to biblical values characterize the Church. Brian Edwards writes, "Revival is always a revival of holiness, and it begins with a terrible conviction of sin." Sometimes, Edwards states, it is "crushing. People weep uncontrollably, and worse...." There is no such thing as a revival without tears of conviction and sorrow. [182]

Consider this moving account from *the First Great Awakening*, and the passionate repentance that came to Scotland.

> I found a good many persons under the deepest exercise of soul, crying out most bitterly of their lost and miserable state, by reason of sin; of their unbelief, in despising Christ and the offers of the gospel; of the hardness of their heart; and of their gross carelessness and indifference about religion, not so much from fear of punishment as from a sense of the dishonor done to God. [183]

Edwards reported what happened toward the end of *the Second Great Awakening* in a meeting in Tuckingmill, England. "Hundreds were crying for mercy at once." In this weeklong gathering, those repenting or crying out for mercy would remain "in great distress from one to fifteen hours, before the Lord spoke peace to their souls." [184]

The New York City Prayer Meeting Revival attracted multiple thousands as people gathered in the prayer meetings, and deep conviction of sin fell across the crowds, and with it, open confession and repentance. J. Edwin Orr wrote:

> The promise of renewal given Solomon in the days of the Kings (2 Chronicles 7:14), has made it clear that the humbling of the people of God, their diligence in intercession, their seeking of the Divine Will, and their turning from recognized sin—these are the factors in Revival, bringing about in God's good time an answer to their prayers, forgiveness of their sin, and a healing of their community. And these were the real factors recognized at the time by authorities qualified to judge, rather than the notions of facetious journalists of the day or opinions of the prejudiced a century or so later. [185]

In the Welsh Revival of 1904, the central message of Evan Roberts came in four clear and confronting statements. As he spoke to crowds from place to place, these statements were the essential standards to be met if revival was going to fall. They were fuel for the fire of the Holy Spirit as the firestorm swept across Wales:

> You must put away any unconfessed sin.
> You must put away any doubtful habit.
> You must obey the Spirit promptly.
> You must confess Christ publicly.

McDow and Reid write, "The burden of Roberts's message was to obey the Holy Spirit, while his rallying cry was 'Bend the Church, save the world.' This bending was about personal brokenness. It was a call to deep repentance. The entire tenor of the nation changed for good and God." [186] This was the case in all five of the post-biblical revivals just as it was in every revival of biblical history.

Accounts from the *Azusa Street Revival* reported that people's "hearts were being searched as with a candle in a dark room. Inner secret motives as well as behavior were being exposed. Nothing could escape God's conviction as Jesus was lifted up." [187]

Mark it! Know it! Spread the word from the platforms of the Church! There will never be a great sweep of revival across America and the world without repentance and a return to holiness and biblical living. A Third Great Awakening—with thousands coming to faith in Christ and cities being transformed—will not happen until the drifting Church becomes anchored again to biblical truth, first love, and personal holiness.

CHARACTERISTIC 8
The Flame of First Love Expressed

Revival brought a return to the offering of blood sacrifices in the Old Testament and a concentration on the death, resurrection and return of Jesus Christ in the New Testament, celebrated in the Lord's Supper.

The disease of drift has infected God's people from the beginning. It began with Adam and Eve in the pristine environment of Eden, when they responded to Satan's temptation and disobeyed God. From this tragic fall of mankind, the pattern of drift has woven its way throughout Israel's history and continued all the way to modern-day congregations. The Church could have learned from history how to avoid Israel's wrong choices, but she didn't. Paul the apostle wrote:

> I do not want you to be ignorant of the fact, brothers, that our forefathers were all under the cloud and that they all passed through the sea. They were all baptized into Moses in the cloud and in the sea. They all ate the

same spiritual food and drank the same spiritual drink; for they drank from the spiritual rock that accompanied them, and that rock was Christ. Nevertheless, God was not pleased with most of them; their bodies were scattered over the desert. Now these things occurred *as examples* to keep us from setting our hearts on evil things as they did. Do not be idolaters, as some of them were. (1 Cor. 10:1–7)

In the Old Testament, the blood sacrifices were a dramatic picture of what would happen to the perfect Lamb of God, Jesus Christ. The night before His death, Jesus instituted the Lord's Supper saying, "Do this...in remembrance of me (1 Cor. 11:25). Jesus gave us the Lord's Supper—communion or the eucharist—as a meaningful way to remember His death and reflect on our sin and God's forgiveness. It was to be central and frequent in the life of the Church.

When God's people Israel were in trouble spiritually, the sacrifices in the Old Testament became rote and religious, if not neglected altogether. Similarly, when the Church has drifted away from her "first love," the observance of communion has become a religious activity that is void of deep passion and reflection.

Before the end of the first century Paul had to write to the Corinthian church about the abuses of this sacred meal. She had become twisted with greed and formality and no longer celebrated the Lord's Supper with reverence, passion, and gratitude.

The memorial meal, communion, is intended to keep God's love and redemption fresh in our hearts. We need it because the heart of the gospel—the death, burial, resurrection, and soon return of Jesus Christ—is too easily forgotten or taken for granted. In times of revival, God's people are deeply moved by conviction and return to an understanding of what it took to rescue and save them. God's people become sensitive to the plight of the people around them, people who are hopelessly lost apart from God's mercy and grace.

In revival, believers are drawn back to the cross, and those who do not know Christ as Savior and Lord, come to the cross, convicted that they have fallen far short of God's righteous requirements. They come to faith in Christ by the thousands. There is an overwhelming conviction that they have been floating anchorless from the God who created them and died for them. All five great revivals are characterized by the preaching of the cross. There is no great awakening apart from a fresh look at what Jesus did for us during the dark days of His torture and sacrificial death. He "is the way, the truth and the life. No one comes to the Father except through [Him]" (John 14:6). It is the eighth characteristic of revival.

Mel Gibson's film, *The Passion of the Christ*, spread across America and the world in 2004, and drew thousands into a new awareness of Christ's sacrifice for sin on the cross and the battle Jesus faced with Satan in the Garden of Eden. The first time I saw the film, it marked my life. I fought back tears and anger until the scene when Mary, the mother of Jesus, got close to where He walked. Bent under the heavy cross, with His blood dripping from His wounds laid bare, Jesus turned to her and said, "I make all things new!" In that powerful moment I could longer hold back my tears. That was when my anger eased and the unspeakable tragic torture made some sense. It was all for me! It was for you!

Paul the apostle explains it to the Christ followers in Rome.

> But God demonstrates his own love for us in this: While we were still sinners, Christ died for us. Since we have now been justified by his blood, how much more shall we be saved from God's wrath through him! For if, when we were God's enemies, we were reconciled to him through the death of his Son, how much more, having been reconciled, shall we be saved through his life! Not only is this so, but we also rejoice in God through our Lord Jesus

Christ, through whom we have now received reconciliation. (Rom. 5:8–11)

According to McDow and Reid, the sad condition of the Church before the *First Great Awakening* was a two headed monster—"deviant orthodoxy and dead orthodoxy or laxity in devotion or compromising the Word of God." [188]

In this setting, Theodore Jackobus Frelinghuysen, a Dutch Reformed pastor, was one of the first preachers to see revival sparks in his ministry. He "determined to bring a fresh vigor to the faith through preaching, church discipline (especially the observance of the Lord's Supper), and zealous visitation." [189]

Brian Edwards, writing from his understanding of historic revival, said that the blood of Jesus and His cross took central stage in preaching. He explained, "Perhaps this is why many records of revival refer to the special blessings experienced at communion services when the blood of Christ is preached both from the Word and through the bread and wine." [190]

Edwards recounted several examples from the First Great Awakening and Wales. In Cambuslang in 1742, Scottish Presbyterians held two consecutive communion services and both events experienced revival. At the second, twenty thousand attended, but only a few thousand were able to participate in communion. Many came to Christ. Edwards wrote, "One writer has concluded that the root of the Methodist revival lay in the Lord's Supper."

The ministries of Whitfield and Wesley, found that although "the preaching of the cross was hated," it was what drew many to faith. Thousands found justification in the blood of Christ, redemption, propitiation, peace, reconciliation, and cleansing, even if they didn't understand those terms. When Joseph Kemp returned from the Welsh revival of 1905, he reported that "the dominating note of the Welsh revival was "redemption through the Blood." [191]

Wesley Duewel gave one of the most exciting accounts of the Lord's Supper in revival. In the first Great Awakening, Whitfield came to Cambuslang, a suburb of Glasgow, on July 8, 1742. He preached several times a day with only two thousand seats provided. Revival fires burned, and for days he preached long hours, even into the night.

On the tenth of July, a communion service was held, and thirty thousand gathered to hear Whitfield. Only seventeen hundred were able to take communion. A second communion service was held in August in three different tents. Three thousand were able to take communion in a crowd estimated to be from thirty to fifty thousand. [192]

Mary Relfe reported similar crowds in *the Second Great Awakening*. Revival broke out after James McGready, a Presbyterian pastor, called for a four-day observance of the Lord's Supper. It was the third community-wide communion service he had held. The meetings were so unusual that another communion service was held a month later. Approximately eleven thousand people flocked to the small church. [193]

In one of the early Methodist revivals, Devereux Jarratt (1733–1801) accepted a call to pastor a church. The theme of his preaching was "man's depravity by the Fall and his inability to be saved by works." He was the product of the powerful preaching of John Wesley and George Whitfield. With the bad news of man's desperate need, His powerful preaching trumpeted the Good News, "salvation in Christ's redemptive work, to be received by faith." Revival broke out in the church in 1776. His ministry illustrates the power of preaching about the cross, one of the primary passions of revival. [194]

The New York City Prayer Meeting Revival of 1857 saw the conversion of approximately one million people in America and one million in Europe. There is no conversion without the Gospel of Jesus Christ. The Lord's Supper, once again, took a prominent place.

Like in the other revivals, *The Welsh* and the *Azusa Street Revivals* were centered on the cross of Christ. The massive sweep of revival in Wales drew God's people back to the churches where services were alive, dynamic, and crowded. As revival moved through the nation, so did the return to the Lord's Supper. It was the same with Azusa Street. Bartleman wrote:

> The "color line" was washed away in the blood. A. S. Worrell, translator of the New Testament, declared the "Azusa" work had rediscovered the blood of Christ to the church at that time. Great emphasis was placed on the "blood" for cleansing, etc. A high standard was held up for a clean life. Jesus was being lifted up, the "blood" magnified, and the Holy Spirit honored once more. [195]

The cross of Christ stands at the apex of human and redemptive history. Is it any wonder that it stands at the apex of revival? Is it any wonder that it was central to the sacrifices of the Old Testament and was restored to its significance when God drew his wandering people back to himself? In revival, people come under a deep conviction of sin by the power of the Holy Spirit. In this state of desperation, thousands rush to receive the good news of salvation and embrace the glorious remedy of God's amazing grace.

CHARACTERISTIC 9
The Thrill of it: Great Celebration and Joy

Revival resulted in an experience of exuberant joy and gladness among the people of God.

"Freedom!"—shouts William Wallace, the mighty warrior played by Mel Gibson in the movie, *Brave Heart*, freedom from the tyranny of his nation's leaders. When people come to Jesus, some of them are ready to shout, "Freedom!" as they explode up out of baptismal waters, especially those who are freed from bondage to a very broken and enslaved past. Few things in life match the deep excitement and joy of being fully forgiven and set free.

To know this deep sense of well-being and renewed hope is to know peace with God, and the peace of God. To know the gift of having eternal salvation and freedom in Christ brings relief and tears of joy. It brings shouts of praise and thanksgiving to God, and deep levels of commitment to serve God. Regardless of how it is expressed—in a celebrative spirit or in the solitude of meditating on the richness of redemption—joy is the ninth characteristic of revival.

Consider this story of great joy from a report on the ministry of Jonathan Edwards in *the First Great Awakening*:

> From day to day, for many months together, might be seen evident instances of sinners brought out of darkness into marvelous light, and delivered out of a horrible pit and from the miry clay, and set upon a rock with a new song of praise to God in their mouths ...The town seemed to be full of the presence of God—it never was so full of love, nor so full of joy, and yet so full of distress as it was then ...It was a time of joy in families on account of salvation being brought to them—parents rejoicing over their children as newborn, and husbands over their wives, and wives over their husbands. [196]

The same thing was going on at the camp meetings of the *Second Great Awakening*. Pastor Barton Stone had gone to Kentucky from the Northwest to see firsthand what was happening. He wasn't used to seeing the manifestations of God's power. He wrote:

The scene was new to me and passing strange. It baffled description. Many, very many, fell down as men slain in battle, and continued for hours together in an apparently breathless and motionless state, sometimes for a few minutes, reviving and exhibiting symptoms of life by a deep groan or a piercing shriek, or by a prayer for mercy fervently uttered. After lying there for hours, they obtained deliverance. The gloomy cloud that had covered their faces seemed gradually and visibly to disappear, and hope in smiles brightened into joy. They would rise shouting deliverance, and then would address the surrounding multitude in language truly eloquent and impressive. With astonishment did I hear men, women, and children declaring the wonderful works of God and the glorious mysteries of the Gospel. [197]

These are the things in revival that cognitive critics and the theologically constrained criticize. They can shout and get crazy at their child's soccer game or when their favorite professional baseball player hits a grand slam in the ninth inning of a close game. They can get very excited when the kicker puts the pigskin between the uprights to win a football game as time is running out. Some can even get a little goofy at a party with friends, but it just doesn't seem right to be emotional about the redemption and long-awaited freedom of a sinner turned saint or at a powerful manifestation of the Holy Spirit!

Revival is sometimes messy, and we may be tempted to fear what people outside of Christ may be thinking. I have nothing against scholarship and educational discipline and excellence, but we who have committed ourselves to the study of theology and the attainment of advanced academic degrees must be careful that these gifts do not quench our openness to God. We must let God be God and allow His people to rejoice and celebrate. God cannot be contained

in a formal box of religion or even in the best of theological con-
structs. The stakes are high when it comes to eternal life—heaven or
hell. Breakthroughs of eternal significance and incredible freedom
call for great joy and celebration. Sometimes God's people fall to
the ground under the power of the Holy Spirit like at the dedication of Solomon's temple and like Saul as he encounters Jesus on
his way to Damascus.

Regardless of how people meet God—emotionally in revival or
in a quiet faith encounter—they enter into the glories of heavenly
hope. Wise leadership must guide revival but must not quench the
work of the Holy Spirit.

I can relate to the more reflective part of God's family. I am
renewed by solitude. I enjoy the grand music of heaven set to music
by God's creative artists or played by a grand symphony orchestra.
I still tear up when singing great historic hymns of faith. However,
I am ready for all styles of God-focused worship and praise. Bring
on the out-of-the-box and exuberant manifestations of the Holy
Spirit in revival. Bring on the loud praise and worship music. I never
want to keep God locked in a box of my experience or preferences!

My older brother, Chas, gave me a statement that has given
direction to me many times. He credited Oswald Chambers for it.
"Don't make a principle out of your experience. Let God be as original with others as He has been with you." This is good revival advice.

Revival brings celebration and exuberant joy. It is time to celebrate, to rejoice in the amazing grace and goodness of God.

J. Edwin Orr, revival historian, recorded firsthand accounts of
many conversions from the *New York City Prayer Meeting Revival*.
If you attended a noontime prayer meeting as a non-Christian, it
nearly guaranteed that someone would pray for you to trust Christ
as your Savior and Lord. Orr included the story of a father who stood
to request prayer for his three unconverted sons. Communication
was slow in those days, but the man, with great joy, later reported

that "each son had written to his father to give an account of his trusting Jesus as their Savior." Another account read:

> The exultant Miller led two other friends to Christ before
> he left Massachusetts for New York City. Upon his return...
> he sought out his cousin in that city and informed him of
> the united prayers of the newly converted family for his
> spiritual condition. The cousin smiled broadly, only to
> say that he, too, had become a disciple of the Master. [198]

An eyewitness report from David Matthews described the meetings of the *Welsh Revival* and the ministry of Evan Roberts: "Confronting and surrounding me was a mass of people, with faces aglow with a divine radiance ...Others, who had received "the blessing," were joyous in their newfound experience." [199] Another observer described the Welsh revival as "a storm center sweeping over Wales like a cyclone, lifting people into an ecstasy of spiritual fervor." [200] Davis described what he observed in Evan Roberts.

> My attention was riveted on Evan Roberts who stood in
> the pulpit and led the music with face irradiated with joy,
> smiles, and even laughter ...He seemed just bubbling over
> with sheer happiness, just as jubilant as a young man at
> a baseball game. [201]

Many firsthand stories of joy and wild excitement were recorded from the *Azusa Street Revival*. Bartleman recounted the time he received a special gift of song from the Holy Spirit. "The Spirit dropped the 'heavenly chorus' into my soul ...It was a spontaneous manifestation and rapture no earthly tongue can describe." [202] Riss recorded the experience of a Baptist pastor who was hit with a similar rush of the Holy Spirit:

> As brother Seymore preached, God's power seemed to be
> increasing ...Near the close of the sermon, as suddenly
> as on the day of Pentecost, while I was sitting in front of
> the preacher, the Holy Spirit fell upon me and literally
> filled me. I shouted and praised the Lord and inciden-
> tally, I began to speak in another language. Two of the
> saints quite a distance apart saw the Spirit fall on me. [203]

Joy and gladness accompanies the restoration of God's people through the Scripture. David danced before the Lord "with all his might" as the Ark of the Covenant came home (2 Sam. 6:14–15). In Psalm 30:11–12, David said to the Lord, "You turned my wailing into dancing...clothed me with joy, that my heart may sing to you and not be silent." It is no wonder the Psalmist wrote in Psalm 85, "Will you not revive us again, that your people may rejoice in you?"

CHARACTERISTIC 10
The Purifying Fire, Social Reform, and Prosperity

Revival was followed by a period of blessing and/or area-wide transformation that produced spiritual, social, and economic reform.

George Otis, of the Sentinel Group, documents moves of God that have produced amazing economic and social change as a part of revivals. The ten characteristics of revival is evident in each one. (See www.Sentinal Group)

Revival begins in the womb of dark and difficult times, and the agonizing labor and travail of prayer and repentance, but in time it brings forth new spiritual life. Each characteristic of revival follows, and in the end, one of the most exciting aspects of revival brings the story to an exciting climax—area-wide, city-wide, national and international transformation. It is the tenth characteristic of revival. Cities and nations are transformed. Economies flourish. The ground produces abundantly.

When *Firestorms of Revival* was first published in 2006, revival was spreading across the Fiji Islands. Social and economic reform were exploding. Warring, insurgent criminals were coming to faith in Christ. War in the streets and insurrection were declining. The government leaders were committing themselves and the nation to Christ and His kingdom. The poor were being fed. Once-polluted streams were flowing clear, and once-dead coral was miraculously returning to life. The depleted fishing industry was restored. The economy was turning around. Crops, once limited, were abundant.

The Sentinel Group has documented other stories. One of them came from Almolonga, Guatemala. Two jails, once overcrowded, were closed. The secular press called Almolonga the "City of God." Over 90 percent of the population became genuinely Christian. Illegal drug traffic and crime became a thing of the past. The Church was unified. The ground was producing mammoth vegetables like carrots the size of a man's forearm. Produce was being shipped to markets further and further away. [204]

In 2 Chronicles 7:14, God promises, not only to forgive His people, but also to heal their land. This is the grand climax of revival—the tenth characteristic. Social reform begins, and societies, nations, and cities are radically transformed. When God's people are revived and living in vital relationship with Him, there is plenty of God's light beamed through His people. It dispels the darkness of Satan's death and destruction.

Mary Stewart Relfe, not only a student of revival, but an authority on economics, reflects on the radical social reformation of revival in her book, *The Cure of All Ills*. Writing on the results of the *First Great Awakening*, Dr. Relfe describes the impact.

> God sought for a man among them, Ezekiel 22:30, and
> found a wealthy German, discerning enough to sense

the need of the Church universal and unselfish enough to organize prayer groups to cry unto God for it. Count Ludwig von Zinzendorf initiated Herrnhut, The Lord's Watch, with a small band of Moravians (persecuted believers who had fled for their faith and found asylum in the Count's estates in Saxony). The rebirth of Western Christian Culture can be traced back to the prayers, which ascended from the altar at Herrnhut. The Wesley brothers and George Whitfield owe their conversion to Moravian Bishop Peter Bohler at Aldersgate.

The revival of 1735 brought about a transformation of conditions which reversed the social, moral, and political declines. The prevailing vain philosophy, Deism, which denied the need of God, was stopped abruptly. Only those dedicated to godly principles were elected to public offices. This Spiritual Awakening returned the reins of the "West" back to God, decency and honesty. [205]

Historian Elie Halevy believed that the stability of eighteenth-century England was the result of the Wesleyan Revival. French-styled revolution did not sweep England like the riots and bloodshed that characterized the continent. A Christian conscience permeated the nation, and there was passion for the poor. National prosperity emerged. There was "such a reversal of conditions, that though their problems were many, the Revival proved to be their solution. [206]

In his book, *Great Revivals and the Great Republic*, Warren A. Candler listed nine results of the First Great Awakening. They include the following transformational developments.

1. A new catholicity was born among churches—unity!
2. Education was promoted and advanced.

3. A new bond of affection between the British Isles and the America colonies was established.
4. There was a unifying of the Anglo-Saxon peoples of the earth.
5. There was a moral revolution that regenerated and unified the colonies. It prepared the way for the political unity of Christian states. [207]

McDow and Reid stated that the Log College, established during the First Great Awakening, was dedicated to training converts, and the forerunner of the modern seminary. Whitfield's tabernacle, which was built for his meetings, was a charity school, and became the home of the University of Pennsylvania. A charity school established for Indians eventually became Dartmouth. Orphanages sprang up to care for homeless children. The revival had a unifying impact on the colonies and changed their moral climate. "The awakening prepared the colonies for the struggle to become a nation later in the century." [208]

The *Second Great Awakening* produced the modern missionary movement and so much more. The abolition of slavery emerged, as well as popular education. Six hundred colleges were founded. Relfe wrote, "Chastity was in vogue again. Honesty and integrity were the rule rather than the exception. Decreased crime, gambling, and drunkenness provided a backdrop for a period of genuine national prosperity." [209]

Many new Christian agencies were born. Among them were The American Bible Society, The New York Missions Society, The Missionary Society of Connecticut, The Massachusetts Society, The American Board of Commissioners for Foreign Missions, The General Missionary Convention of the Baptist Denomination, The American Home Missions Society, The Sunday School Union in Philadelphia, The New York Sunday School Union, and The American Sunday School Union. Christian magazines were birthed from the revival, particularly to support the growing Christian Education movement. [210]

The Second Great Awakening, particularly the Methodist movement, changed people's thinking and their hearts. It was a spiritual revolution. Chandler commented:

> It affected the destiny of the Great Republic, and in fact, the history of all mankind...reinvigorating the moral and religious life of the nation...inspiring invention, quickening industrialism and saving it from revolutionary tendencies, by averting perils from within and turning back dangers from without. [211]

What would social transformation look like today? Without exaggeration, I believe we would see a return to the Ten Commandments as the ethical base for civic life. Biblical marriage would be rooted in obedience to God and centered in men loving their wives and women respecting their husbands (Eph. 5:21–33). Thousands of couples living together outside of marriage would get married. The tragic infanticide of babies would come to an end. The epidemic of pornography would be seriously crippled. Churches across the nation would be packed once more and would mobilize God's people to meet the crying needs of the hungry, the imprisoned, the homeless, and the addicted. America would return to a Judeo-Christian consensus. She would return to being a spiritual and moral light at home and abroad.

The New York City Prayer Meeting Revival changed the social and financial landscape of America, and it had the same impact when it jumped across the ocean. Mary Stewart Relfe described it as a cure for social ills.

> The Revival of 1857 restored integrity to government and business in America once again. There was renewed

obedience to the social commandments. An intense sympathy was created for the poor and needy. A compassionate society was re-birthed. The reins of America were returned to the godly. Yet another time, revival became the solution to the problems, the remedy for the evils, and the cure of the ills. [212]

The international impact was similar.

> "Virtues of honesty, sobriety and integrity were kindled. Courtesies were reborn. Gentle, modest restraints kept men in order again ...Women were able to blush again and children were taught obedience. Around the globe, decency returned to government and business. Values for good and for God arose in the hearts of mankind everywhere as God wiped the spit from off the face of the earth once more. [213]

Relfe described the social changes as a moral revolution. Pornography was nearly eliminated. Illegitimate births declined. Morally destructive theatrical companies were shut down, Bible sales escalated, enemies became friends, and the ministries of women and men were honored equally. [214]

J. Edwin Orr tells us more. Think of what this would mean for America today. Think about what historians would be writing.

> Socially, the Nineteenth Century Awakening gave birth to a litter of active religious and philanthropic societies, which accomplished much in human uplift, the welfare of children, the reclamation of prostituted women, of alcoholics, of criminals, and the development of social virtues. Certain effects of the Awakening were not immediately apparent—the relationship between the

conversion of hundreds of thousands who developed an insatiable desire for education, and the passing of the 1870 Education Act, or the evangelical conversion of Keir Hardie under Moody's ministry and the introduction of that evangelical spirit into the Labor Movement in contrast to the atheism of Continental socialism. The great Evangelical Revival...was also effective in all three spheres of life: it saved Britain from the bloody Revolution; it produced the Evangelical order within the Church of England and Methodism, and revived Nonconformity without; and it changed the social order by stages, spectacularly in the abolition of slavery. [215]

In a later book, *The Fervent Prayer: The Worldwide Impact of the Great Awakening of 1858,* Orr included two chapters on social impact. He gave England the lead in social reform while America struggled through the Civil War. "However, in the post-war years, American Evangelicals began to address social problems related to the homeless and hungry, the drunkard, criminal and the harlot." There was more. "A school of Christian philanthropists soon arose, seeking to go straight to the heart of the slums with its practical Samaritans, yet always ready to cooperate in all wise legislative improvements." [216]

Industrial Extension Acts brought educational reform, the establishment of orphanages, reform on behalf of incarcerated criminals, the rehabilitation of prostitutes, and efforts to remove slavery. The impact on world missions was revolutionary. Orr wrote, "No other voluntary agency in all the world has achieved so much good and so little harm. Hence missionaries have stayed on where civil power evacuated." He highlighted great achievements in industrialization, medical services and hygiene, education, and agriculture. [217]

The impact of *the Welsh Revival* of 1904 followed the same pattern. Riss wrote that employers were amazed at the improvement in the quality of work that their employees produced. Waste was reduced, and there was less drinking, idleness, and gambling. As others have reported, the mine ponies in Wales could no longer understand the commands of the miners because their language had improved so much. They had quit cussing and kicking the ponies. The poor little burden bearers didn't know what to do. [218]

Another account of transformation was given by the chief constable of Cardiff and recorded in Judge Gilym William's quarterly report. It said there was a decrease of 1,364 in the number of people brought in for "nonindictable offenses." This improvement arose mainly from the decrease of drunkenness, especially in quarters where Mr. Evan Roberts had held revival services." [219]

Although it has been more difficult to define the social impact of *The Azusa Street Revival of 1906,* it has been concluded that the impact was without measure. Pratney stated that there were 100,000 recorded healings in the first five years of the revival and this was certainly a major impact. Recorded accounts also tell how people were raised from the dead. Beyond this immediate result, the impact of Azusa Street was like time-released social salt scattered across the world with fifty million Pentecostal adherents by 1980 and many more Charismatic followers scattered throughout many denominations and were some of the largest, most rapidly growing, and most impacting mission societies and mega congregations. [220]

Revival changes history, and its social and economic impact is immeasurable.

Will the Church in America arise to pray and care for their towns and cities? It is never too late.

George Otis Jr., whose videos have presented story after story of revival and transformation, has compiled a list of transformational markers. As the Church humbles herself in prayer and repentance, she can expect these results.

1. Political leaders publicly acknowledge their sin and dependence on God (2 Kgs. 11:17–18; 23:2; Jon. 3:6–9).
2. New laws and business practices are put into effect (2 Chron. 19:10; Neh. 10:31).
3. The natural environment is restored to its original life-nurturing state (Lev. 26:4–5; 2 Chron. 7:14; Ezek. 34:27; 36:29–30).
4. Economic conditions improve and lead to a discernable lessening of poverty (2 Chron. 17:3–5; Ps. 144:14; Isa. 60:5; Amos 9:13).
5. There is marked change in social entertainment and vices as kingdom values are integrated into the rhythm of daily life (Ezra 10:4; Neh. 8:10; Eccles. 10:17; Acts 19:17–20).
6. Crime and corruption diminish throughout the community (2 Kgs. 12:13–15; Neh. 5: 6–12; Isa. 60:17–18).
7. Volunteerism increases as Christians recognize their responsibility to heal and undergird the community (Isa. 58:10–12; 61:104).
8. Restored hope and joy lead to a decline in divorce, bankruptcy, and suicide (Neh. 12:27–28, 43; Isa. 54:11–14; 62:3, 7; Jer. 30:17–19; 31:11–13; Hos. 2:15).
9. The spiritual nature of the growing sociopolitical renewal becomes a hot topic in the secular media (2 Chron. 20:29; Neh. 6:16; Isa. 55:5; Ezek. 36:36; Acts 19:17).
10. Overwhelmed by the goodness of God, grateful Christians take the embers of revival into surrounding communities and nations (2 Chron. 17:9; Isa. 61:6; Acts 11:20–26). [221]

This list fans the flame for revival and transformation in our time. Can you picture how your area would look if these things were happening? George Otis, Jr.'s list inspires hope.

In late December 2004, one of history's greatest natural disasters occurred after a powerful earthquake centered in the Indian Ocean. A massive Tsunami hit the surrounding nations in wave after wave of destruction. Over three hundred thousand people lost their lives. One island in the Indian Ocean was moved one hundred feet. The newspapers were full of reports about generous financial support, as individuals, organizations, and nations began to provide aid and relief. Penetrating questions were asked. Was it a natural disaster? Was it God's judgment for the purpose of returning the nations to righteousness? David Wilkerson, the pastor of Times Square Church in New York City, reflected on America's response to the disaster in a January 17, 2005, letter he sent to his national constituents.

> America is a giving nation and very compassionate. Thank God for the response of so many who are praying, giving and going to help. But something deep within my soul troubles me. The magnitude of the disaster in not sinking in ...If we cannot be brought to our knees—if we cannot humble ourselves before such unleashed power, after witnessing the worst natural disaster in world history, our entire globe trembling—what will it take to silence the God-mockers? [222]

As I pondered the of the tsunami disaster, I recalled the description of the end times that Jesus gave in Luke 21:25–28:

> There will be signs in the sun, moon and stars. On the earth, nations will be in anguish and perplexity at *the roaring and tossing of the sea*. Men will faint from terror, apprehensive of what is coming on the world, for the heavenly bodies will be shaken. At that time they will see the Son of Man coming in a cloud with power and great glory. When these things begin to take place, stand up and lift up your heads, because your redemption is drawing near.

No one knows the exact time of the Lord's return, but scriptures like this stop me in my tracks. What kinds of disasters will come next? How bad will they be? Is the pandemic of 2020 and 2021 a wakeup call? Mary Stewart Relfe urges us to take action:

> Now is the time to respond like the King of Nineveh, when he called his nation to prayer, humility and fasting. "Who can tell? He cried. Perhaps even yet God will have pity on us and hold back his fierce anger from destroying us" (Jonah 3:9). The Revival of 1857 restored integrity to government and business in America once again. There was renewed obedience to the social commandments. An intense sympathy was created for the poor and needy. A compassionate society was re-birthed. The reins of America were returned to the godly. Yet another time, Revival became the solution to the problems, the remedy for the evils and the cure of the ills. [223]

Malcolm McDow and Alvin L. Reid's book, *Fire Fall: How God Has Shaped History Through Revivals,* was a call to prayer. Commenting on revival between 1901 and 1910, they said: "The story of revival...offers hope for our generation. Surely we can follow the example of those before us to set aside special times of prayer and fasting to seek the Lord" [224]

Church of Jesus Christ, followers of Jesus, it is time to gather for prayer across our cities. It's time for a historic move of God in our time. Let's take the initiative to gather God's people around us in our congregations, our neighborhoods, and our cities. We know how revival happens and will happen again. Our times are difficult. Our God is omnipotent. The pattern of history is clear. Our instructions in 2 Chronicles 7:14 call us to passionate prayer. God promises to answer.

Chapter 11

A TALE OF THREE CITIES

You say the little efforts that I make will do no good,
They never will prevail to tip the hovering scale
Where justice hangs in the balance?
I don't think I ever thought they would,
But I am prejudiced beyond debate
In favor of my right to choose which side
Shall feel the stubborn ounces of my weight.
(Boraro Overstreet) [225]

CHARLES DICKENS GAVE our world a well-known novel, *A Tale of Two Cities.* He wrote during the French Revolution. His first line was been better known. "It was the best of times—it was the worst of times." [226] It has described our times.

Some good things are happening in the "best" of our times. A prayer movement is growing across America. Large multi-campus congregations of thousands have been birthed and continue to grow. Many are coming to faith in Christ as they worship and teach in ways that emerging cultures can understand. These fellowships are characterized by intentional efforts to meet the needs of their communities.

Thousands are coming to Christ in Iran, China, Africa, and Latin America. Modern technology gives the Church an unprecedented ability and opportunity to communicate the gospel around the globe.

In spite of this, many believe that we have been facing the "worst" of times. The contrast between darkness and light has been increasing. Secularism and sensuality have become the norm. A biblical consensus on morality in America and the Western post-Christian world has been diminished. The Ten Commandments, as well as public manger scenes, have been removed from public settings. Traditional Christmas carols and any reference to the birth of Jesus have been removed from public schools. Christmas vacation has been renamed winter break. America has led the world in gambling, out-of-wedlock births, the use of alcohol and illicit drugs, and the number of people incarcerated. The LGBTQ+ agenda has been gaining acceptance and promoted, taught as viable choices, and protected. Millions have been hooked on pornography, and porn has been a rapidly growing industry for years, now an industry making billions of dollars annually.

Schools have become centers of violence and death. Armed police have been patrolling public school hallways to prevent violence. Security checks are set up in most public venues. Congregations have been quietly adding armed security people to be stationed at their gatherings. The increase of mass shootings has been alarming. With the pandemic that began in early 2020, crime and homicide have doubled. Depression, suicides, domestic violence, and alcoholism have increased.

The Importance of Our "Little Efforts"

I introduced this chapter with a brief statement by Bonaro Overstreet. It came to me years ago on a small card enclosed in a birthday note from Dr. Vernon Grounds, the former present of Denver Seminary.

He was a godly model and mentor to me. At the time I received it, I was wondering if the sacrifices of radical discipleship were worth the struggles and pain I was feeling. I decided they were—even to death—and I have cherished Overstreet's words about the importance of "little efforts." They have been framed in a prominent place in my study and in my soul for a long time.

We have the power to radically transform our nation and our cities. We have the power to answer Jesus's prayer for unity in John 17:20–23, and we can embrace the instructions for revival in 2 Chronicles 7:14. If we will unify, our nation and our communities will know that the Father sent Jesus, His Son. Some say unity is impossible. But wait! Nothing is possible for God. A pastor friend says we must pray for the harmony produced by a great symphony made up of many diverse instruments. Unity sometimes has the connotation that we all have to be the same, to give up our distinctives or uniqueness, but it's not true. Ephesians 4:1–16 describes the Church as a body of Christ followers who have unity in diversity and stand together in mutuality. As we practice speaking the truth to each other in love, we grow up to look like Jesus, the second incarnation, Jesus alive on earth again where we live and serve.

Couldn't we obey the apostle Paul's passionate teaching on unity in his letters? Enough can never be said about the importance of obedience. In 1 Samuel 15:22, we are advised that it is better to obey than to practice religious rituals or sacrifices. Dare I suggest that this includes the things that keep us from pursuing unity in our cities and towns, and our Great Commandment and Great Commission?

> I pray also for those who will believe in me through their message, that all of them may be one, Father, just as you are in me and I am in you. May they also be one in us so that the world may believe that you have sent me. (John 17:20–21)

Love the Lord your God with all your heart and with all your soul and with all your mind. This is the *first and greatest commandment.* And the second is like it: Love your neighbor as yourself. All the Law and the Prophets hang on these two commandments." (Matt. 22:36–40)

Jesus said, "All authority in heaven and on earth has been given to me. *Therefore go* and make disciples of all nations, baptizing them in the name of the Father and of the Son and of the Holy Spirit, and teaching them to obey everything I have commanded you. And surely I am with you always, to the very end of the age. (Matt. 28:16–20)

Jesus said that we would be His friends if we would obey (John 15:14). Obedience characterized the incarnate life of Jesus, and it must characterize the Church (John 15:1–11). Have you noticed the desire of God's heart for His people, "Oh, that their hearts would be inclined to fear [revere] me and keep all my commands always, so that it might go well with them and their children forever" (Deut. 5:29)?

Let's begin to passionately pray for another great move of God through the Church of our time. We have discussed the ten characteristics of revival, and we have learned how revival happens.

Tommy Tenney, of *God Chasers* fame, reminded me of two Bible stories that illustrate two different responses to God, like Jesus's hometown of Nazareth did when He returned for a visit, or like Nineveh did when Jonah finally obeyed God and called the city to repentance. Our response will have determined if revival will sweep our nation, and perhaps even the world.

Nazareth

Nazareth was the home of Mary and Joseph. The angel Gabriel had spoken to Mary to tell her that by the Holy Spirit of God she would miraculously conceive the Lord Jesus, the Messiah, in her womb. The angel also appeared to Joseph to tell him to take Mary, the woman to whom he was engaged, to be his wife.

Mary was "highly favored" (Luke 1:28), and her song of praise to God in Luke 1:46–55 demonstrated amazing maturity, wisdom, and intimacy with God. Her heart was full of love and adoration for God. She was submitted to His will. Joseph came from the royal line of King David, the man after God's own heart. Like David, his heart was sensitive to hear and obey the voice of God through the angel that appeared to him. Did the villagers see this in them? Did they know the story?

Jesus grew up in Nazareth with his earthly parents and family. They would have been well known in the village. Jesus spent thirty years of His life there. The village had a synagogue, and that is where the family would have attended on the Sabbath. It's where Jesus went when He came home after His ministry had begun (Luke 4:16–30). Jesus's reputation for performing miracles and speaking with wisdom had spread through the entire countryside (Luke 4:14). He had visited many synagogues, and everyone was praising Him.

When He stood up to read the Scripture in Nazareth, He chose Isaiah 61:1–2, a prophecy about the Messiah. He read it to show that the Spirit of the Lord was on Him. He was the Messiah of Israel, anointed to "preach good news to the poor." He was sent by God to "proclaim freedom for the captives and the release of prisoners from darkness."

Jesus's hometown crowd knew what He was saying. He was the Messiah? All eyes were glued on Him as He announced, "Today [right now] this Scripture is fulfilled in your hearing." The people of Nazareth could not believe it. They knew Jesus and His family. "Isn't this Joseph's son?" they asked.

Jesus responded by saying, "No prophet is accepted in his hometown" (Luke 4:24). He knew what they were thinking, and He let them know that disbelief had closed the door of opportunity to know His messianic, spirit-filled, miraculous ministry among them. He reminded them of other times in Israel's history when a lack of faith had stopped the wonderful work of God. It had happened in Elijah's day, when the widow of Zarephath in Sidon—not the people from Israel—saw God's miracles during the great years of famine. Many in Israel had leprosy in Elisha's time, but it was Naaman, a Syrian leader, who was healed. At the reminder of their faithless history, the hometown folks were enraged and drove Jesus out of town to kill him. "He walked right through the crowd and went on his way" (Luke 4:30).

Jesus made it clear in John 14:6, "I am the way and the truth and the life. No one comes to the Father except through me." It's been thieves and robbers who have tried to come to Him in other ways (John 10:1). They have either believed Jesus, or they haven't, and if not, they remain lost and separated from God. The consequences have always been presently and eternally significant.

Unbelief put a lid on the miraculous opportunity for Jesus to minister in His hometown. Did familiarity breed contempt? It certainly stopped a move of the Holy Spirit, a revival of hearts, and the thrill of receiving their long-awaited Messiah—Jesus. After centuries of waiting for Him, they tried to kill Him.

Nineveh

Nineveh was the second city in our tale, the capitol of the Assyrian Empire (known as Iraq today). It was pagan and famous for war crimes and violence, known for making monuments out of the decapitated heads of their enemies. They were long standing enemies of Israel. Nineveh was large for its day, with a population of 120,000. It would have taken Jonah three days to go through the city (Jonah 3:3).

God told Jonah, a patriot of Israel, to go to Nineveh and tell the people they must repent of their sin or destroyed. He knew about Nineveh, their brutality and paganism. How did Jonah feel? He found a ship headed in the opposite direction and booked passage, all to avoid God's call. God sent a great storm that could have sunk the ship and destroyed the lives of all on board. The sailors were fearing death. As they cried out to their gods, the weather-beaten veterans of the sea noticed that Jonah was not in the prayer meeting. He was sound asleep below the deck. The sailors awakened the sleeping missionary in their panic and asked, "Hey, man, why are you sleeping? We're going down. Pray! And, by the way, do you know who is responsible for this storm?" Jonah had to "come clean." He confessed running from God. Jonah realized that his only hope to save the ship and crew was to cast himself on God's mercy—overboard. The storm was his fault.

At this point, the story became a little "fishy." God created a large fish to swallow His rebellious missionary. In the digestive system of the fish—I can't imagine it—Jonah decided that obeying God was not a bad idea after all. The large fish spit Jonah up on shore, and he headed to Nineveh.

There was an amazing response to Jonah's preaching. From the king in sackcloth and ashes, with his face to the ground, to all of Nineveh's people—all the way down the social ladder—even including the animals, the city responded to Jonah's message. They fasted in repentance and turned to God, even with an unwilling preacher and his threatening, hard message. God has always responded with grace and mercy when people repent and turn to Him.

Can you imagine the king of Nineveh sitting in dust and calling for everyone to fast and repent? When you read Jonah 3:1–10, can you picture the mayor of your city calling out to God in similar humility and repentance at a time of riots, anarchy in the streets, or an economic or other disaster? What would happen if the president of the United States, his cabinet, and the Congress would follow this example?

Revival in history is predictable; the pattern is given in 2 Chronicles 7:14. When God's people do their part, God does His. He hears from heaven, forgives their sin, and heals their land. Psalm 145:13 says, God is "faithful to all his promises and loving toward all he has made." It's about Nineveh-style, dust-driven humility, calling out to God, and seeking His face with passionate, no-excuses repentance. It's turning from sin. It's the pathway to revival. There can be no room for "business as usual."

Who has prevented God from moving in revival? It has not been drug dealers, other criminals, or governments. It has been God's people. It was easier to convert pagan Nineveh than Nazareth where people knew about Jesus. God's calls out to His people when times are stormy and when they are living in fear of dying, when conditions are bad socially, spiritually, and economically. When God's people respond in obedience, the far side of revival has always been a vibrant Church, a healed land, great joy, and social change.

The City Where We Live

There is a third city in our tale. What will happen in your city? What will happen in my city? Will it be like Nazareth or Nineveh? The tale is ours to tell; we must decide. God is calling the Church to unified, passionate prayer and repentance. If we will we lay aside some of our personal agendas to embrace the unity of the city-wide Church (John17: 20–23), and if we will embrace 2 Chronicles 7:14 for our time, God will respond, and in His time, He will visit us with revival, a historic move of His Spirit.

In West Texas, playa lakes dot the landscape. These shallow, unconnected lakes are normally dry and barren because the area usually receives little rainfall. They do little to change the climate of the region but only reflect it. However, after a good rainfall, they are full of water and provide nourishment for thirsty creatures and birds, but they soon become dry again. They appear to be a picture of the ups and downs of Church history. When congregations in a city or a region function independently of each other, they are like the playas in Texas. The atmosphere of the area is unchanged, merely a reflection of the dry climate conditions, with some exceptions.

On the other hand, ocean currents called gyres, are full of life and impact the climates of the entire globe, especially those in their immediate proximity. It is time for the Church across the United States and the world to turn from being playas and become gyres, flowing in a current of the Holy Spirit that transforms the spiritual climate of our regions, our nation, and even the world.

We know how revival happens. The ten characteristics of revival are consistent throughout history. If we do our part, God will certainly do His as He promised in 2 Chronicles 7:14. He will respond to our passionate prayers as we seek His face. He will honor our humility. He will honor our unity for which He prayed in John 17:20–26. He will honor our repentance and mobilize us to transform the world in which we live.

I urge you to be intentional about joining with others who are gathering in prayer for revival. Together we will see another great firestorm of revival sweep through our land and the world.

Litany of Dedication: Jesus as Lord and King over Rockford

A S MEMBERS OF the city-wide Church of Rockford, Illinois, we are gathered at our city's crown jewel, the Coronado. In this place of coronation, we declare that Jesus Christ, the eternal Son of God, is Lord over Rockford. Together we crown you, Lord Jesus, as King over our city. We beseech You, Lord Jesus Christ—come in Your manifest presence. May Your kingdom come and Your will be done in Rockford as in heaven. For Thine is the kingdom, and the power, and the glory forever. Amen!

Revised and repeated on April, 2005, at an area-wide prayer rally held in the Coronado Theater

We, the area-wide Church of Rockford, Illinois, gathered at our area's crown jewel, the Coronado, the place of coronation, declare that Jesus Christ, the eternal Son of God, is Lord over our Rockford area. Together we crown you, Lord Jesus, King over our city. We beseech You, Lord Jesus Christ—come in Your manifest presence. May Your kingdom come and Your will be done in the Rockford area as it is in heaven. Bring revival to Your Church. Bring area-wide Great Awakening—thousands coming to faith in Christ. Transform, O God, the greater Rockford area for Your kingdom's sake, for Thine is the kingdom, and the power, and the glory for-ever. Amen!

ROCKFORD RENEWAL MINISTRIES: WHO WE ARE (A FOURTEEN-POINT STRATEGY)

THE VISION OF ROCKFORD RENEWAL MINISTRIES is a sweeping revival of the Church of Jesus Christ in the city of Rockford, Illinois, and a Great Awakening across the city, both accomplished by effectual fervent prayer and personal and corporate holiness.

THE MISSION OF ROCKFORD RENEWAL MINISTRIES is to call the Church of Jesus Christ across the city to repentance and to seek God through humble prayer for revival and a Great Awakening according to 2 Chronicles 7:14. The results shall be personal and corporate righteousness, people and congregations on fire for God and His kingdom, and dramatic social change—the transformation of the city.

We exist to serve:

Jesus Christ

Prayer is an expression of our total dependence on a God who loves us extravagantly. Every area of Rockford Renewal

Ministries passionately seeks to serve Jesus Christ and fulfill His kingdom purposes.

The City

1. GRIPP (Greater Rockford in Prayer & Praise) monthly gatherings in local churches for worship and prayer.
2. A Pastor's Prayer Summit, held annually or more frequently for area-wide clergy, organized in partnership with Bridge Ministries.
3. Two weekly prayer meetings will be held downtown to pray for revival in the city-wide Church.
4. Lighthouses of Prayer will be established across the city in as many neighborhoods as possible. The goal is 3,000.
5. Special prayer meetings are held each month at the school district office, city hall, the courthouse, and in the jail.
6. Rockford Renewal Ministries will encourage the establishment of a twenty-four hour a day, seven days a week prayer effort, focused on praying for the needs of the city, the revival of the Church, and a Great Awakening.

The Church

1. Speaking across the city as opportunities are presented. Common subjects are prayer, revival, repentance, and the ten characteristics of revival found in the Scripture and in major revivals of post-biblical history.
2. A city-wide servant leader team will be established to seek God's direction for the spiritual transformation of the city and to engage the city-wide Church to follow His direction. The team will direct revival when it sweeps the area.
3. The Prayer Team of Rockford Renewal Ministries will be committed to pray daily for revival, the transformation of the city,

and for the ministry of Bob and Connie Griffin. Intercessors on several different levels will meet at scheduled prayer times each week. The Board of RRM will meet with the Griffins once a month to pray for personal concerns, for the RRM ministry, and for revival and area-wide transformation.

Christian Leaders

1. Fellowship dinners of denominational and racial diversity will be held regularly for pastoral couples and singles to build unity and friendship, and to pray for revival in the Church, healing in the city, and a Great Awakening.
2. The leaders of Rockford Renewal Ministries will make individual appointments with clergy in the city to encourage unity and participation in city-wide prayer efforts.
3. The leaders of Rockford Renewal Ministries will offer personal pastoral counseling for the encouragement, freedom, and revival of individual Christians, especially focused on leaders.
4. As resources allow, a quarterly publication, *Reflections on Revival: Fanning the Flame,* will be mailed to congregations and area leaders. It will report revival news and promote area-wide unity and prayer. *A Partner's Perspective* will be mailed quarterly to ministry wives.
5. Rockford Renewal Ministries will publish a city-wide prayer list of civic leaders and needs in the city. The list will be distributed to the Prayer Team, identified intercessors, and those who request it.

DEFINITION OF REVIVAL

Revival is a spontaneous spiritual awakening by God the Holy Spirit among His people. It comes in answer to their humble prayers as they passionately seek His face and repent of their sins. The awakening results in deepened intimacy with God, passion for Him, holy living, evangelism, and citywide or area-wide transformation, expressed through social reform.

Appendix III

TIPS ON PRAYER

Dr. Bob Griffin ~ Renewal Ministries
Prayer is quality talk, conversation, and time with our Heavenly Father.

1. It is 98 percent discipline and hard work. *Strategic weapons* take lots of learning and skill to use effectively.
2. There are at least three beastly barriers: time, sleep, and location. You need to block out a time when you can be awake, a quiet place without distraction, and a STRATEGIC PLAN for prayer, approach, what and when.
3. There are at least five beastly barriers to *answered* prayer:
   Motives James 4:6
   Patience/God's timing Isaiah 55:8–9
   Sin Psalm 66:18–20
   Faith Hebrews 10:23; 35–39; 11:1–2, 6; Romans 4:16–22
   Abiding/intimacy with Him John 15:5–8
4. Everyone's plan will be different, and the plan will change over time. When the plan no longer works, change it. "Don't make a principle out of your experience; let God be as original with others as He has been with you."
5. A fundamental approach: Begin with *adoration* or worship— praise God for who He is. Then go to *confession*. Be specific.

Confess through the fruit of the Holy Spirit in Galatians 5 or the Beatitudes in Matthew 5. I find it helpful to ask the Holy Spirit to reveal to me *thoughts* that need to be confessed, *attitudes* that were out of line with His Truth, and *things that I said* or did that were out of line. *Thanksgiving* comes next—all you can think about (You won't have enough time). Conclude with *supplication*—ask! (Memorize the Lord's Prayer and pray it daily, Matt. 6:9–13.)

6. When you feel under spiritual attack, pray through the armor of Ephesians 6. For example, "Lord I take the *sword of the Spirit*, the Word of God. Give me great skill today in using the Word as Jesus did in the wilderness. Add Scripture that comes to mind. For example, "Without faith it is impossible to please God." "Faith is the substance of things hoped for, the evidence of things not seen" (Heb. 11).

7. List praying can be very boring, but it is critically important: Churches, friends and family, missionaries, government officials, and so forth. *Try to find a time when you are active doing something else like working out on the treadmill (paste lists to the wall to see when working out), walking, commuting to work, and so on.*

8. One of the most effective ways of praying is to write a letter to God. You can follow the ACTS outline (see No. 5). Then *stop* to listen to what God wants to say. Ask Him to speak. Write down your impressions. Test what you hear with biblical truth. If it is unusual, check it with another mature trusted Christian.

9. If there are special things or needs, you can pray at special times, at every stoplight or at a certain common intersection, the ninth hole on the golf course, long trips in the car, exercising, and the like.

10. Learn about fasting, different kinds and ways. Fasting enriches your prayer life. It helps you focus.

11. If you are married, block out time to pray with your partner. It is one of the secrets of intimacy. Many Christians find a small prayer group or prayer partner. Praying with others is exciting and powerful. Accountability can help you stay focused and sometimes is essential to breaking old patterns.

12. Many have found that thoughtfully praying the Lord's Prayer is a very enriching daily habit.

Group prayer can quickly become routine and boring. Here are guidelines that are intended to keep group prayer alive and dynamic:

GUIDELINES FOR PRAYER

- Listen for the Holy Spirit's direction.
- Blend songs and prayer together
- Be long on praise and worship.
- Pray brief passages of Scripture.
- Lead in song as the Holy Spirit leads you.
- Allow for silence and listen.
- Pray shorter prayers so many can pray.
- Stay with a subject until the Holy Spirit is finished with it.
- **Be sensitive to diversity: gifts, volume, worship style.**
- **Pray along with others as they pray.**
- Rather than taking time to list requests, weave worship and prayer together. Let the requests come as someone prays for something. Others can join in praying for the concern as they hear it.
- Give announcements about events at other times, not in prayer.

Corrie ten Boom wrote, "Don't pray when you feel like it. Make an appointment with the King and keep it. The devil smiles when we make plans. He laughs when we get too busy, but he trembles when we pray." She says, "Ask yourself: Is prayer my steering wheel or my spare tire?" (1) https://quotefancy.com/quote/786978/Corrie-ten-Boom-Don-t-pray-when-you-feel-like-it-Corrie ten Boom

Martin Luther said: "Tomorrow I plan to work, work, work, from early until late. In fact, I have so much to do that I shall spend the first three hours in prayer." (2) https://www.goodreads.com/quotes/35269-i-have-so-much-to-do-that-i-shall-spend Martin Luther

Appendix IV

BREAKING GENERATIONAL CURSES
AND OTHER STRONGHOLDS

I F YOUR SPIRITUAL journey is extremely difficult, you may have some spiritual house cleaning to do. The most helpful approach to me has been to review my personal history and the patterns of struggle in my life. List them. There could be strongholds in these areas. Often these relate to lies of the *culture*, the world. An example would be telling yourself or believing that you have to have certain things to be happy, a thin body or a certain size, not short or stocky, and so forth. The next source of deceit is *yourself*, things you have been told that are not true, such as you are dumb or just good, average, and so on. Finally, and especially important, is to understand that *Satan* wants to destroy you with deceit. He lies to you daily about many things. Test common concerns against the truth of the Scripture. For example, I can't do anything well. Not so. The Bible promises that you can do all things through Christ who strengthens you. Replace the lie. Having identified the patterns and/or lies, renounce them in the name of Jesus Christ, and write down or speak out the truth from the Word of God. In Jesus's name, renounce and cast away any perpetuating demons.

Can you identify patterns from your past generations? How about sensuality, drug or alcohol abuse, child abuse, divorce, rage and anger, lack of boundaries with people, or co-dependency, and the like. These are more than likely generational curses or strongholds. Identify them. Write them down. This is the same process with strongholds in your life. Recall what Paul said in Ephesians 4:26, "Be angry but don't sin. Don't let the sun go down on your anger." If you do, you will give the devil a foothold or stronghold.

I suggest that you find a few discerning fellow believers who are wise and mature in Christ, people of prayer, people who hear God speaking or who have the gift of discernment or knowledge. Block out some hours to pray with them, asking God to show you what generational curses and/or strongholds are operative in your soul. Take careful notes to refer back to at times. The following is an approach to prayer that will break them. Modify it as the Holy Spirit leads you. Do not do strategic warfare praying by yourself, unless you are very strong and led by God to do it. Always work with a group of other believers who are confident of their faith in Christ and His protection.

1. Bind Satan, principalities, and powers from your location and within you. By faith, apply the blood of Jesus Christ, the eternal Son of God who came in human flesh, to yourself, body, soul, and spirit, and to all prayer partners (Some demons use the name, Jesus, to fool or deceive us). Put on the full armor of God from Ephesians 6. Pray through these, not just name them.
2. Renounce each stronghold or curse by name and break it in the name of Jesus Christ.
3. Renounce and break all negative soul ties to anyone involved, from conception forward, past, present and future to the third and fourth generation, a parent, former sexual partner, and so on.
4. Cover the curse or stronghold with the Satan-death-and-hell–defeating blood of Jesus Christ from conception to the third and fourth generation.

5. Bind up and cast all associated demons, principalities, and powers out to the feet of Jesus or wherever He wants them to go. (He knows what to do with them.)

6. Cleanse each place in your soul or body by faith with the blood of Jesus Christ, which have been occupied or influenced by the stronghold and/or demons. Ask and thank God for soul healing; then ask the Holy Spirit to fill that place that had been formerly occupied.

7. As you do this for each stronghold or curse one at a time, replace each one with biblical truth. For example, if it was a stronghold of anger, replace it with God's patience and peace. If it was a stronghold of sensuality, replace it with God's purity.

Appendix V

TEN CHARACTERISTICS OF REVIVAL
IN THE SCRIPTURES

T WELVE IN THE Old Testament—Jacob: Genesis 35:1–15; Asa: 2 Chronicles 15:1–15; Jehoash: 2 Kings 11–12, 2 Chronicles 23–24; Hezekiah: 2 Kings 18:4–7, 2 Chronicles 29–31; Josiah: 2 Kings 22–23; Ezra: Ezra 5–6; Nehemiah/Ezra: Nehemiah 8:9, 12:44–47; Jonah; Jehoshaphat: 2 Chronicles 17:6–9, and chapter 20; Moses: Exodus 32–33; Samuel: 1 Samuel 7:1–13; Elijah: 1 Kings 18

Eight in the New Testament—John the Baptist: Matthew 3:1–12; Pentecost: Acts 2:1–4, 14–47; the Church: Acts 4:23–37; Ananias and Sapphira: Acts 5:1–16; Stephen's sermon and death: Acts 7:54–8:25; Cornelius: Acts 10:23–48; Pisidian Antioch: Acts 13:44–52; Ephesus: Acts 19:1–20

Confirmed in Post-biblical History

Confirmed in post-biblical history through the First and Second Great Awakenings—1726 and 1776, the New York City Prayer Meeting Revival—1857, the Azusa Street Revival—1906 and the Welsh Revival of 1904 (See chapters 6, 8, and10)

1. Revival occurred in times of personal or national crisis and great spiritual need, and in times of moral darkness and spiritual decline among God's people, Israel, or his Church.

2. Revival began in the heart(s) of one or more consecrated servants of God, who became the agent(s) God used to lead His people back to faith and obedience.

3. Prayer was central to revival. Leaders called out to God in prayer, passionately seeking His face in repentance and in the confession of their personal and national sins. They ignited prayer among God's people.

4. Revival rested upon the powerful proclamation—preaching and teaching—of the law of God and His Word. Many of the revivals were the result of a return to the Scripture.

5. Revival in the Old Testament reflected the work of God the Father to awaken his people, Israel, to a restored relationship with Him, to obey Him, and serve his redemptive purpose. Revival in the New Testament and post-biblical history reflected the work of the Holy Spirit in miracles and in the equipping of people for ministry. It resulted in the spread of the gospel and the growth of the Church.

6. Revival was marked by a return to the worship of God.

7. Revival led to repentance and the destruction of idols and ungodly preoccupations, and to turning away from personal and corporate sin.

8. Revival brought a return to the offering of blood sacrifices in the Old Testament and a concentration on the death, resurrection, and return of Jesus Christ in the New Testament—celebrated in the Lord's Supper.

9. Revival resulted in an experience of exuberant joy and gladness among the people of God.

10. Revival was followed by a period of blessing and area-wide transformation that produced spiritual, social, and economic reform.

Appendix VI

THE GOOD NEWS:
THE MESSAGE OF THE CHURCH

T HE PROBLEM OF "drift" among God's people has been a
pattern through history (Ps. 96:10b). In recent times, theological and philosophical perspectives have added to it. The Church
must remain firmly anchored to her primary message, the Good
News, the Gospel of Jesus Christ. It is the message of her Great
Commission (Acts 1:8; Matt. 28:19–20). It's the message to take
into the world day by day as she loves her neighbors as herself, and
loves each other like Jesus did (Luke 10:27; John 13:34). Without a
clear biblical understanding of the Gospel, there will not be a clear
message. In fact, if we get it wrong, there will be no redemption.
Certainly, as we share God's truth, we will have to communicate it
in a way that cultures can understand it, contextualizing it, but we
must never change the truth of the Word of God.

New theological and philosophical perspectives have detracted
from the Great Commission to share the Gospel. In mainline
denominations and others, universalism has declared that everyone
will make it to heaven. It discredits Jesus's teaching about heaven
and hell. It removes the biblical teaching that "all have sinned and
fall short of the glory of God" (Rom. 3:23) and must embrace John
3:16–17. Those two texts tell of our need and how to be saved.
Romans 6:23 tells us: "For the wages of sin is death, but the gift of

God is eternal life in Christ Jesus our Lord" (NIV). And John 1:12 teaches what to do about our sin. "Yet to all who receive him [Jesus], to those who believed in his name, he gave the right to become children of God." Eternal salvation "is by grace … through faith—and this not from yourselves, it is the gift of God—not by works so that no one can boast" (Eph. 2:8–9). One who tries to get to heaven in some other way is "a thief and a robber" (John 10:1).

Let's begin with mankind's basic need. All have sinned and the wages of sin is death, eternal separation from God. The message of the Bible is that only Jesus Christ can radically change the human heart. It is changed by conversion.

WHAT IS CONVERSION?

Conversion or eternal salvation occurs when one hears the truth about their lost condition, acknowledges it, and embraces the Gospel, the good news of eternal salvation through Jesus Christ. They are redeemed by embracing the price paid for their salvation through the death and resurrection of Jesus. Most people do not need to be convinced of their need. They know internally that they cannot even live up to their own standards, not to mention God's holiness. With the invitation to receive God's gift of salvation through the payment of their sin, they must come to a place of decision. They must choose to receive God's gift of salvation or reject it. The decision to receive Christ as Savior results in a changed life, sometimes rather suddenly, sometimes more slowly. It begins the life of spiritual growth and sanctification that Paul the apostle personifies as he shares his commitment to growth in Philippians 3. Speaking of knowing Christ and His power, Paul says, "Not that I have already obtained all this, or have already been made perfect, but I press on to take hold of that for which Christ Jesus took hold of me …Forgetting what is behind and straining toward what is ahead, I press on toward the goal to win the prize for which God has called me heavenward in Christ Jesus. All of us who are mature should take such a view of things" (vv. 12–15). Christian growth and discipleship is not about arriving, but being on the way, intentionally living a life of spiritual growth.

Paul gives us two essentials of conversion in Acts 20:21: "I have declared to both Jews and Greeks" that they must (1) *turn to God in repentance*, and (2) have *faith* in our Lord Jesus." Here is the turning from, and the turning to, that shapes conversion. The need for *faith* in God's gracious provision is explained in Ephesians 2:6–9, as well as in many other passages of Scripture. Jesus declared in Luke 18:3, "Unless you *repent*, you will all perish." The need for repentance is woven throughout the Scripture.

Conversion comes from the Hebrew verb, *shubh,* and the Greek verb, *epistrepho,* both meaning "to turn or return." The simple verb, *strepho,* which means to turn, is used by Jesus in Matthew18:3 where He says, "I tell you the truth. Unless you change and become like little children, you will never enter the kingdom of Heaven." *Epistrepho,* to turn about or to turn toward, is used in James 5:19–20 and in other places like Matthew 13:15, Mark 4:12, and Luke 22:32— turning a sinner from the error of his way. The Greek noun is used in Acts 15:3, which requires a turning from and a turning to.

When Paul writes to the Ephesian church, in chapter two, he expresses what Jesus has done for us as "incomparable … [the] riches of His grace, expressed in his kindness to us in Christ Jesus" (v. 7). It is "by grace you have been saved through faith—and this not from yourselves, it is the gift of God—not by works, so that no one can boast" (vv. 8–9). John and Paul are writing about individual conversion.

Paul the apostle's individual story of conversion is repeated three times (Acts 9:1–9; 22:3–21; 26:4–20), making it a significant example of personal conversion. The "whoever" in John 3:16 makes conversion an individual choice. Jesus likens it to birth in John 3:1 and following. From this text comes the popular description of conversion, "being born again." Paul likens it to creation or re-creation in 2 Corinthians 5:17: "Therefore, if anyone is in Christ, he is a new creation; the old has gone; the new has come." Conversion blends God's sovereignty with human responsibility in a divine creative tension. "Whoever believes in the Son has eternal life" (John 3:36; 5:24) is blended in a divine matrix with, "In him we were chosen, having been predestined according to the plan of him who works out everything in conformity with the purpose of his will" (Eph. 1:11, NIV). These truths stand as poles of biblical truth. To embrace one and neglect the other is to embrace an unbalanced extreme.

The cross of Jesus Christ stands at the apex of redemptive history. It is the watershed. One slope leads to eternal separation from God in a place prepared for Satan and his demons, the other to eternal life and salvation with Jesus. The contemporary mind struggles with the "wrath of God" against unrighteousness taught by Paul in the first five chapters of Romans. God lays the sin of Adam and Eve on all people of all time (Rom. 5:21–21). Then in grace and mercy, God lays all that sin on Jesus Christ as He suffers and dies on the cross. Satan, death, and hell are defeated in His resurrection. Jesus is the eternal Lamb of God, killed and sacrificed for the sin of the entire world. Then in grace and mercy, God lays or imputes the righteousness of Christ to those who receive His gift of salvation. Jesus died for all of us.

Dallas Willard describes conversion and Christian discipleship with fresh contemporary language in his book, Renovation of the Heart:

> The revolution of Jesus is in the first place and continuously a revolution of the human heart or spirit. It did not and does not proceed by means of the formation of social institutions and laws, the outer forms of our existence, intending that these would then impose a good

order of life upon people who come under their power. Rather, his is a revolution of character, which proceeds by changing people from the inside through ongoing personal relationship to God in Christ and to one another. It is one that changes their ideas, beliefs, feelings and habits of choice, as well as their bodily tendencies and social relations. It penetrates to the deepest layers of their soul. External, social arrangements may be useful to this end, but they are not the end, nor are they a fundamental part of the means.

On the other hand, from those divinely renovated depths of the person, social structures will naturally be transformed so that "justice roll[s] down like the waters and righteousness like an ever-flowing stream" (Amos 5:24). Such streams cannot flow through corrupted souls. Conversely, a renovated "within" will not cooperate with public streams of unrighteousness. It will block them— or die trying. It is the only thing that can do so. (Dallas Willard, *Renovation of the Heart: Putting on the Character of Christ,* (Colorado Springs: CO: NavPress, 2002), 15).

How will our family, friends, neighbors and the entire world know and understand the Gospel? We must tell them. We must fulfill the Great Commission. The stakes are high. The love of Christ and the Word of God compel us to spread this Good News! (For a more thorough treatment of this subject, see David Larson's *The Evangelism Mandate,* p 22.)

Appendix VII

SOME OF BOB'S SPECIAL VERSES

WHAT GOD IS LIKE; His point of view and our ever-present help

1 John 4:8 God is love.

Zephaniah 3:17 The LORD your **God is** with you, the Mighty Warrior who saves. He will take *great delight in you; in his **love** he will no longer rebuke you but will rejoice over you with singing."*

Isaiah 41:9–10 I took you from the ends of the earth, from its farthest corners I called you. I said, 'You are my servant; *I have chosen you and have not rejected you. So do not fear, for I am with you* with my righteous right hand.

Isaiah 30:15 This is what the Sovereign LORD, the Holy One of Israel, says: "In repentance and rest is your salvation, *in quietness and trust is your strength*, but you would have none of it ...Yet *the LORD longs to be gracious to you; therefore, he will rise up to show you compassion.* For the LORD is a God of justice. Blessed are all who wait for him!"

Isaiah 40:11 He tends his flock like a shepherd: He *gathers the lambs [you] in his arms and carries them close to his heart*; he gently leads those that have young.

Deuteronomy 33:7 The eternal God is your refuge, and underneath [you] are the everlasting arms.

Psalm 16:5–8; 11 LORD, You alone are my portion and my cup; you make my lot secure. The boundary lines have fallen for me in pleasant places; surely, I have a delightful inheritance ...I will praise the LORD, who counsels me; even at night my heart instructs me. I keep my eyes always on the LORD. With him at my right hand, I will not be shaken. You make known to me the path of life; you will fill me with joy in your presence, with eternal pleasures at your right hand.

Psalm 62:1–2; 5–8; 11–12 Truly my soul finds rest in God; my salvation comes from him. Truly he is my rock and my salvation; he is my fortress; I will never be shaken. Yes, my soul, find rest in God; my hope comes from him. Truly he is my rock and my salvation; he is my fortress; I will not be shaken. My salvation and my honor depend on God; he is my mighty rock, my refuge. Trust in him at all times, you people; pour out your hearts to him, for God is our refuge.

Psalm 17:7 Show me the wonders of your great love, you who save by your right hand those who take refuge in you.

Psalm 84: 5–7 Blessed are those whose strength is in you, whose hearts are set on pilgrimage. As they pass through the Valley of Baka, they make it a place of springs; the autumn rains also cover it with pools. They go from strength to strength, till each appears before God in Zion.

SPIRITUAL DISCIPLINES—growing in faith

1 Chronicles 28:20 Be strong and courageous, and <u>do the work</u>. Do not be afraid or discouraged, for the LORD God, my God, is with you. He will not fail you or forsake you until <u>all the work</u> [to which I called you is completed].

Colossians 3...<u>set your heart</u> things above...<u>set your mind</u>...<u>put to death</u>, therefore, whatever belongs to your earthly nature;...<u>rid yourselves</u> of all such things as these: anger, rage, malice, slander, and filthy language from your lips. Do not lie to each other ...Whatever you do, <u>work at it with all your heart</u>. **4:2** <u>Devote</u> yourself to prayer.

2 Peter 1:5 <u>Try your hardest</u> (NEB); <u>Make every effort</u>; (NIV);...to add to your faith, goodness, knowledge, self-control, perseverance, godliness, brotherly kindness, love....

Romans 8:12–13...if by the Spirit you <u>put to death</u> the misdeeds of the body, you will live ...(Grace is not opposed to effort, but to earning. The air is free, but you have to breathe.)

1 Corinthians 9:24–27 Do you not know that in a race all the runners run, but only one gets the prize? Run in such a way as to get the prize. Everyone who competes in the games goes into strict <u>training</u>. They do it to get a crown that will not last; but we do it to get a crown that will last forever. Therefore I do not run like a man running aimlessly; I do not fight like a man beating the air. No, <u>I beat my body and make it my slave</u> so that after I have preached to others, I myself will not be disqualified for the prize.

1 Thessalonians 1:3...<u>work</u> produced by faith...<u>labor</u> prompted by love...<u>endurance</u> inspired by hope.

Philippians 2:12...<u>work out</u> your own salvation with fear and trembling, for it is God who works in you.... **3:13–14**...<u>strain toward</u> what is ahead...<u>press on</u> toward the goal.

1 Timothy 4:7–8...<u>train</u> yourself to be Godly. **16** Watch your life and doctrine closely...pay close attention to yourself and to your teaching; <u>persevere</u> in these things.

2 Timothy 2:15...<u>a workman</u> who does not need to be ashamed and who correctly handles the word of truth.

Hebrews 11:6 And without faith it is impossible to please God, because anyone who comes to him must believe that he exists and that he rewards those who <u>earnestly seek him</u>.

Proverbs 4:23 Above all else...<u>guard</u> your heart...watch over your heart with <u>all diligence</u> for <u>the sources of our life lie in it...it is the well spring of life.</u>

1 Corinthians 15:10 <u>I worked harder</u> than all of them, yet not I, but the grace of God that was with me.

57–58 *But thanks be to God! He gives us the victory through our Lord Jesus Christ.* Therefore, my dear brothers, <u>stand firm</u>. Let nothing move you. Always <u>give yourselves fully</u> to the <u>work</u> of the Lord, because you know that your <u>labor</u> in the Lord is not in vain. **16:13** Be on your <u>guard; stand firm</u> in the faith; be men of <u>courage</u>; <u>be strong</u>. Do everything in love.

James 1:2–8 Consider it pure joy, my brothers, whenever you face trials of many kinds, because you know that the <u>testing of your faith develops</u> **perseverance.** **Perseverance** must finish its work so that <u>you may be mature and complete, not lacking anything.</u> If any of you lacks wisdom, he should ask God, who gives generously to all without finding fault, and it will be given to him. But when he asks, he must believe and not doubt, because he who doubts is like a wave of the sea, blown and tossed by the wind. That man should not think he will receive anything from the Lord; he is a double-minded man, unstable in all he does. (No heat, no refining; no irritation, no pearl; no pain, no gain.

Galatians 5:22–23 The fruit of the Spirit is...<u>self-control</u>....

MANAGING THE MIND—the truth will set us free

Proverbs 23:7 (KJ)...as a man thinks in his heart, so is he.

2 Corinthians 10:4 The weapons we fight with are not the weapons of the world. On the contrary, they have divine power to demolish strongholds. We demolish arguments and every pretension that sets itself up against the knowledge of God, and <u>we take captive every thought</u> to make it obedient to Christ. John 8:32: You will know the truth, and <u>the truth will set you free.</u>

1 Corinthians 14:20 Brothers, stop <u>thinking</u> like children. In regard to evil be infants, but in your <u>thinking</u> be adults.

2 Peter 3:1 I write to stimulate you to <u>wholesome thinking</u>....

Philippians 4 Whatsoever things are true, noble, right, pure, lovely, admirable...<u>Think on these things</u>. (Let your <u>mind dwell on these things.</u> What you have learned from me, put into <u>practice</u>...and the God of peace will be with you.

Philippians 2 Have this <u>mind</u> which was in Christ Jesus....

Isaiah 26:3–4 You will keep in perfect peace him whose <u>mind is steadfast</u>, (focused/stayed on you) because he trusts in you. <u>Trust in the LORD forever, for the LORD, the LORD, is the Rock eternal</u>.

Matthew 14:28–33 Peter walking on the water: When his <u>eyes were on Jesus...his gaze,</u> he did well. When he looked at the waves, he sank. He need to just glance at the water and get his gaze back.

Hebrew 3:1 <u>Fix your thoughts</u> on Jesus ...(Hymn lyric: "Turn your eyes upon Jesus. Look full in His wonderful face, and the things of earth will grow strangely dim in the light of His glory and grace.")

1 Peter 1:13 <u>Prepare your minds</u> for action...be self-controlled...set your hope...don't conform...be holy....

Romans 12:2 Be transformed by the renewing of you <u>mind</u>.

Colossians 3:2 <u>Set your minds</u> on things above, not on things of earth.

Hebrews 4 (old self, deceitful desires) Put off your old self ...Be made new in the <u>attitude of your minds.</u> Put on the new self. (Who am I? God's lavished loved, adopted, gifted, child.)

Lamentations 3:19–26 I remember my affliction and my wandering, the bitterness and the gall. I well remember them, and my soul is downcast (depressed) within me. Yet <u>this I call to mind</u> and therefore I have <u>hope</u>: Because of the LORD's great love we are not consumed, for his compassions never fail. They are new every morning; great is your faithfulness. I say to myself, "The LORD is my portion; therefore I will wait for him." The LORD is good to those whose hope is in him, to the one who seeks him; it is good to wait quietly for the salvation of the LORD.

Psalm 73...my feet had almost slipped; I had nearly lost my foot-hold. I envied the arrogant when I saw the prosperity of the wicked ...Surely in vain have I kept my heart pure; in vain have I washed my hands in innocence. All day long I have been plagued; I have been punished every morning ...When I tried to understand all this, it was oppressive to me, until I entered the sanctuary of God. Then I understood their final destiny. Yet I am always with you; you hold me by my right hand. You guide me with your counsel, and after-ward you will take me into glory. Whom have I in heaven but you? And earth has nothing I desire besides you. My flesh and my heart may fail, but God is the strength of my heart and my portion forever.

Psalm 77 I cried out to God for help; I cried out to God to hear me. When I was in distress, I sought the LORD ...I mused, and my spirit grew faint...I was too troubled to speak ...Will the LORD reject forever? Has his unfailing love vanished forever? Has his promise failed for all time? Has God forgotten to be merciful? Has He in anger withheld His compassion? **Then I thought,** "To this I will appeal: I will remember the deeds of the LORD; yes, I will remember your miracles of long ago. I will meditate on all your works and consider all your mighty deeds."

2 Timothy 4:5 But you, **keep your head in all situations**, endure hardship, do the work of an evangelist, discharge all the duties of your ministry.

Psalm 116:3–7 The cords of death entangled me, the anguish of the grave came upon me; I was overcome by trouble and sorrow. *Then I called on the name of the LORD*: "O LORD, save me!" The LORD is gracious and righteous; our God is full of compassion. The LORD protects the simple-hearted; when I was in great need, he saved me. Be at rest once more, O my soul, for the LORD has been good to you.

Psalm 55:1–18 Listen to my prayer, O God, do not ignore my plea; hear me and answer me. My thoughts trouble me and I am distraught at the voice of the enemy, at the stares of the wicked; for they bring down suffering upon me and revile me in their anger. My heart is in anguish within me; the terrors of death assail me. Fear and trembling have beset me; horror has overwhelmed me. I said, "Oh, that I had the wings of a dove! I would fly away and be at rest—I would flee far away and stay in the desert; I would hurry to my place of shelter, far from the tempest and storm." Confuse the wicked, O Lord, confound their speech, for I see violence and strife in the city. Day and night they prowl about on its walls; malice and abuse are within it. Destructive forces are at work in the city; threats and lies never leave its streets. If an enemy were insulting me, I could endure it; if a foe were raising himself against me, I could hide from him. But it is you, a man like myself, my companion, my close friend, with whom I once enjoyed sweet fellowship as we walked with the throng at the house of God. Let death take my enemies by surprise; let them go down alive to the grave, for evil finds lodging among them. But I call to God, and the LORD saves me. Evening, morning and noon I cry out in distress, and he hears my voice.

Romans 8:5–6 Those who live according to the sinful nature have their minds set on what that nature desires; but those who live in accordance with the Spirit have their minds set on what the Spirit desires. The mind of sinful man is death, but the mind controlled by the Spirit is life and peace;

Isaiah 46:8–11 Remember this, fix it in your mind, take it to heart, you rebels. Remember the former things, those of long ago; I am God, and there is no other; I am God, and there is none like me. I make known the end from the beginning, from ancient times, what is still to come. I say: "My purpose will stand, and I will do all that I please. From the east I summon a bird of prey; from a far-off land, a man to fulfill my purpose. <u>What I have said, that will I bring about; what I have planned, that will I do.</u>"

WITH WHAT SHALL I MANAGE MY MIND AND EMOTIONS? THE TRUTH, THE WORD OF GOD, THE MANUAL ON DOING LIFE!

Acts 20: 30–32 From your own number men will arise and distort the truth …I commit you to God and the <u>word</u> of his grace which can build you up and give you an inheritance among all those who are sanctified.

Joshua 1:5–8 No one will be able to stand up against you all the days of your life. As I was with Moses, so <u>I will be with you; I will never leave you nor forsake you</u>. "Be strong and courageous, because you will lead these people to inherit the land I swore to their forefathers to give them. Be strong and very courageous. Be careful to **obey** all the law my servant Moses gave you; do not turn from it to the right or to the left, that you may be successful wherever you go. <u>Do not let this Book of the Law depart from your mouth; meditate on it day and night</u>, so that you may be careful to do everything written in it. Then you will be **prosperous and successful**.

John 8:31–32 If you <u>hold to my teaching</u>, you are really my disciples. You shall know the <u>truth</u>, and the <u>truth</u> will set you free.

Colossians 3:16 Let the <u>word of Christ dwell in you richly</u> as you teach and admonish one another.

Hebrews 4:12 For the <u>word of God</u> is living and active, sharper than any double-edged sword. It <u>penetrates</u> even to dividing soul and spirit, joints and marrow; <u>it judges the thoughts and attitudes</u> of the heart.

2 Timothy 2:15 Do your best to present yourself to God as one approved, a workman who does not need to be ashamed and who <u>correctly handles the word of truth</u>.

Psalms 130:5 I wait for the LORD, my soul waits, and in <u>his word</u> I put my hope.

Jeremiah 15:16 When <u>your words</u> came, I ate them; they were my joy and my heart's delight, for I bear your name, O LORD God Almighty.

Titus 1:1 The *knowledge of the truth* that leads to godliness....

Psalm 119:11 I have hidden <u>your word</u> in my heart that I might not sin against you. **18** Open my eyes that I may see wonderful things in <u>your law</u>. **24** <u>Your statutes</u> are my delight; they are <u>my counselors</u>. **28** My soul is weary with sorrow; strengthen me according to <u>your word</u>. **37** Turn my eyes away from worthless things; preserve my life according to <u>your word</u>. **50** My comfort in my suffering is this: <u>your promise</u> preserves my life. **71** It was good to be afflicted so that I might <u>learn your decrees</u>. **(KJV) 89** Forever, O Lord, your word is settled in heaven). **92** If <u>your law</u> had not been my delight, I would have perished in my affliction. **105** <u>Your word</u> is a lamp to my feet and a light for my path. **113** You are my refuge and my shield; I have put my hope in <u>your word</u>. **130** The unfolding of <u>your words</u> gives light; it gives understanding to the simple. **144** <u>Your statutes</u> are forever right; give me understanding that I may live. **165** Great peace have they who love <u>your law</u>, and nothing can make them stumble.

Psalm 1 Blessed...is the one whose delight is the <u>law of the LORD</u> ...In <u>His law</u> he meditates day and night ...He will be <u>like a tree firmly planted by streams of water</u>...[that] yields its fruit in season. Its leaf does not wither ...Whatever he does prospers.

2 Thessalonians 2:13 God chose you to be saved through the sanctifying work of the Spirit and through <u>belief in the truth.</u>

2 Peter 1:3–11 His divine power has given us everything we need for life and godliness through our knowledge of him who called us by his own glory and goodness. Through these he has given us his very great and precious promises, so that through them you may participate in the divine nature and escape the corruption in the world caused by evil desires. For this very reason, make every effort to add to your faith goodness; and to goodness, knowledge; and to knowledge, self-control; and to self-control, perseverance; and to perseverance, godliness; and to godliness, brotherly kindness; and to brotherly kindness, love. For if you possess these qualities in increasing measure, they will keep you from being ineffective and unproductive in your knowledge of our Lord Jesus Christ. But if anyone does not have them, he is nearsighted and blind, and has forgotten that he has been cleansed from his past sins. Therefore, my brothers, be all the more eager to make your calling and election sure. For if you do these things, you will never fall, and you will receive a rich welcome into the eternal kingdom of our Lord and Savior Jesus Christ.

1 Peter 1:23–25 You have been born again, not of perishable seed, but of imperishable, through the <u>living and enduring word of God</u>. For, "All men are like grass, and all their glory is like the flowers of the field; the grass withers and the flowers fall, but <u>the word of the Lord stands forever.</u>

2 Peter 3:1–2 I have written both of them as reminders to stimulate you to <u>wholesome thinking</u>. I want you to <u>recall the words spoken</u> in the past by the holy prophets and the command given by our Lord and Savior through your apostles.

Psalm 37:31 The <u>law of the LORD</u> is in his heart, his feet do not slip.

Psalm 40:11 May your love and your <u>truth</u> always protect me…for troubles without number surround me.

Isaiah 66:2 This is the one I esteem: he who is humble and contrite in spirit and trembles at my <u>word</u>.

2 Samuel 22:31 As for God, His way is perfect; <u>the word</u> of the LORD is flawless.

Ephesians 6 The sword of the Spirit is the <u>word of God</u>.

Jeremiah 23:28–29 <u>Let the prophet who has a dream tell his dream</u>, but let the *one who has my word speak it faithfully.* "For what has straw to do with grain?" declares the LORD. "Is not *my word like fire,*" declares the LORD, "and like **a hammer** that breaks a rock in pieces?

James 1:21 (Be quick to listen, slow to speak, slow to become angry . . .) Therefore, get rid of all moral filth and the evil that is so prevalent and humbly accept <u>the Word</u> planted in you, which can save you. Vs. 22 Do not merely listen to <u>the Word, and so deceive yourselves. Do what it says.</u> Vs. 25 But the man who looks intently (like at himself in a mirror) into the perfect law that gives freedom, and continues to do this, not forgetting what he has heard, but doing it…he will be blessed in what he does.

HEALING SCRIPTURES AND PERSPECTIVE

Exodus 15:26
There the LORD made a decree and a law for them, and there he tested them. He said, "If you listen carefully to the voice of the

LORD your God and do what is right in his eyes, if you pay attention to his commands and keep all his decrees, I will not bring on you any of the diseases I brought on the Egyptians, for I am the LORD, who heals you."

Exodus 23:25–26

Worship the LORD your God, and his blessing will be on your food and water. I will take away sickness from among you, and none will miscarry or be barren in your land. I will give you a full life span.

Deuteronomy 7:15

The LORD will keep you free from every disease. He will not inflict on you the horrible diseases you knew in Egypt, but he will inflict them on all who hate you.

Deuteronomy 28:1–14, 61

(1–13, A list of all the blessings of God which imply health, especially given the curses which include disease, etc.) Do not turn aside from any of the commands I give you today, to the right or to the left, following other gods and serving them. However, if you do not obey the LORD your God and do not carefully follow all his commands and decrees I am giving you today, all these curses will come upon you and overtake you…. (A list follows) He will bring upon you all the diseases of Egypt that you dreaded, and they will cling to you.

Deuteronomy 30:19–20

This day I call heaven and earth as witnesses against you that I have set before you life and death, blessings and curses. Now choose life, so that you and your children may live and that you may love the LORD your God, listen to his voice, and hold fast to him. For the LORD is your life, and he will give you many years in the land he swore to give to your fathers, Abraham, Isaac and Jacob. The same promise is in 11:8–9, 21

Psalm 41:1–3 For those who have regard for the weak

Blessed is he who has regard for the weak; the LORD delivers him in times of trouble. The LORD will protect him and preserve his life; he will bless him in the land and not surrender him to the desire of his foes. The LORD will sustain him on his sickbed and restore him from his bed of illness.

Psalm 30:1–5

I will exalt you, O LORD, for you lifted me out of the depths and did not let my enemies gloat over me. O LORD my God, I called to you for help and you healed me. O LORD, you brought me up from the grave; you spared me from going down into the pit. Sing to the LORD, you saints of his; praise his holy name. For his anger lasts only a moment, but his favor lasts a lifetime; weeping may remain for a night, but rejoicing comes in the morning.

Psalm 91:1–16

He who dwells in the shelter of the Most High will rest in the shadow of the Almighty. I will say of the LORD, "He is my refuge and my fortress, my God, in whom I trust." Surely he will save you from the fowler's snare and from the deadly pestilence. He will cover you with his feathers, and under his wings you will find refuge; his faithfulness will be your shield and rampart. You will not fear the terror of night, nor the arrow that flies by day, nor the pestilence that stalks in the darkness, nor the plague that destroys at midday. A thousand may fall at your side, ten thousand at your right hand, but it will not come near you. You will only observe with your eyes and see the punishment of the wicked. If you make the Most High your dwelling—even the LORD, who is my refuge—then no harm will befall you, no disaster will come near your tent. For he will command his angels concerning you to guard you in all your ways. They will lift you up in their hands, so that you will not strike your foot against a stone. You will tread upon the lion and the cobra; you will trample the great lion and the serpent. "Because he loves me," says the LORD, "I will rescue him; I will protect him, for he acknowledges my name. He will call upon me, and I will answer him; I will be with him in trouble, I will deliver him and honor him. With long life will I satisfy him and show him my salvation."

Psalm 103

Praise the LORD, O my soul, and forget not all his benefits—who forgives all your sins and heals all your diseases, who redeems your life from the pit and crowns you with love and compassion, who satisfies your desires with good things so that your youth is renewed like the eagles.

Psalm 107:19–21

Then they cried to the LORD in their trouble, and he saved them from their distress. He sent forth his word and healed them; he rescued them from the grave. Let them give thanks to the LORD for his unfailing love and his wonderful deeds for men.

Psalm 118:16–18

The LORD's right hand is lifted high; the LORD's right hand has done mighty things!" I will not die but live, and will proclaim what the LORD has done. The LORD has chastened me severely, but he has not given me over to death.

Proverbs 4:20–22

My son, pay attention to what I say; listen closely to my words. Do not let them out of your sight, keep them within your heart, for they are life to those who find them and health to a man's whole body.

Isaiah 57:14–19 (For those with a contrite and humble spirit)
And it will be said: "Build up, build up, prepare the road! Remove the obstacles out of the way of my people." For this is what the high and lofty One says—he who lives forever, whose name is holy: "I live in a high and holy place, but also with him who is contrite and lowly in spirit, to revive the spirit of the lowly and to revive the heart of the contrite. I will not accuse forever, nor would will I always be angry, for then the spirit of man grow faint before me—the breath of man that I have created. I was enraged by his sinful greed; I punished him, and hid my face in anger, yet he kept on in his willful ways. I have seen his ways, but I will heal him; I will guide him and restore comfort to him, creating praise on the lips of the mourners in Israel. Peace, peace, to those far and near," says the LORD. 'And I will heal them.' "

Jeremiah 30:17; 33:6 (The promise for restoration of Israel)
But I will restore you to health and heal your wounds, declares the LORD, because you are called an outcast, Zion for whom no one cares. 33:6. Nevertheless, I will bring health and healing to it; I will heal my people and will let them enjoy abundant peace and security. I will bring Judah and Israel back from captivity and will rebuild them as they were before.

Isaiah 53:4–5
Surely he took up our infirmities and carried our sorrows, yet we considered him stricken by God, smitten by him, and afflicted. But he was pierced for our transgressions, he was crushed for our iniquities; the punishment that brought us peace was upon him, and by his wounds we are healed. (This text is not just redemption as confirmed in Matthew 8:16–17 below, and 1 Peter 2:24. When evening came, many who were demon-possessed were brought to him, and he drove out the spirits with word and healed all the sick. This was

to fulfill what was spoken through the prophet Isaiah: "He took up our infirmities and carried our diseases."

1 Peter 2:24
He himself bore our sins in his body on the tree, so that we might die to sins and live for righteousness; by his wounds you have been healed.

Matthew 8:2–3; (with a centurion—vv. 7–8)
A man with leprosy came and knelt before him and said, "Lord, if you are willing, you can make me clean." Jesus reached out his hand and touched the man. "I am willing," he said. "Be clean!" Immediately he was cured of his leprosy. Jesus said to him, "I will go and heal him." The centurion replied, "Lord, I do not deserve to have you come under my roof. *But just say the word*, and my servant will be healed.

Matthew 8:16
When evening came, many who were demon-possessed were brought to him, and he drove out the spirits with a word and healed all the sick.

Ezekiel 34:4 You have not strengthened the weak or healed the sick or bound up the injured. You have not brought back the strays or searched for the lost. You have ruled them harshly and brutally.

Matthew 10:1, 7–8
He called his twelve disciples to him and gave them authority to drive out evil spirits and to heal every disease and sickness. As you go, preach this message: 'The kingdom of heaven is near.' Heal the sick, raise the dead, and cleanse those who have leprosy, drive out demons. Freely you have received, freely give.

Matthew 14:34–36
When they had crossed over, they landed at Gennesaret. And when the men of that place recognized Jesus, they sent word to all the surrounding country. People brought all their sick to him and begged him to let the sick just touch the edge of his cloak, and all who touched him were healed.

Matthew 21:21–22 (the power of faith and the promise of God)
Jesus replied, "I tell you the truth, if you have faith and do not doubt, not only can you do what was done to the fig tree, but also you can say to this mountain, 'Go, throw yourself into the sea, and it will be done. If you believe, you will receive whatever you ask for in prayer.'"

Romans 4:17–22 As it is written: "I have made you a father of many nations." He is our father in the sight of God, in whom he believed—the God who gives life to the dead and calls things that are not as though they were. Against all hope, Abraham in hope believed and so became the father of many nations, just as it had been said to him, "So shall your offspring be." Without weakening in his faith, he faced the fact that his body was as good as dead—since he was about a hundred years old—and that Sarah's womb was also dead. Yet he did not waver through unbelief regarding the promise of God, but was strengthened in his faith and gave glory to God, being fully persuaded that God had power to do what he had promised. This is why it was credited to him as righteousness."

Hebrews 11:1 1 Now faith is being sure of what we hope for and certain of what we do not see.

Matthew 18:18–19 "I tell you the truth, whatever you bind on earth will be bound in heaven, and whatever you loose on earth will be loosed in heaven. Again, I tell you that if two of you on earth agree about anything you ask for, it will be done for you by my Father in heaven. For where two or three come together in my name, there am I with them."

Luke 9:1–2
When Jesus had called the Twelve together, he gave them power and authority to drive out all demons and to cure diseases, and he sent them out to preach the kingdom of God and to heal the sick.

Luke10:9 (Sending out the 72)
Heal the sick who are there and tell them, "The kingdom of God is near you."

Romans 8:11
And if the Spirit of him who raised Jesus from the dead is living in you, he who raised Christ from the dead will also give life to your mortal bodies through his Spirit, who lives in you.

1 Corinthians 12:8–9 To one there is given through the Spirit the message of wisdom, to another the message of knowledge by means of the same Spirit, to another faith by the same Spirit, to another gifts of healing by that one Spirit.

GOD KEEPS HIS PROMISES

Hebrews 10:23
Let us hold unswervingly to the hope we profess, for he who promised is faithful.

Jeremiah 1:12
The LORD said to me, "You have seen correctly, for I am watching to see that my word is fulfilled."

1 Kings 8:56

Praise be to the LORD, who has given rest to his people Israel just as he promised. Not one word has failed of all the good promises he gave through his servant Moses.

Psalm 145:13b

Your kingdom is an everlasting kingdom, and your dominion endures through all generations. The LORD is faithful to all his promises and loving toward all he has made.

Number 23:19–20

God is not a man, that he should lie, nor a son of man, that he should change his mind. Does he speak and then not act? Does he promise and not fulfill? I have received a command to bless; he has blessed, and I cannot change it.

Hebrews 4:17

By two unchangeable things in which it is impossible for God to lie, we who have fled to take hold of the hope offered to us may be greatly encouraged. We have this hope as an anchor for the soul, firm and secure.

1 Samuel 15:29

He who is the Glory of Israel does not lie or change his mind; for he is not a man, that he should change his mind.

WITH GOD, ALL THINGS ARE POSSIBLE; NOTHING IS TOO DIFFICULT FOR HIM

Matthew 19:26

Jesus looked at them and said, "With man this is impossible, but with God all things are possible."

Jeremiah 32:17

"Ah, Sovereign LORD, you have made the heavens and the earth by your great power and outstretched arm. Nothing is too hard for you."

SOURCES OF ILLNESS

1. The fall of mankind into sin/general sin; we live in a fallen suffering world. Romans 8:18–22 affirms that our broken world is in bondage to decay waiting to be liberated—genetic defects, deterioration of the gene pool, due to environment and pollution, such as black lung of a miner, or results of lead poisoning, asbestos, etc.

2. Personal sin and disobedience—like those in 2 Corinthians who had sinned at the communion service; the curses that come with disobedience as in Deuteronomy 28 and when we do not obey in (see Mal. 3:7b-10).

3. Human choices—some dangerous activities without protection—athletics—poor eating habits and lack of exercise or good health habits, and the abuse of tobacco, alcohol and drugs.

4. Satanic attack and/or curses.

5. Generational curses and sins passed on through generations (see Exod. 34:6–7).

6. God is allowing suffering to make us holy and/or to refine us. (1 Pet. 1:6–9; Job 23:10; 43:5–6; Isa. 48:10).

7. It is a mystery sometimes. Paul left Trophimus sick in Miletus (2 Tim. 4:20), and Paul told Timothy to take some wine for his stomach problems and frequent illnesses (1 Tim. 5:23). Paul preached the Gospel to the Galatians and was concerned that his illness would be a concern to them (Gal. 4:13–14; 6:11 eyes?).

8. The natural aging process is described by Paul as a tent in which we live and so we long to be clothed with immortality (2 Cor. 5:1–10).

HEALING MYTHS

1. If only you have enough faith you will be healed. Of course, faith is central to healing (Matt. 9:22; Heb. 11:6), but Jesus healed some where there was no evidence of faith, such as in John 9:1–5. Healing ministry becomes hurtful when people feel they are responsible for not having enough faith. After all, faith the size of a mustard seed can move a mountain (Matt. 17:20).
2. If you really trust God to heal you, you will stop taking your medication. This would assume that medical healing is not healing. Physicians are allies in healing.
3. Healing must be instantaneous and dramatic, or it isn't real. Evidence for many is that they are healed over a period of time. The instantaneous healings by Paul and Jesus are sometimes repeated in our times, but there was also something foundational about their work (Eph. 2:20).
4. The Bible does not describe healing ministry as vested in an individual traveling from place to place, using their gift. James calls the elders of the Church to pray for the sick. Congregations are told to pray for each other. It is wonderful when someone has this gift, but there is no biblical illustration of the gift being used on its own apart from other ministry.
5. Only "yes" answers come from God (2 Cor. 12:8–9). Psalm 115:3 puts the responsibility on the sovereignty of God. In His wisdom and sovereign plan, He may say no, yes, wait, or I have a better idea or plan.

THEREFORE

It is clear from Scripture that God desires to bless us with health and healing, for example, Isaiah 53:5 and 1 Peter 2:24—by the stripes of Jesus we are healed. We must remember that although His love for us is completely unconditional and incomprehensible in its greatness, His blessing is not. God's blessing is conditioned on growing obedience unless He heals unbelievers to draw them to Himself (Phil. 3:12ff) as in the covenant blessings of Deuteronomy 26–28. So, listen for the voice of the Holy Spirit as you seek God for healing; pray and obey as He directs (John 10:2–5; 1 John 5:18–19). God knows us and works with us individually and personally. His healing plan will be tailored to our uniqueness. No two situations or people are identical.

Confession of sin is central to healing in James 5:14–18. The exception, as above, may be when God chooses to heal an unbeliever as a means of drawing them to himself for salvation. This kind of healing demonstrates the significance of miracles. Experience proves that sin, hate and/or bitterness, or too much stress, are significant sources of illness. Generational sins or curses (Exod. 34:6–14) may be the source and need to be identified and renounced, their powers broken.

Do you want to be healed? In obedience to James 5:14–16, call for the elders of the Church to anoint you with oil and pray for your healing, or ask those in your community of faith with the gift of healing to pray for you. Then daily, trust the Word of God: "By His stripes [I am] healed," or, "He heals all [my] diseases" (Ps. 103:3). God loves me (Rom. 5:8; Ps. 103:11). Other verses may be God's specific words to you. Remember, sometimes healing is instantaneous, and sometimes it takes place over time. I believe God uses the medical profession as well. He has in my life.

God may not heal us in areas of illness or physical weakness for which we are responsible as a steward. Yet, in his mercy and grace, he may. Our responsibility includes exercise, weight management, a healthy diet, and emotional health (John 8:32; 2 Cor. 10:4). In areas of emotional needs related to illness, we may need to take responsibility to get counseling help.

SELECTED BIBLIOGRAPHY

Anderson, Leith and Elmer Towns, *Rivers of Revival.* Ventura, CA: Regal Books, 1997.

Anderson, Neil, *The Bondage Breaker.* Eugene, OR: Harvest House Publications, 2000.

_____, *A Way of Escape: Freedom from Sexual Strongholds.* Eugene, Oregon: Harvest House Publications, 1994.

_____, *Victory Over the Darkness: Realizing the Power of Your Identity in Christ.* Ventura, CA: Regal Books, 2000.

Autrey, C. E. *Revivals of the Old Testament.* Grand Rapids, MI: Zondervan, 1960.

Avant, John, Malcolm McDow, and Alvin Reid, eds. *Revival: The Story of the Current Awakening in Brownwood, Ft. Worth, Wheaton, and Beyond.* Nashville: Broadman and Holman, 1996.

Baker, Ernest. *The Revivals of the Bible.* Capetown, South Africa: Miller Publishing, 1906.

Barna, George, *The Frog in the Kettle.* Ventura, CA: Regal Books, 1990.

_____, *The Second Coming of the Church.* Nashville: Word Publishing Group, 1998.

_____, *Revolution* (Special Reader Preview: Unedited Manuscript). Wheaton, IL: Tyndale House Publishers, Inc. 2005.

Bartleman, Frank. *Azusa Street: The Roots of Modern-day Pentecost.* South Plainfield, N.J.: Bridge Publishing, 1980.

Blackaby, Henry T., and Claude V. King. *Fresh Encounter: Experiencing God in Revival and Spiritual Awakening.* Nashville: Broadman and Holman, 1996.

Blumhofer, Edith L. and Randall Balmer. 1993. *Modern Christian Revivals.* Chicago: University of Illinois Press, 1993.

Bready, John Wesley. *England: Before and After Wesley: The Evangelical Revival and Social Reform.* New York: Russell and Russell, 1971.

Bright, Bill. *The Coming Revival: America's Call to Fast, Pray, and 'Seek God's Face,'* Orlando, FL: Baker Book House, 1995.

Bryant, David. *The Hope at Hand: National and World Revival for the Twenty-First Century.* Grand Rapids, MI: Baker Book House, 1995.

Burns, James, Ed. *The Laws of Revival,* by Tom Phillips. Wheaton, IL: World Wide Publications, 1904.

Cairns, Earle E. *An Endless Line of Splendor.* Wheaton, IL: Tyndale House Publishers, 1986.

Candler, Warren A. *Great Revivals and the Great Republic.* Nashville: Publishing House of the M. E. Church, 1904.

Cho, Paul Y. *Prayer: Key to Revival.* Dallas: Word Publishing, 1984.

Coleman, Robert E. *The Coming World Revival.* Wheaton, IL: Crossway Books, 1995.

Cymbala, Jim. *Fresh Wind, Fresh Fire: What Happens When God's Spirit Invades the Hearts of His People.* Grand Rapids, MI: Zondervan Publishing House, 1997.

_____, *Breakthrough Prayer: The Secret of Receiving What You Need From God.* Grand Rapids, MI: Zondervan, 2003.

Damazio, Frank. *Seasons of Revival: Understanding the Appointed Times of Spiritual Refreshing.* Portland, OR: B. T. Publishing, 1996.

Davis, George T. B. *When the Fire Fell*. Philadelphia PA: The Million Testaments Campaigns, 1945.

Dickerson, John S. *The Great Evangelical Recession: 6 Factors That Will Crash the American Church...and How to Prepare* Grand Rapids, MI: Baker Books, 2013.

Drummond, Lewis. *Eight Keys to Biblical Revival*. Minneapolis, MN: Bethany, 1994.

Duewel, Wesley. *Revival Fire*. Grand Rapids, MI: Zondervan, 1995.

Dye, Colin. *Revival Phenomena*. Tonbridge, England: Sovereign World Publishing, 1996.

Edwards, Brian H. *Revival! A People Saturated With God*. Durham, England: Evangelical Press, 1990.

Emerson, Michael O. and Christian Smith. *Divided by Faith: Evangelical Religion and the Problem of Race in America*. New York, NY: Oxford University Press, 2000.

Fereday, William Wollreidge. *Josiah and Revival*. Kilmarnock: J. Ritchie Publishers, 1940.

Finney, Charles G. *Lectures on Revivals of Religion*. Cambridge, MA: Harvard University Press, 1960.

Finney, Charles G., and Louis Gifford Parkhurst, Jr., eds. *Principles of Revival*. Minneapolis, MN: Bethany House, 1987.

Foster, Richard J. *Prayer: Finding the Hearts True Home*. San Francisco, CA: Harper, 1992.

Frangipane, Francis. *The Three Battlegrounds: An in-depth View of the Three Arenas of Spiritual Warfare: The Mind, the Church and the Heavenly Places*. Cedar Rapids, IA: Arrow Publications, 1989.

Frizzell, Gregory R. *How to Develop a Powerful Prayer Life*. Memphis, TN: The Master Design, 1999.

_____, *Returning to Holiness: A Personal and Church-wide Journey to Revival.* Memphis, TN: The Master Design, 2000.

Gillies, John. *Historical Collections of Accounts of Revival.* Edinburgh: Banner of Truth Trust, 1981.

Goetzman, Martha. Anomalous Features in the Chicago Prayer Meeting Revival as Revealed in Contemporary Newspaper Accounts. M.A. Thesis, Trinity Evangelical Divinity School, 1985.

Hardman, Keith J. *Seasons of Refreshing: Evangelism and Revival in America.* Grand Rapids, MI: Zondervan, 1994.

Hayden, Eric W. *Spurgeon on Revival.* Grand Rapids, MI: Zondervan Publishing House, 1996.

Henson, Al. *Practical Theology of Revival.* Canadian Revival Fellowship. Cassette, 1998.

Hempy, Robert W. *A Comparative Study of Selected Revivals in America.* M.Div. thesis, Western Evangelical Seminary, 1960.

Hill, S.J. *Enjoying God: Experiencing Intimacy with the Heavenly Father.* Lake Mary, FL: Relevant Media Group, Lake Mary, 2001.

Hughey, Rhonda. *Desperate for His Presence: God's Design to Transform Your Life and Your City.* Minneapolis, MN: Bethany House, 2004.

Hunt, Alfred Leedes. *Evangelical By-paths: Studies in the Religious and Social Aspects of the Evangelical Revival of the Eighteenth Century and a Reply to its Critics.* London: Charles J. Thynne and Jarvis, 1927.

Johnson, Henry. *Stories of Great Revivals.* London: The Religious Tract Society, 1906.

Kaiser, Walter. *Quest for Revival.* Chicago, IL: Moody Press, 1986.

Kilpatrick, John. *When the Heavens Are Brass: Keys to Genuine Revival.* Shippensburg, PA: Revival Press, 1997.

Kopp, Robert R. *Fifteen Secrets for Life and Ministry*. Kirkwood, MO: Impact Christian Books, 2004.

Ladd, George. *The Gospel of the Kingdom*. Grand Rapids, MI: William B. Eerdmans Publishing Company, 1959.

Larsen, David L. *The Evangelism Mandate: Recovering the Centrality of Gospel Preaching*.

Westchester, IL: Crossway Books, 1992.

Lewis, Robert with Rob Wilkins. *The Church of Irresistible Influence: Bridge Building Stories to Help Reach Your Community*. Grand Rapids, MI: Zondervan, 2001.

Lloyd-Jones, Martyn G. *Revival*. Westchester, IL: Crossway Books, 1987.

Lutzer, Erwin. *Flames of Freedom*. Chicago, IL: Moody Press, 1976.

Lyrene, Edward Charles. *The Role of Prayer in American Revival Movements, 1740 to 1860*. Ph.D. diss., Southern Baptist Theological Seminary, 1985.

McDow, Malcolm and Alvin L. Reid. *Fire Fall: How God has Shaped History through Revivals*. Nashville, TN: Broadman and Holman Publishers, 1997.

McKenna, David L. *The Coming Great Awakening: New Hope for the Nineties*. Downers Grove, IL: InterVarsity Press, 1990.

Minshall, Britt. *Renaissance or Ruin: The Final Saga of a Once Great Church*. Baltimore, MD: Renaissance Institute Press, 1994.

Olford, Stephen F. *Heart-Cry for Revival*. Westwood, NJ: Fleming H. Revell, 1962.

Orr, J. Edwin. *The Fervent Prayer: The Worldwide Impact of the Great Awakening of 1858*. Chicago: Moody Press, 1974.

_____. *The Second Great Awakening in America*. London: Marshall, Morgan and Scott, 1952.

_____. *The Second Evangelical Awakening*. London: Marshall, Morgan and Scott, 1964.

_____. *The Flaming Tongue: The Impact of Twentieth Century Revivals*. Chicago, IL: Moody Press, 1973.

Owens, Jimmy and Carol. *Heal Our Land: Securing God's Blessing on America*. Grand Rapids, MI: Zondervan, 1997.

Phillips, Tom and Mark Curshall. *Revival Signs*. Gresham, OR: Vision House Publishing, 1995.

Pratney, Winke. *Revival*. Springfield, PA: Whitaker House, 1983.

Randall, Christie J. *The Revival Under Hezekiah*. M.A. Thesis, Trinity Evangelical Divinity, 1991.

Ravenhill, Leonard. *Revival God's Way: A Message for the Church*. Minneapolis, MN: Bethany House Publishers, 1986.

_____. *Why Revival Tarries*. Minneapolis, MN: Bethany Fellowship, 1959.

Relfe, Mary Stewart. *Cure of All Ills*. Montgomery, AL: League of Prayer, 1988.

Rhee, Yoon-Ho. *Towards a Theory of Revival: A Case Study of the Biblical and Korean Revivals*. M.A. Thesis, Fuller Theological Seminary, 1988.

Riss, Richard M. *20th Century Revival Movements in North America*. Peabody, MA: Hendrickson Publications, 1988.

Roberts, Richard Owens. *Revival*. Wheaton, IL: Richard Owen Roberts Publishers, 1982.

Shearer, John. *Old Time Revival: How the Fire of God Spread in Days Now Past and Gone*. London: Pickering and Inglis, 1930.

Sheets, Dutch. *Intercessory Prayer: How God Can Use Your Prayers to Move Heaven and Earth*. Ventura, CA: Regal Books, 1996.

Silvoso, Ed. *That None Should Perish.* Ventura, CA: Regal Books, 1994.

Smith, Timothy L. *Revivalism and Social Reform: American Protestantism on the Eve of the Civil War.* Baltimore: MD: Johns Hopkins University Press, 1980.

Smith, Wilbur. *Nine Characteristics of Great Revivals in the Old Testament: The Glorious Revival Under King Hezekiah,* Grand Rapids, MI: Zondervan, 1937.

Smyth, Charles and Hugh Eggerton. *Simeon and Church Order: A study of the Origins of the Evangelical Revival in Cambridge in the Eighteenth Century.* Cambridge, England: University Press, 1940.

Sprague, William B. *Lectures on Revivals of Religion.* Edinburgh, Scotland: Banner of Truth Trust, 1978.

Thornbury, John F. *God Sent Revival: The Story of Asahel Nettleton and the Second Great Awakening.* Grand Rapids, MI: Evangelical Press, 1977.

Towns, Elmer and Warren Bird. *Into the Future: Turning Today's Church Trends into Tomorrow's Opportunities.* Grand Rapids, MI: Revell, 2000.

Wagner, C. Peter. *Prayer Shield: How to Intercede for Pastors, Christian Leaders and Others on the Spiritual Front Lines.* Ventura, CA: Regal Books, 1995.

_____ *Praying With Power: How to Pray Effectively and Hear Clearly From God.* Ventura, CA: Regal Books, 1995.

_____ (See other books in this series by C. Peter Wagner, published by Regal Books, Ventura, CA: *Warfare Prayer; Breaking Strongholds in Your City; Churches that Pray; Engaging the Enemy: Wrestling With Dark Angels)*

Wallis, Arthur. *In the Day of Thy Power: The Scriptural Principles of Revival.* London, England: Christian Literature Crusade, 1956.

Walton, Harold W. *A Study of the Principles in Revival.* Abstract, D.Min. Project, Trinity

Evangelical Divinity School, 1995.

White, Tom. *City-wide Prayer Movements: One Church, Many Congregations.* Ann Arbor, MI: Vine Books, Servant Publications, 2001.

Woods, Arthur Skevington. *The Indistinguishable Blaze: Spiritual Renewal and Advance in the Eighteenth Century.* Grand Rapids, MI: Eerdmans, 1960.

Endnotes

1   John S. Dickerson, *The Great Evangelical Recession: 6 Factors That Will Crash the American Church . . . and How to Prepare* (Grand Rapids, MI: Baker Books, 2013), 26.

2   Ibid, 28.

3   Elmer Towns and Warren Bird, *Into the Future: Turning Today's Church Trends into Tomorrow's Opportunities* (Grand Rapids, MI: Revell, 2000), 37.

4   Andy Stanley, *Irresistible: Reclaiming the New that Jesus Unleashed for the World* (Grand Rapids, MI: Zondervan, 2018), 267–268.

5   John O'Sullivan, "Christianity, Post-Christianity, and the Future of the West," *National Review*, December 14, 2013.

6   https://www.ligonier.org/learn/articles/essentials-unity-non-essentials-liberty-all-things/

7   Ronda Hughey, *Desperate for His Presence: God's Design to Transform Your Life and Your City* (Minneapolis, MN: Bethany House, 2004), 79.

8   Ibid., 93.

9   https://www.pewresearch.org/social-trends/2018/04/25/the-changing-profile-of-unmarried-parents/

10   "The Impossible Dream" from Man of La Mancha (1972); music by Mitch Leigh and Lyrics by Joe Darion.

11   Richard J. Mouw, "Is Tolerance the Enemy of Religious Freedom?" *Evangelicals: the Magazine of the National Association of Evangelicals*, fall 2015, Vol. 1, No. 1, page 14.

12   Alexander Tyler, googlereads.com/quotes/108530-a-democracy-cannot-exist-as-a-permanent-form-of-government

13 George Barna, 2005, *Revolution*, (Special Reader Preview: unedited Manuscript), Wheaton, IL: Tyndale House Publishers, Inc.

14 Bill Bright, *The Coming Revival: America's Call to Fast and Pray*, and *Seek God's Face* (Orlando, FL: Life Publications, 1994), 19.

15 Brian H. Edwards, *Revival! A People Saturated with God* (Durham, England: Evangelical Press, 1990), 73–74

16 Ibid, 84.

17 Paul Y. Cho.1984, *Prayer: Key to Revival* (Dallas, TX: Word Publishing, 1984).

18 Dutch Sheets, *Intercessory Prayer: How God Can Use Your Prayers to Move Heaven and Earth* (Ventura, CA: Regal Books, 1930), 11–12.

19 "The Lausanne Covenant," 1974, 1989, Page 1. The Lausanne Covenant is a declaration agreed upon by more than 2,300 evangelicals during the <u>1974 International Congress,</u> to be more intentional about world evangelization. Since then, the covenant has challenged churches and Christian organizations to work together to make Jesus Christ known throughout the world. (See Web page: www.lausanne. org/Brix?pageID=12891).

20 www.allamerica.org; All.America—Praying for and connecting with every person in America.

21 Jim Stewart, *CBS Evening News*, Washington, D.C., January 6, 2005.

22 Rhonda Hughey, *Desperate for His Presence: God's Design to Transform Your Life and Your City*, 69–79.

23 George Ladd, *The Gospel of the Kingdom* (Grand Rapids, MI: Wm. B. Eerdmans Publishing Company, 1959), 114.

24 Nicholson and Lee, eds., Francis Thompson, "Hound of Heaven," *The Oxford Book of English Mystical Verse*, (New York: Bartleby.com, 2000), 239.

25 W. E. Vine, *An Expository Dictionary of New Testament Words* (Old Tarpan, NJ: Fleming H. Revell Company, 1996), 146–147.

26 David Larsen, *The Evangelical Mandate: Recovering the Centrality of Gospel Preaching* (Westchester, IL: Crossway Books, 1992), p. 171–172.

27 G. Campbell Morgan in Stephen F. Olford, *Heart-Cry for Revival* (Westwood, N.J.: Fleming H. Revell, 1962), 68.

28   Arthur Wallis, *Rain From Heaven,* (Minneapolis, MN: Bethany Fellowship, 1979), 17.

29   J. Edwin Orr, *The Second Evangelical Awakening in Britain* (London: Marshall, Morgan, and Scott, 1949), 118–119.

30   Ibid.

31   Earle E. Cairns, *An Endless Line of Splendor: Revivals and Their Leaders from the Great Awakening to the Present* (Wheaton, IL: Tyndale House Publishers, 1986), 319–321.

32   Ibid., 322.

33   R. A. Torrey, quote available online at http://www.bible.org/page.asp?page_id=59

34   Eric W. Hayden, *Spurgeon on Revival* (Grand Rapids, MI: Zondervan Publishing House, 1962), 73–74.

35   Lewis Drummond, *Eight Keys to Biblical Revival* (Minneapolis, MN: Bethany House Publishers, 1994), 15.

36   Brian H. Edwards, *Revival! A People Saturated with God,* 31, 73–74.

37   Elana Lynse, *Fames of Revival* (Wheaton, IL: Crossway Books, 1989), 47–48.

38   Stephen Olford, *Heart-Cry for Revival* (Westwood, NJ: Fleming H Revell, 1962), 80.

39   James Burns, ed., *The Laws of Revival* (Wheaton, IL: World Wide Publications, 1993), 23–24.

40   Ibid., 28.

41   Arthur Wallis, *Rain From Heaven,* 32.

42   Walter Kaiser, *Quest for Revival* (Chicago, IL, Moody Press, 1986), 13.

43   Ibid., 13–14.

44   Ibid.

45   Ibid.

46   Ibid., 14–15.

47   Wilber Smith, *Nine Characteristics of Great Revivals in the Old Testament: The Glorious Revival under King Hezekiah* (Grand Rapids, MI: Zondervan, 1937), 7–8.

48   Brian H. Edwards, *Revival! A People Saturated With God,* 18, 30.

49   Elana Lynse, *Flames of Revival,* 23–28.

50   Arthur Wallis, *Rain From Heaven,* 101–102.

51 Malcolm McDow and Alvin L. Reid, *Fire Fall: How God Has Shaped History Through Revivals* (Nashville: Broadman and Holman Publishers, 1997), 69.

52 Lyle Shaller, "Jesus for Peoria," *The Community Builders Foundation*, June 2002, 3.

53 John S. Dickerson, *The Great Evangelical Recession: 6 Factors That Will Crash the American Church . . . and How to Prepare* (Grand Rapids, MI: Baker Books, 2013), 137–138

54 Arthur Wallis, *Rain from Heaven*, 101–102.

55 Stephen F. Olford, *Heart-Cry for Revival*, 67–76.

56 E. D. Head, *Revivals in the Bible* (Fort Worth, TX: Southwestern Baptist Seminary, 1951), 15–40.

57 Mission America Telephone Conference Call, *City Impact Round Table*, Interview with George Otis, Jr., February 8, 2005, Mission America Coalition: A Collaborative movement of Christians promoting unity, evangelism and revival.

58 Earle E. Cairns, *An Endless Line of Splendor: Revivals and Their Leaders from the Great Awakening to the Present*, 32, 83.

59 Mary Stewart Relfe, *Cure of All Ills* (Montgomery, AL: League of Prayer), 1988, 71.

60 Earle E. Cairns, *An Endless Line of Splendor: Revivals and Their Leaders from the Great Awakening to the Present* (Wheaton, IL: Tyndale House Publishers, 1986), 196–197.

61 Frank Bartleman, *Azusa Street: The Roots of Modern-day Pentecost* (South Plainfield, NJ: Bridge Publishing, 1980), ix

62 Ibid, xx.

63 Richard M. Riss, *20th Century Revival Movements in North America* (Peabody, MA: Hendrickson Publications, 1988), 47.

64 Malcolm McDow and Alvin L. Reid, *Fire Fall: How God Has Shaped History Through Revivals*, 184–204.

65 Ibid.

66 Ibid.

67 Ibid.

68 Ibid.

69   Henry Johnson, *Stories of Great Revivals* (London: the Religious Tract Society, 1906), 21–22.

70   Ibid., 22–23.

71   Winkie Pratney, *Revival* (Springfield, PA: Whitaker House, 1983), 111.

72   Malcolm McDow and Alvin L. Reid, *Fire Fall: How God Has Shaped History Through Revivals,* 228.

73   Warren A. Chandler, *Great Revivals and the Great Republic* (Nashville: Publishing House of the M. E. Church, 1904), 43–45.

74   Ibid.

75   J. Edwin Orr, *The Fervent Prayer: The Worldwide Impact of the Great Awakening of 1858* (Chicago: Moody Press, 1974). 1.

76   Warren A. Chandler, *Great Revivals and the Great Republic,* 43–45.

77   Ibid.

78   Earle E. Cairns, *An Endless Line of Splendor: Revivals and Their Leaders from the Great Awakening to the Present,* 147.

79   Ibid.

80   Henry Johnson, *Stories of Great Revivals* (London: the Religious Tract Society, 1906), 348.

81   Malcolm McDow and Alvin L. Reid, *Fire Fall: How God has Shaped History Through Revivals,* 276.

82   George T. Davis, *When the Fire Fell* (Philadelphia: The Million Testaments Campaigns, 1945) 66-67.

83   Frank Bartleman, *Azusa Street: The Roots of Modern-day Pentecost,* x-xi

84   Ibid., 18–19.

85   Ibid., 20.

86   Mary Stewart Relfe, *Cure of All Ills,* 63.

87   Ibid., 66.

88   Ibid.

89   Malcolm McDow and Alvin L. Reid, *Fire Fall: How God Has Shaped History Through Revivals,* 282–283.

90   Earle E. Cairns, *An Endless Line of Splendor: Revivals and Their Leaders from the Great Awakening to the Present,* 31–33.

91   Malcolm McDow and Alvin L. Reid, *Fire Fall: How God Has Shaped History Through Revivals,* 167–168.

92 Edith L. Blumhofer and Randall Balmer, *Modern Christian Revivals*, 84.

93 Malcolm McDow and Alvin L. Reid, *Fire Fall: How God Has Shaped History Through Revivals*, 229–231.

94 Ibid., 231.

95 Ibid., 235–239.

96 Malcolm McDow and Alvin L. Reid, *Fire Fall: How God Has Shaped History Through Revivals*, 235–239.

97 Earle E. Cairns, *An Endless Line of Splendor: Revivals and Their Leaders from the Great Awakening to the Present*, 148–150.

98 Mary Stewart Relfe, *Cure of All Ills*, 47–49.

99 Ibid.

100 Ibid., 45

101 Malcolm McDow and Alvin L. Reid, *Fire Fall: How God Has Shaped History Through Revivals*, 225.

102 Earle E. Cairns, *An Endless Line of Splendor: Revivals and Their Leaders from the Great Awakening to the Present*, 194–197.

103 Malcolm McDow and Alvin L. Reid, *Fire Fall: How God Has Shaped History Through Revivals*, 277.

104 Ibid., 276.

105 Richard M. Riss, *20ᵗʰ Century Revival Movements in North America*, 47.

106 Ibid., 49.

107 Ibid., 51–52.

108 Brian H. Edwards, *Revival! A People Saturated with God*, 73–84.

109 Ibid., 73–84.

110 Winkie, Pratney, *Revival*, 68.

111 Ibid., 70.

112 Wesley Duewel, *Revival Fire*, 52–54.

113 Ibid.

114 Malcolm McDow and Alvin L. Reid, *Fire Fall: How God Has Shaped History Through Revivals*, 205.

115 Henry Johnson, *Stories of Great Revivals*, 24.

116 Mary Stewart Relfe, *Cure of All Ills*, 27–28.

117 Ibid.

118 Ibid., 28

119 Winkie Pratney, *Revival,* 112–114.

120 Malcolm McDow and Alvin L. Reid, *Fire Fall: How God Has Shaped History Through Revivals,* 231.

121 Ibid., 229.

122 Earle E. Cairns, *An Endless Line of Splendor: Revivals and Their Leaders from the Great Awakening to the Present,* 92.

123 Ibid., 178–179.

124 Ibid.

125 Frank Bartleman, *Azusa Street: The Roots of Modern-day Pentecost,* ix.

126 Ibid., 8–9.

127 Ibid., 13.

128 Ibid., 36.

129 Ibid., 47.

130 Richard Dresselhaus, "Three Miles from the Coffee," Enrichment (summer, 2004), 36.

131 E. M. Bounds quote: www.cybernation.com/quotationcenter/quote-show.php?type=author&id-1078

132 Ibid.

133 Martin Luther quote: www.cybernation.com/quotationcenter/quote-show.php?type=author&id-1078

134 E. M. Bounds, see www.cybernation.com/quotationcenter/quote-show.php?type=author&id-1078

135 Dr. Walter Kaiser, *Quest for Revival: Personal Revival in the Old Testament* (Chicago: Moody Press, 1986), 15.

136 Dallas Willard, *Hearing God: Developing a Conversational Relationship with God* (Downers Grove, IL, 1999), 134.

137 Timothy Keller with Kathy Keller, *The Songs of Jesus: A Year of Daily Devotions in the Psalms,* (Viking, New York: NY, 2015), 195.

138 Vance Havner, *Day by Day,* (Westwood, NJ: Fleming H. Revell, 1953), 15.

139 Brian Edwards, *Revival! A People Saturated With God,* 73–84.

140 Brother Lawrence, *The Practice of the Presence of God* (Grand Rapids, MI: Baker Book House, Spire), 1994.

141 E. M. Bounds, see www.cybernation.com/quotationcenter/quote-show.php?type=author&id-1078

142 Oswald Chambers, *My Utmost for His Highest* (Dodd Mead & Co. NY, NY, 1935), 291.

143 Dr. Martin Lloyd Jones, see www.ravenhill.org/index, Maxims #3, Page 1.

144 E. M. Bounds, see www.cybernation.com/quotationcenter/quote-show.php?type=author&id-1078

145 Richard Dresselhaus, "Three Miles from the Coffee," Enrichment (Summer, 2004). 36.

146 Dutch Sheets, *The River of God* (Regal Books, 1998), 194.

147 J. Edwin Orr, *The Second Evangelical Awakening*, 20

148 Ibid., 130.

149 Ibid., 154.

150 Ibid., 19–64.

151 Ibid., 155.

152 Earle E. Cairns, *An Endless Line of Splendor*, 194–197

153 Ibid.

154 Mary Stewart Relfe, *Cure of All Ills*, 95.

155 George T. Davis, *When the Fire Fell*, 65.

156 Ibid, 72–73.

157 C.S. Lewis: http(s://www.azquotes.com/quote/1560611)

158 Malcolm McDow and Alvin L. Reid, *Fire Fall: How God Has Shaped History Through Revivals*, 225- 226

159 Mary Stewart Relfe, *Cure of All Ills*, 23.

160 Winkie, Pratney, *Revival*, 106–107.

161 Henry Johnson, *Stories of Great Revivals*, 192–193.

162 Warren A. Chandler, *Great Revivals and the Great Republic*, 88–89.

163 Ibid., 100.

164 Ibid., 189.

165 Winkie, Pratney, *Revival*, 115, 134–135.

166 Mary Stewart Relfe, *Cure of All Ills*, 35.

167 Malcolm McDow and Alvin L. Reid, *Fire Fall: How God Has Shaped History Through Revivals*, 247.

168 J. Edwin Orr, *The Second Evangelical Awakening*, 20

169 Ibid., 66.

170 Warren A. Chandler, *Great Revivals and the Great Republic*, 66.

171 J. Edwin Orr, *The Second Evangelical Awakening,* 114–115.

172 Ibid., 116.

173 Ibid.

174 George T. Davis, *When the Fire Fell,* 72–73.

175 Winkie, Pratney, *Revival,* 178.

176 Frank Bartleman, *Azusa Street: The Roots of Modern-day Pentecost,* ix.

177 Winkie, Pratney, *Revival,* 107.

178 Brian H. Edwards, *Revival! A People Saturated with God,* 140–141.

179 Winkie, Pratney, *Revival,* 137

180 Brian H. Edwards, *Revival! A People Saturated with God,* 137.

181 Ibid., 132, 140.

182 Ibid., 116–117.

183 Ibid., 118.

184 Ibid., 116–117.

185 J. Edwin Orr, *The Fervent Prayer: The Worldwide Impact of the Great Awakening of 1858,* (Chicago, Moody Press, 1974), 5.

186 Malcolm McDow and Alvin L. Reid, *Fire Fall: How God Has Shaped History Through Revivals,* 278.

187 Ibid. 64.

188 Ibid. 204.

189 Ibid. 207.

190 Brian H. Edwards, *Revival! A People Saturated with God,* 108.

191 Ibid., 32.

192 Wesley Duewel, *Revival Fire,* 65–66.

193 Mary Stewart Relfe, *Cure of All Ills,* 28–29.

194 Earle E. Cairns, *An Endless Line of Splendor: Revivals and Their Leaders from the Great Awakening to the Present,* 97.

195 Frank Bartleman, *Azusa Street: The Roots of Modern-day Pentecost,* 80.

196 Warren A. Chandler, *Great Revivals and the Great Republic,* 50.

197 Ibid., 179.

198 J. Edwin Orr, *The Second Great Awakening in America,* 41–42.

199 _____, *The Fervent Prayer: The Worldwide Impact of the Great Awakening of 1858* (Chicago: Moody Press, 1974). 38.

200 George T. Davis, *When the Fire Fell,* 74.

201 Ibid., 74, 78.

202 Frank Bartleman, *Azusa Street: The Roots of Modern-day Pentecost,* 56.

203 Richard M. Riss, *20th Century Revival Movements in North,* 5–7.

204 "Transformations," and "The Quickening," © The Sentinel Group, www.transformations.com, Global Net Productions.

205 Mary Stewart Relfe, *Cure of All Ills,* 20–22.

206 Ibid., 23.

207 Warren A. Chandler, *Great Revivals and the Great Republic,* 87–100.

208 Mary Stewart Relfe, *Cure of All Ills,* 35–36.

209 Ibid., 225–226.

210 Warren A. Chandler, *Great Revivals and the Great Republic,* 150.

211 Mary Stewart Relfe, *Cure of All Ills,* 49.

212 Ibid., 62.

213 Ibid., 87–94.

214 J. Edwin Orr, *The Second Great Awakening in America,* 156–157.

215 J. Edwin Orr, *The Fervent Prayer: The Worldwide Impact of the Great Awakening of 1858,* 176.

216 Ibid.

217 Richard M. Riss, *20th Century Revival Movements in North America,* 40.

218 Henry Johnson, *Stories of Great Revivals,* 370.

219 Winkie, Pratney, *Revival,* 191.

220 George Otis, Jr., unpublished teaching notes, reported in Hughey, *Desperate for His Presence: God's Design to Transform Your Life and Your City,* 196.

221 David S. Wilkerson, *America's Last Call* (Lindale, TX: Wilkerson Trust Publications, 1998), Letter to Constituents.

222 Mary Stewart Relfe, *Cure of All Ills,* 49.

223 Malcolm McDow and Alvin L. Reid, *Fire Fall: How God Has Shaped History Through Revivals,* 297.

224 Bonaro W. Overstreet, "Stubborn Ounce," in book of poetry, "Hands Laid Upon the Wind," http://www.letrs.indiana.edu/cgi/f/findaid/findaid-idx?type=simple;view=text;subview=fulltext;c=fa-lilly;id=InU-Li-VAA1283

225

226

CPSIA information can be obtained
at www.ICGtesting.com
Printed in the USA
LVHW052233300621
691582LV00014B/753

9 781662 821349